THE CAR RESTORER'S WORKSHOP COMPANION

THE CAR RESTORER'S WORKSHOP COMPANION

The complete guide to techniques and tools for vehicle restoration and repair

GEOFF PURNELL

PSL

PATRICK STEPHENS LIMITED

First published in 1989

British Library Cataloguing in Publication Data

Purnell, Geoff.
The car restorer's workshop companion
1. Cars. Maintenance & repair - Manuals
I. Title
629.28'722

ISBN 1-85260-224-4

Cover illustrations courtesy of Haymarket Publications.

Patrick Stephens Limited is part of the Thorsons Publishing Group, Wellingborough, Northamptonshire NN88 2RQ, England.

Typeset by Burns & Smith, Derby

Printed by Bath Press, Bath, Avon

10 9 8 7 6 5 4 3 2

Contents

Introduction

The primary purpose in writing this book is to provide a simple guide to tackling the basic metalwork and woodwork processes required to restore, renovate or repair your motor vehicle or motorcycle, whatever its age.

Many enthusiasts will have had the opportunity of receiving instruction in these subjects while at school, but the passage of time may have dimmed the memory of the finer details of these processes or they may have been lost altogether. I hope that the following pages will enable you to successfully complete those jobs that so many books assume you can accomplish without any guidance at all.

Should you be in the position of having, as so many people do, a great deal of enthusiasm, some skill, but little or no equipment, your local evening classes may provide the answer. Most schools, and certainly local colleges, are well enough equipped to satisfy most of the small machining needs of the enthusiast, plus possibly casting and welding. If there is no suitable class in your area, then try approaching your local Education Authority. If a need can be shown, they are usually willing to run a course, which may provide an ideal opportunity for local clubs to get together.

Lastly, don't be afraid to attempt jobs that you have put off in the past; with careful thought, planning and ingenuity, it is surprising what can be achieved. The sense of satisfaction that can come from a job well done, especially if it is something attempted for the first time, is one of life's real pleasures. If this book helps you achieve that satisfaction, it will have been well worth the writing.

CHAPTER 1

A place to work and tools to work with

Unfortunately not many people are blessed with the ideal situation of plenty of space, light and heat to work on their vehicle.

However, a great deal can be accomplished in a small space with a little care and thought. The most important item is a strong, rigid bench of a height best suited to you; 33 ins (840 mm) is the height of the average bench which you can use as a guide if you are making one from scratch. The top should be at least 1½ in (38 mm) thick and firmly attached to the legs, which in turn should be bolted or screwed to the floor or wall. The top should also extend beyond the underframe by at least 1½ in (38 mm) so that work can be clamped to the top by a G clamp or similar. It is also beneficial to let into the edge of the top a piece of angle iron fixed with countersunk screws; this will be found useful for bending sheet metal as described in the relevant chapter. Another useful tip is to cover the top with hardboard, well varnished it to prevent it soaking up liquids, to protect the main bench top from damage. When this becomes too tatty, it can be removed and a fresh piece put in its place.

Figure 1 shows the basic plan of a suitable bench. As its construction does not have any woodworking joints, it can be made quickly and easily. If a long bench is made, the number of legs should be increased, 4 ft (1200 mm) being the furthest they should be apart for rigidity.

The essential engineer's vice should be bolted, not screwed to the bench, as they invariably come loose, and as near to a leg as possible to give extra support. The top of the jaws of the vice should be level with your elbow. The height of the vice

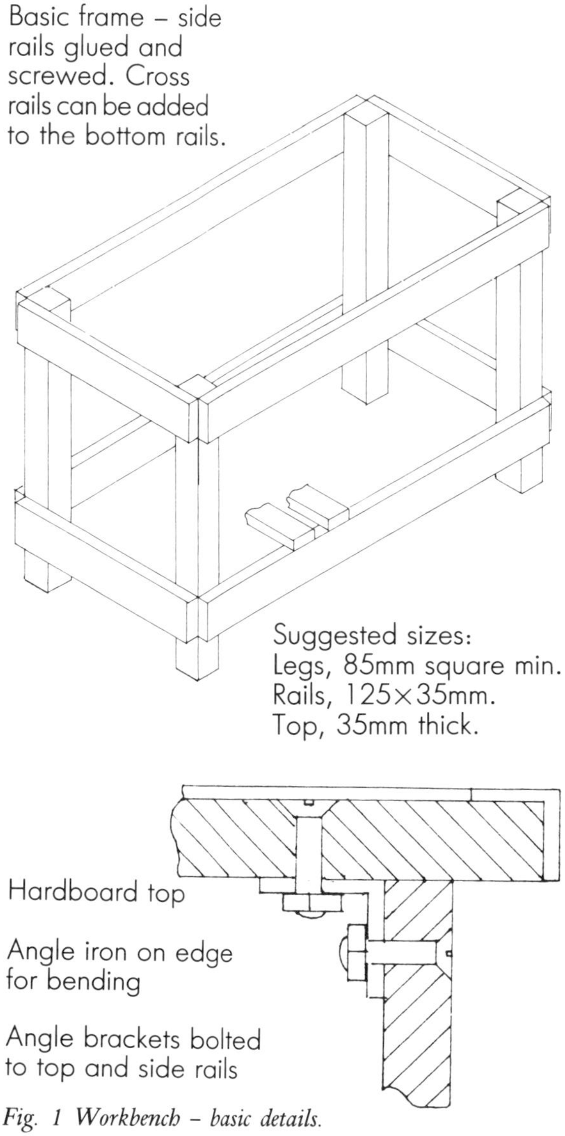

Fig. 1 Workbench – basic details.

subtracted from this dimension will give you the ideal height for the top of the bench. When fixing the vice make sure that the fixed jaw is beyond the edge of the bench top; this will enable you to hold long pieces of work vertically in the vice.

While on the subject of vices, buy the best you can afford; cheap vices are often made from an inferior grade of iron and will not stand up to heavy usage. If you intend doing a great deal of heavy hammering on the vice, it is important to buy one designed for that purpose; these usually incorporate an anvil in their design, otherwise you could find the casting cracked after use.

The jaws of the vice will be serrated and, though this is very useful for gripping work very securely, it will leave marks in it. To prevent this a pair of fibre soft jaws can be bought to clip over the vice jaws. Another method is to remove the jaws and place thin sheet steel or aluminium behind them; the jaws are bolted back in place and the thin sheet folded over the front of the jaws, covering the serrations.

As far as tools go, there is no end to achieving a full set. Perhaps the most important thing is to ensure that those you buy are the best you can afford. Resist the temptation to buy a full set of, for example, reamers or taps and dies, unless you have plenty of spare money. Some of these you will probably never use and the money would be better spent on your vehicle.

While on the subject of these tools, I would not advise anyone to buy second-hand taps, dies or reamers unless you are sure they have not had much use. Tools such as these are useless when they are blunt and cannot easily be sharpened without special equipment. When buying cutting tools, it is preferable to buy those made from high speed steel (H.S.S.); they are more expensive than those made from carbon steel (C.S.), but they will keep their edge much longer. The only exception I would make would be taps and dies if they are not likely to be used very often.

A set of drills 1/16 in to ½ in or 1 mm to 13 mm is ideal and if kept sharp and stored carefully will last for years. The old letter and number drills have now been superseded by metric sizes and are more expensive to buy. The tables at the end of the chapter on drills show that many of these have a metric equivalent.

Files come in a bewildering array of shapes and sizes and for a start the following will be most useful:

10″ Hand file (second cut) one edge safe
10″ Half round (second cut)
8″ Round
8″ Three square
6″ Half round
6″ Flat
¼″ Round
10″ Millencut or Dreadnought
A set of needle files

Make sure you use good-quality file handles such as the 'Python'; these are much stronger and there is less chance of the handle splitting.

A senior and junior hacksaw complete with adaptor clips for 'Abra' saw blades will satisfy most of your sawing needs. For marking out and measuring, the following are the minimum necessary: scriber, centre punch, 4 in engineer's square, 6 in (150 mm) or 12 in (300 mm) steel rule, and 4 in (100 mm) or 6 in (150 mm) dividers. For accurate measuring, a micrometer or a pair of vernier callipers are needed. Micrometers are either metric or imperial, whereas vernier callipers are usually dual measurement.

As for the rest of the tools, apart from the basic ones you need to dismantle the vehicle, they are probably best bought as and when you need them. Power tools are an invaluable help to the restorer and anyone who tackles any major work without the minimum of an electric drill is going to find the work that much harder. An electric drill with a ½ in (13 mm) chuck is ideal, preferably with a variable speed control as even two-speed drills revolve too quickly for large diameter drills on their slowest speed. For accurate drilling, a drill stand is very useful, together with a good quality drill press vice. When buying such a vice check that the moving jaw is a good fit where it slides on the base and does not lift up as it tightens onto the work, so presenting it to the drill out of true. Obviously a pedestal drill is the ideal solution and these can be found at auctions and second-hand machine dealers. A small bench grinder is a very useful piece

Right *An angle grinder, a very useful tool to have in the workshop.*

Below *A small bandsaw for sawing straight or curves.*

of equipment, not only for grinding pieces of work but for sharpening drills, cold chisels etc. If you are contemplating doing a lot of welding then an angle grinder is invaluable for dressing up the welds; with a cutting disc instead of the grinding wheel it will cut through body panels with ease.

The ultimate machine tool is of course a lathe, a most versatile machine that can be a boon to the restorer. If you are in the position to be able to afford a lathe, careful consideration must be given to the work you hope to achieve with it. A modelmaker's lathe is excellent for small work, but does not have the capacity to handle anything of any size, whereas a 7½ in lathe capable of turning a 15 in diameter flywheel takes up a great deal of space and will most likely need three-phase electricity to run it. Perhaps the best size of lathe is 5 in or 6 in and the chapter on lathes includes a check list of points to look for when buying second-hand.

Should your car have a wooden-framed body in need of repair, you will need some basic woodworking tools. The following are probably the minimum you will require:

14″ Jack plane
Panel or cross-cut saw
Tenon saw
Marking gauge
Marking knife
½″ (13 mm) and 1 in (25 mm) bevelled edge chisels
Try square
4″ (100 mm) and 6″ (150 mm) G cramps

A power saw is an obvious tool to have if you have a considerable amount of wood to cut. Power saws fall into two groups: circular saws, which can be hand-held, table-mounted or in the form of a radial arm saw, and band saws. In recent years, several manufacturers have produced small, reasonably priced band saws. Of the two, my personal preference would be for the band saw as it is the more versatile, being able to cut curves as well as straight. With suitable blades it will also cut metal and plastic. The main drawback of the small bandsaw is the difficulty of sawing long lengths of timber accurately unless a fence is used and the saw is clamped to a firm surface.

Some of this equipment is expensive and if it is not going to be used very often, there will be a lot of money tied up in its purchase which could be better spent on your vehicle. In this case hiring may be the best solution. There are now many hire shops which can supply a wide range of equipment. Only you can decide which is best—purchase or hire—and that will depend on the amount of use the equipment will receive. Obviously the more frequent your need for a certain piece of equipment, the more cost-effective it will be to buy it.

CHAPTER 2

Metals for motor vehicles

Composition, usage, forms of supply

All metals, whatever their composition, have physical properties which make them suitable or unsuitable for particular applications on a motor vehicle.

Brittleness is the property of breaking without much permanent distortion. Cast iron is a brittle metal because its structure is split up by flakes of graphite, which is a brittle material. Shortness is another expression used instead of brittleness. Hot or red-shortness in a metal is when it is brittle in the red-hot state. Cold shortness means that a metal is brittle when cold.

Toughness is the resistance to fracture or deformation. Toughness decreases as metals become hot.

Elasticity The elasticity of a metal is its ability to return to its original shape after being deformed by a force, e.g. a road spring. The elastic limit of a metal is expressed in tons per square inch or newtons per square millimetre. If the elastic limit of a metal was 20 tons per square inch and this force was exceeded, the bar could take on permanent stretch, often called permanent set.

Hardness This is the resistance of the metal to being scratched, worn or indented by harder materials. There are a number of standard tests (e.g. Brinell) by which hardness of metals can be compared.

Malleability The property which allows a metal to be rolled or hammered without breaking. Lead, for instance is a very malleable metal.

Plasticity This is a similar property to malleability and involves permanent deformation without rupture. Plasticity is necessary for forging and most metals become plastic when hot.

Ductility The ability to be drawn into fine wire. Ductility often increases with heat. It bears little relation to malleability,. e.g. lead is very malleable but not ductile as it does not have the strength to be drawn.

Strength The strength of a metal is its ability to resist the application of a force without rupture. In use, a metal may have to withstand forces in compression, torsion, tension, shear or a combination of these. The ultimate tensile strength (U.T.S.) of a metal is the load necessary to fracture a sample 1 square inch (25 mm square) in cross-section. It is expressed in pounds or tons per square inch or newtons per square millimetre.

Cast Iron This is an alloy of iron and carbon where the carbon content is in the range of 2% to 4½%. Other elements present in much smaller percentages are silicon, manganese and phosphorus.

Cast iron is a brittle metal that has relatively little strength except in compression, and care should be taken when working on this metal. Its great advantage is its good fluidity in the molten state, making it ideal for complex castings such as cylinder blocks and cylinder heads. It is easily machined, once the hard outer layer is cut through, and it is also good as a bearing surface, i.e. cylinder bores, where the free graphite in its structure seems to act as a lubricant.

Cast iron engines are often quieter than those of aluminium alloy because the density of the metal reduces noise transmission.

Special alloy cast irons have been developed in recent years; these contain small percentages of nickel, copper, chromium or molybdenum. This produces a tough metal which casts well, resists shock loadings and is ideally suited for crankshafts.

Cast iron is not normally available at retail outlets. Typical uses include: cylinder blocks, cylinder heads, brake drums, water pump bodies, clutch pressure plates, exhaust manifolds, crankshafts.

Steel This is also an alloy of iron and carbon but in this case the carbon content ranges between 0.05% and 1.4%. Above this figure, carbon cannot be contained in the combined state with the iron and will exist as free graphite, and the metal merges into the group of cast irons.

Carbon steels fall into five main groups: dead mild 0.05%–0.15% carbon, mild steel 0.1%– 0.3% carbon, medium carbon 0.3%–0.6%, high carbon 0.6%–0.9% and tool steel 0.9%–1.4% carbon. Typical uses of these steels may be seen in Fig. 2.

Alloy Steel

To improve the properties of these plain carbon steels, they are frequently alloyed with small quantities of other elements. Nickel, for example, improves tensile strength and toughness. Chromium in small quantities will increase the hardness of the steel and in large quantities will produce stainless steel, which is corrosion resistant. 18/8 stainless steel refers to 18% chromium and 8% nickel in the composition of the metal.

Molybdenum reduces the brittleness of the steel and improves machinability. Among the alloy steels, the nickel-chrome-molybdenum steels possess perhaps the best all-round combination of properties useful for vehicle work.

Vanadium in small quantities improves the forging and stamping properties of the alloy, and chrome-vanadium steels are widely used for drop forgings, i.e. drop-forged spanners and sockets.

Fig. 2 Typical uses of various carbon steels.

TYPE OF STEEL	% CARBON	USES
DEAD MILD	0.05–0.10	RIVETS, NAILS, CHAIN. HOT AND COLD ROLLED STRIP, SEAM WELDED PIPE.
MILD	0.10–0.20	RSJ, SCREWS, MACHINE PARTS, STAMPINGS, SHEET, DROPS FORGINGS.
	0.20–0.30	FREE CUTTING STEELS, SHAFTING, GEARS, FORGINGS, STRUCTURAL WORK.
MEDIUM CARBON	0.30–0.40	HIGH TENSILE TUBES, AXLES, CON-RODS, FORGINGS, CRANE HOOKS, WIRE.
	0.40–0.50	CRANKSHAFTS, GEARS, AXLES, SHAFTS, DIE-BLOCKS, HEAT TREATED MACHINE PARTS.
	0.50–0.60	LAMINATED SPRINGS, WIRE ROPES, RAILS.
HIGH CARBON	0.60–0.70	SCREWDRIVERS, SAWS, SET SCREWS.
	0.70–0.80	HAMMERS, LAMINATED SPRINGS, CAR BUMPERS.
	0.80–0.90	COLD CHISELS, PUNCHES, SOME HAND TOOLS.
TOOL STEELS	0.90–1.00	SPRINGS, KNIVES, DIES, SILVER STEEL.
	1.00–1.10	DRILLS, TAPS, SCREWING DIES.
	1.10–1.20	BALL BEARINGS, LATHE AND WOOD TOOLS.
	1.20–1.30	FILES, REAMERS, BROACHES.
	1.30–1.40	SAWS, RAZORS, MACHINE PARTS WHERE RESISTANCE TO WEAR IS ESSENTIAL.

TYPE OF STEEL	B.S. 970. DESIGNATION	USES
LOW CHROME 1%	530 M 40	AXLES, CON-RODS, STEERING ARMS.
LOW NICKEL LOW CHROME	653 M 31	HIGHLY-STRESSED PARTS IN AUTO-ENGINEERING, E.G. CON-RODS, DIFFERENTIAL SHAFTS.
LOW CHROME LOW NICKEL	640 M 40	CRANKSHAFTS, CON-RODS, DIFFERENTIAL GEARS, AXLES.
1% CHROME MOLYBDENUM	709 M 40	CRANKSHAFTS, CON-RODS, STUB AXLES ETC.
1½% NICKEL CHROME MOLYBDENUM	817 M 40	DIFFERENTIAL SHAFTS, ETC, WHERE FATIGUE AND SHOCK RESISTANCE ARE IMPORTANT.
4½% NICKEL CHROME MOLYBDENUM	835 M 30	AIR-HARDENING STEEL FOR HIGHLY-STRESSED PARTS CAN BE SURFACE-HARDENED BY CYANIDE.

Fig. 3 Typical uses of some alloy steels.

Fig. 3 gives some alloy steels and their uses.

Steels are readily available in a great variety of sections: round, square, hexagonal, rectangular (known as flats), angles, sheet and tube of different sections. Black mild in flat or square form has rounded corners and comes coated with scale which looks like a dark brown skin. It is softer than bright drawn mild steel (B.D.M.S.) which is pickled in a 3% to 10% solution of sulphuric acid to remove the oxide and then drawn through a series of dies. This produces a more accurately sized metal and the flats and squares have 90° square corners. The metal is harder because of the drawing process.

Freecutting mild steel (F.C.M.S.) is produced by the addition of small quantities of lead to the metal which improves machinability.

The standard lengths of these sections is 10 ft (3 metres) and most steel stock holders are loathe to cut bars into smaller lengths. If you only want small quantities, then local engineering works are probably the best place to try.

Steel tubes are available in a variety of sections and properties but they fall into two main groups: Firstly seamed, which is made by forming a flat sheet into the shape required, then electrically welding the seam; these tubes are known as electric resistance welded (E.R.W.). Secondly, cold drawn seamless (C.D.S.) tube, which is drawn from a solid block of metal through dies to the required shape. This type of tube is stronger than E.R.W. and should be used for such items as track rods and drag links.

Sheet steel comes in two basic sizes 8 ft x 4 ft (2,400 mm x 1,200 mm) and 6 ft x 3 ft (1,800 x 900 mm). Its thickness, and that of any sheet metal, is measured in standard wire gauge (S.W.G.); Fig 4 shows the imperial and metric equivalents. It can also be obtained coated in various materials to provide a corrosion resistant or decorative surface.

S.W.G.	IMP.	METRIC	S.W.G.	IMP.	METRIC
6	.192	4.90	16	.064	1.60
7	.176	4.50	17	.056	1.45
8	.160	4.10	18	.048	1.23
9	.144	3.70	19	.040	1.05
10	.128	3.30	20	.036	0.92
11	.116	2.95	21	.032	0.82
12	.104	2.65	22	.028	0.72
13	.092	2.35	23	.024	0.61
14	.080	2.05	24	.022	0.56
15	.072	1.85	25	.020	0.51

Fig. 4 Imperial and metric equivalents to S.W.G.

A standard wire gauge for measuring sheet metal.

Steel coated with tin is known as tinplate and is widely used for petrol tanks. Lead-coated steel is also used for this purpose and is known as terne plate. Galvanised steel has a zinc coating. It is also possible to buy steel sheet coated with plastic.

Non-ferrous metals Aluminium in its pure state is a relatively soft and weak metal. For use in industry, it is usually alloyed with other elements, mainly copper, to increase its hardness and strength. Aluminium has two main uses in motor vehicles: sheet material for body panels and castings of various types. Extrusions are also available in a wide variety of shapes for many different purposes.

Sheet aluminium is available in the same sizes and thicknesses as sheet steel but a basic difference is that it can be ordered in various stages of hardness, soft, half-hard and hard. In the soft condition, it can be easily shaped but it is perhaps too prone to denting to be useful for bodywork. Half-hard will still work fairly easily and is much more resistant to dents, while hard sheets are best used for panels that need little or no shaping. Aluminium sheet is also available with a variety of raised patterns to produce a non-slip surface — often referred to as tread plate.

Aluminium casting alloys fall into two main groups: sand casting and die casting. To increase their strength, some of these alloys can be heat-treated. The table in Fig. 5 gives some of the most widely used alloys.

Magnesium alloys, often referred to as Elektron, are found in the form of castings on some vehicles, particularly high performance machines where the extra cost can be offset by the advantage of saving weight.

Zinc-based alloys, often known by their trade name 'Mazak', are mainly used for gravity or pressure die-castings of components which have to take relatively little stress, e.g. carburettors, door handles, light fittings, etc. The alloy can easily be chrome-plated, but suffers from a major drawback, that is the swelling and cracking of the casting during use. This is most noticeable in the earlier forms of zinc casting before metallurgists discovered that the presence of impurities in the zinc were causing the problem. The situation has improved in recent years by the use of 'Four Nines' zinc, i.e. 99.99% pure metal.

Other metals used in motor vehicles include: copper, mainly used for electrical wiring and gaskets, and brass, often used for decorative mouldings, hinges in earlier cars and some small castings. Both these metals can be obtained in sheets or tube. Brass can also be bought in the usual range of sections while copper is not usually available in these forms because of its soft nature and cost.

Bearing metals will be dealt with separately in a later chapter.

Fig. 5 Some typical uses of common aluminium casting alloys.

TRADE NAME	CHARACTERISTICS AND USES
LM 4	GENERAL PURPOSES. WITHSTANDS MODERATE STRESSES.
LM 9	SUITABLE FOR INTRICATE CASTINGS. GOOD CORROSION RESISTANCE.
LM 13	LOW THERMAL EXPANSION. USED FOR PISTONS FOR HIGH-PERFORMANCE ENGINES.
LM 14 Y-ALLOY	PISTONS AND CYLINDER HEADS FOR LIQUID AND AIR COOLED ENGINES. GENERAL PURPOSES.
LM 16	USEFUL FOR INTRICATE SHAPES AND PRESSURE TIGHTNESS. CYLINDER HEADS; VALVE BODIES; WATER JACKETS.

CHAPTER 3
Heat treatment

Although heat treatment of metal is often considered beyond the scope of the amateur restorer, there is a certain amount that can easily be accomplished in the home workshop.

Annealing

All metals, when they are worked in the cold state by bending or hammering, harden as the work progresses. The metal has to be re-softened or annealed, as it is called, so that work can continue without the metal cracking. Annealing involves heating the metal to a certain temperature, then allowing it to cool slowly.

Steel Should be heated to red heat, held at that temperature until the heat has soaked right through the metals then left to cool slowly, preferably in a container of vermiculite granules or, failing this, dry sand.

Aluminium Must first be coated with a thin film of soap, the reason for this being that aluminium does not change its appearance when it is heated until it begins to melt, making it very difficult to judge the temperature of the metal. The layer of soap will turn a dark brown colour when the annealing temperature has been reached, then the metal should be left to cool.

Copper This should be heated until a rainbow effect of colours appears on the surface; this indicates that the correct temperature has been reached. It can then either be left to cool or can be quenched in water without affecting its softness.

Brass This should be heated to red hot and allowed to cool slowly.

Hardening

The only metal that can be hardened in the home workshop is steel; the two methods depend on its carbon content. Steel with more than 0.3% carbon can be hardened by heating to red heat and quenching vertically, with a swirling figure-of-eight movement, in water or brine. This will produce an extremely hard brittle metal that is of little use in this state; some of this brittleness must be removed by the process known as tempering.

Tempering

Tempering requires the metal to be re-heated to a specific temerature, then quenched. Fortunately, it is possible to assess the temperature of the metal by observing the changing colour of the oxide film on the surface of the metal as it is heated. Obviously the surface must be cleaned up with emery cloth after it has been hardened so that this change in colour can be seen. When the correct colour is reached, the metal is again quenched in water or brine. Care must be taken not to heat the metal too quickly as the oxide film changes rapidly and it is very easy to overheat the work. The table in fig. 6 shows the correct colour and temperature for different applications.

Case hardening

It is not possible to harden steel with less than .3% carbon in its structure, i.e. mild steel, by heating and

TEMPER COLOUR	TEMP. CENT.	ARTICLES
PALE STRAW	230	TURNING TOOLS, SCRAPERS.
DARK STRAW	240	DRILLS, MILLING TOOLS.
BROWN	250	TAPS, SHEAR BLADES.
BROWNISH-PURPLE	260	PUNCHES, REAMERS.
PURPLE	270	AXES, PRESS TOOLS.
DARK PURPLE	280	COLD CHISELS.
BLUE	300	SPRINGS, SCREWDRIVERS.

Fig. 6 Tempering temperatures.

quenching. In this instance it is necessary to introduce extra carbon into the outer layer of the metal.

This is achieved by heating the steel to red heat and rolling it in carbon powder (available commercially under the trade name 'Kasenite'). The metal has to be re-heated and then rolled again. After this process has been repeated two or three times, the surplus powder should be brushed off with a wire brush, the metal heated to bright red heat and then quenched. This will leave a case of high carbon steel around a tough mild steel core.

In commercial operations, the parts to be case hardened are packed in special refactory boxes full of carbon powder and heated in a furnace for several hours before being quenched.

Normalising

This process returns work-hardened steel to its normal condition after forging or bending. The metal has to be heated to red heat and allowed to cool naturally in still air.

CHAPTER 4

Bearings and bearing materials

Wherever moving parts come into contact with each other or with a stationary surface, friction will try to prevent the movement between them. Heat is generated and efficiency will be impaired unless an attempt is made to reduce the friction.

The purpose of a bearing is to reduce this friction to an acceptable amount, usually in conjunction with some kind of lubrication.

Bearings can be separated into two main groups; plain bearings and rolling element bearings. Plain bearings are the simplest type of bearings, ranging from a bronze bush that carries a slow moving shaft to a high-performance white metal shell that can support a crankshaft revolving thousands of times a minute.

Bronze is used for bushes that carry a moderate load ut medium speeds. The bush can be machined from cast bronze bar and, to save a large amount of waste, bar above one inch diameter can be bought hollow in a range of sizes.

Hollow bronze bar for making plain bushes.

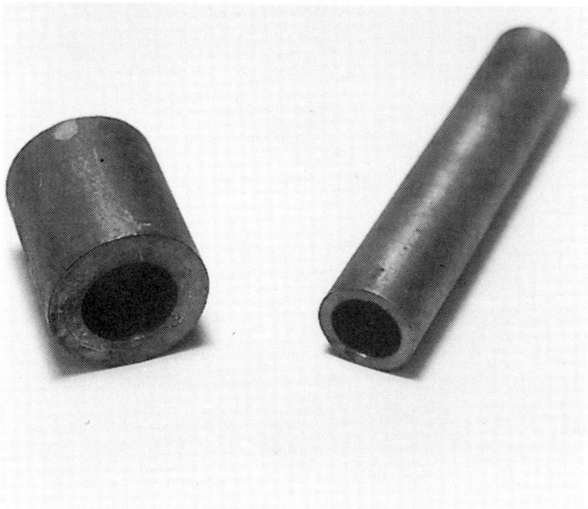

Self-lubricating or porous bronze bushes are used in situations where regular lubrication would be difficult and an excess of oil undesirable. These bushes are made from bronze powder which is formed to the required shape in a die on a hydraulic press. The bronze powder is cold welded together under the pressure of the press. The bush is then sintered in an oven to give it its final strength. These bushes should be soaked in oil for 24 hours before fitting; the lubrication should then last the lifetime of the bush.

Plain bearings for high speed and high loadings are made from white metal - this is a blanket description which covers a range of different alloys of lead and tin. The original alloy was called 'Babbit' metal, the name of the original patentee, and it contained a large proportion of lead. As crankshaft speeds became higher, the lead was replaced by tin to form an alloy of 88% tin, plus 8% antimony and 4% copper.

In the mid 1960s lead-indium bearings were developed for high speed engines. This bearing material consists of a bronze layer on the steel shell, then a layer of pure lead is plated onto the bronze. Finally a layer of indium is electrolytically and thermally infused over the bearing surface to give it good anti-frictional qualities.

In recent years the rising price of tin has forced bearing manufacturers to experiment with other metals, particularly aluminium. Reticular tin aluminium bearings have been developed which do not require the overlay of indium or other materials. The crystals of aluminium are coated with tin and the material is bonded onto the steel strip. This is followed by a heat treatment process during which

Left *Moulded white metal big-end and big-end shells.*

Right *Fig. 7 Some typical rolling element bearings.*

Middle right *A rigid ball bearing.*

Bottom right *A rigid roller bearing.*

the tin aluminium structure is modified and the tin forms a continuous network throughout the aluminium.

Fitting moulded bearings

Up until the late 1930s big end bearings were cast direct onto the con-rod and then machined to size. This type of bearing must be carefully fitted by hand-scraping to match the corresponding crankshaft journal. The process of scraping is not difficult but it requires care and patience to achieve a good result. The crankshaft journal must be clean and then a thin coating of engineer's blue should be applied to the whole of the journal. The con-rod should then be bolted to the journal and the crankshaft rotated for one or two revolutions by hand. The con-rod should then be removed and the white metal inspected; the high spots of the bearing will show blue where they have rubbed the crankshaft journal, and these must be carefully removed using a half round scraper; only a very small amount of metal should be removed at a time as it is easy to go too far. The bearings should then be bolted up again, after the journal has been cleaned and re-coated with the engineer's blue, and the crankshaft rotated. The scraping of the bearing should continue until an even coating of blue is transferred to the whole surface of the big-end bearing. The con-rod should also rotate freely round the journal. Don't forget that there should also be clearance between the sides of the bearing and the cheeks of the crankshaft to allow for expansion when the engine gets warm. It is foolish to cheat at this stage and add a little extra engineer's blue to the con-rod to make the bearing appear a better fit. You are only storing up trouble for later on. If the crankshaft has been re-ground at the same time as the bearings have been re-metalled, there should not be much scraping needed to provide a perfect fit.

More modern engines are fitted with shell bearings and their replacement is a simple matter. If the bearing shows any sign of heavy scoring or uneven wear it should be replaced. Naturally the crankshaft must also be checked visually for signs of scoring or ridging and with a micrometer for any signs of ovality or taper.

Manufacturer's workshop manuals usually give the maximum allowance for ovality and there should be no taper from one end of the journal to the other. If the journal is oval or scored, the crankshaft should be reground and the next undersize big end bearings fitted.

Plastics, particularly nylon, have been used as plain bearings for some years. Their use is limited to medium speed, low load applications where heat will not be a problem. Plastics technology is progressing rapidly and it may not be long before new plastics will be able to take over the role of more traditional materials.

Though plain bearings have many uses in motor vehicles, they are quite inefficient compared to

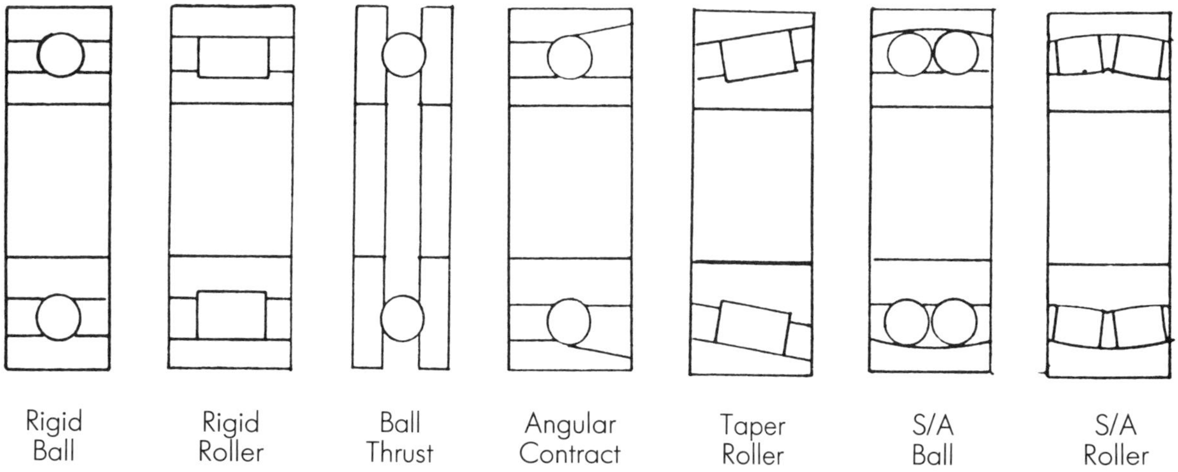

rolling element bearings. These bearings convert the sliding friction of plain bearings to rolling friction, which requires less power to overcome.

There are many types of rolling element bearings available and Fig. 7 shows the main types of anti-friction bearings found on motor vehicles. The rigid ball bearing shown is probably in greater use than any other type. It will carry radial and axial loads with combinations of both, and has many uses in gear-boxes, rear wheel bearings, etc.

Rigid roller bearings are capable of carrying very high radial leads but they cannot take axial loads. They also cannot be used to locate a shaft as the design of the bearing permits free lateral movement of the shaft.

The ball thrust bearing is designed to take axial loads only and is most suited for use at, slow speeds. It can be found in some types of steering box to take the end thrust from the steering column.

The angular contact bearing is a dual purpose bearing; it is capable of taking thrust in one direction only or combined thrust and radial loads. Ideally two such bearings should be fitted to the shafts, set in opposite directions. Because it is the axial load that keeps the balls in their tracks, it must be carefully adjusted to eliminate end play. The pre-war Austin Seven used two of these bearings to support the front end of its crankshaft.

The tapered roller bearing is designed to take high axial loadings in one direction only. Two of these

Left *A ball thrust bearing.*

Middle left *Angular thrust bearings, showing thrust and non-thrust faces.*

Bottom left *A tapered roller bearing.*

bearings are used in normal front wheel hubs. Older type bearings are adjusted so that there is a small amount of play in the system. Some newer types of these bearings are designed to be set up with some pre-load on the system.

All the bearings described so far rely on the accurate alignment of shaft and bearing housing to work correctly. Where this cannot be achieved or where the shaft is likely to deflect, a self-aligning bearing should be chosen. The self-aligning ball bearing should not be used where axial loading is present though it will take moderate radial loads. Where higher radial loads are anticipated, the self-aligning roller bearing should be used.

Whenever a component is stripped down that has a ball or roller bearing in it, the bearing should be inspected carefully for signs of wear or damage.

Wash the bearing carefully in white spirit, making sure it is completely clean. Examine the tracks and rolling elements for pitting or scoring. Also look for any signs of overheating. Hold the outer ring firmly and turn the inner ring with pressure first on one side then the other. If there is any gritty or rough feeling as it is turned, it should be scrapped, similarly if any other signs of wear are present it should also be scrapped.

If you are in any doubt, scrap the bearing anyway — it has probably been in place for years and the cost of a new one is worth the peace of mind it brings.

Take care when removing bearings from their shafts or housings. A sustained attack with a large hammer will only serve to ruin what could have been a perfectly serviceable bearing. A press or a set of claw extractors are the right tools for the job but if you cannot borrow or hire them, then, with care, a hammer can be used.

It is usual for the rotating part of the bearing to be an interference fit and the stationary part of the bearing a push fit. In the majority of cases where a shaft rotates, the inner race must be an interference fit on

Right *A needle roller bearing.*
Middle right *A self-aligning ball bearing.*
Bottom right *A self-aligning roller bearing.*

the shaft, and the outer race a sliding push fit into the housing. In this instance the inner ring of the bearing must be used to drive the bearing off the shaft. Use a brass drift and a heavy hammer, working round the ring to even out the pressure. It is essential that the bearing is kept square to the shaft to prevent damage to either. Obviously the outer ring of the bearing will be driven out of the housing in the same way.

Re-fitting bearings must also be done with carc. A press is the best method but if one is not available, a hammer can be used. When fitting a bearing onto a shaft, a short length of thick walled tube, slightly larger than the diameter of the shaft, will help to drive the bearing on square.

Where a bearing is being fitted into a housing, it is often a good idea to warm the housing first. If it is small, it can be warmed in a domestic oven or a small blow lamp can be used. Take care with the heating, particularly if the housing is made of aluminium or other low melting point alloy. If the housing is small enough, it may be possible to use the bench vice as a small press to fit the bearing. Obviously it is essential to keep everything very clean during this operation, to prevent dirt or grit finding their way into the bearing.

If the outer or inner ring of the bearing has been rotating in the housing or on the shaft, the fault will have to be rectified before reassembly. Should the wear be small, it is possible to use an adhesive such as 'Perma Bond AllB' retainer; correctly applied this will give up to four times the shear strength of an interference fit. Where the wear is too great, the shaft or housing will have to be built up either by metal spraying or electro-plating. Under no circumstances try to rectify the problem by using a centre punch to raise the surface of the shaft or housing. It may appear to work but the bearing will soon fret loose again.

Most bearings located in the external casing

of a component are fitted with an oil seal of some description. These should always be renewed before re-assembly; their low cost does not warrant trying to make do with a worn seal. Ensure that the new seal is fitted the correct way round and that it is seated squarely in its housing.

The older type of felt seal which was used to retain grease should be renewed if it shows any signs of hardening or leakage. New felt seals should be soaked in oil before fitting.

CHAPTER 5

Hand tools for metal working

This chapter describes some of the more common hand tools that could be useful to the car restorer; it is not intended as a comprehensive guide to all hand tools — to achieve that would require a book in itself.

Marking out and measuring tools

Steel rule Available in a range of sizes and choice of graduations. Much preferred to a wooden rule for measuring.

Scriber Made of high carbon steel and available in several sizes and types. The point should be ground to a 30° angle and kept sharp for accuracy.

Centre punch Made of high carbon steel. The point should be ground to 90°. Used for marking the position of a hole before drilling. A dot punch is similar in shape and size but the point is ground to 60°. Used to define a line that has to be worked to.

Engineer's square Used for checking squareness and marking lines at right angles to an edge.

Combination set A combination set is four tools in one — a grooved steel rule that three other tools can slide along. The square head has one face at 90° to the rule, another at 45°. It also incorporates a spirit level. This can be used as a mitre square, square, or depth gauge, etc. The protractor head enables the rule

A scriber and dot punch.

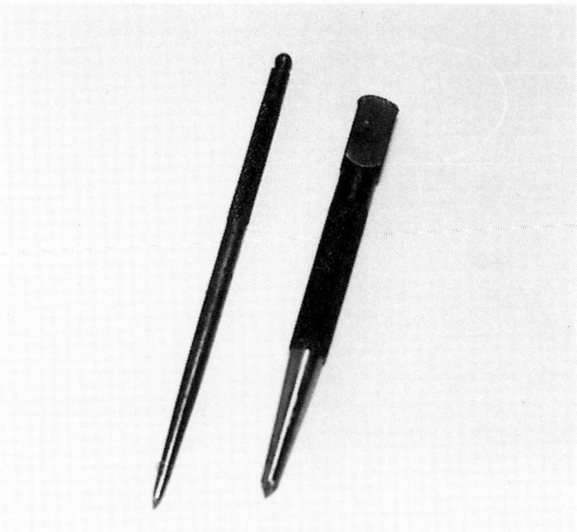

A transfer centre punch. This is very useful for marking centres through one component into another.

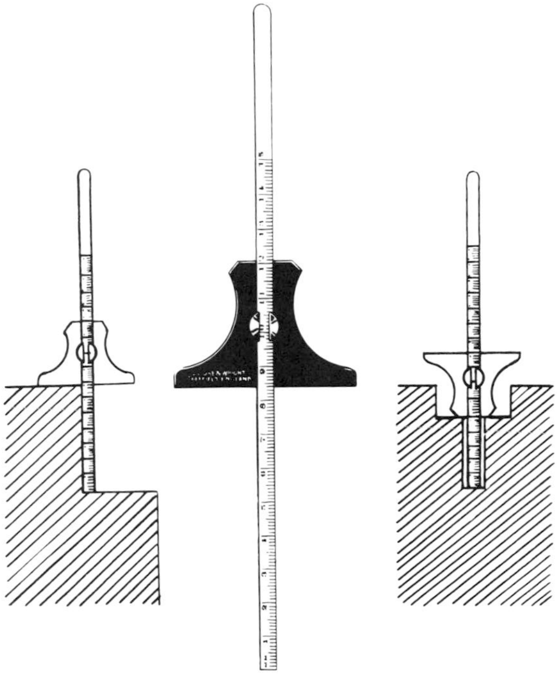

to be set at any angle for marking out or measuring angles. The centre square is used to locate the centre of a round bar.
All the heads can be locked to the rule with knurled nuts; the spirit levels can be used for setting up work before machining.

Depth gauge This tool consists of a steel body with a narrow rule running through the centre of it. The rule can be locked in any position by means of a knurled nut. It is used to measure the depth of holes, recesses, etc.

Dividers For scribing arcs and circles, also for stepping off measurements.

Trammel For drawing large diameter circles and stepping off measurements beyond the scope of dividers.

Two heads are used on a beam of suitable length and some types have a fine adjustment mechanism on one head for accurate setting.

Inside callipers Used for measuring inside diameters or slots. One leg is held in contact with the metal while the other is rocked through an arc to get the right 'feel'.

Outside callipers Used for measuring outside diameters. They must be held square to the work or a false reading will be obtained.

Odd-leg callipers These are used for scribing a line parallel to an edge. Care must be taken to ensure that they are held square to the edge otherwise the line will be inaccurate. They can also be used to find the centre of a bar by estimation from four positions. Also known by the name Jenny or hermaphrodite callipers.

Micrometer The appearance and construction principles of the micrometer are the same whether it is for imperial or metric measurement. The micrometer consists of the frame which is roughly semi-circular in shape and carries in its left hand end the anvil and in its right the barrel. The barrel is

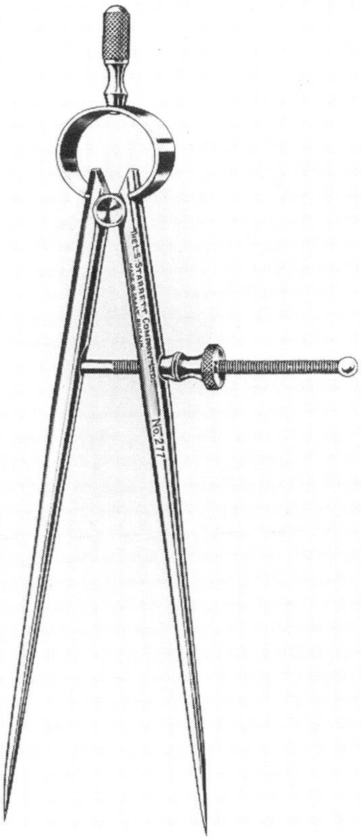

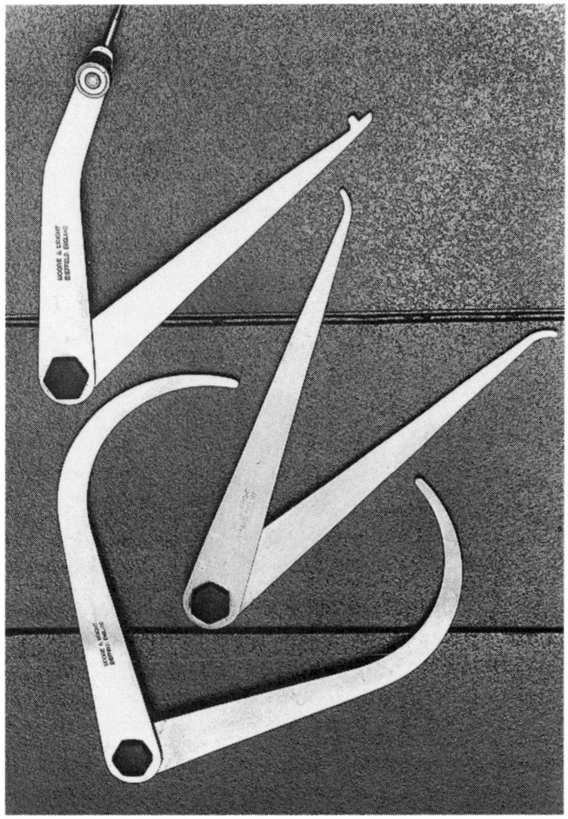

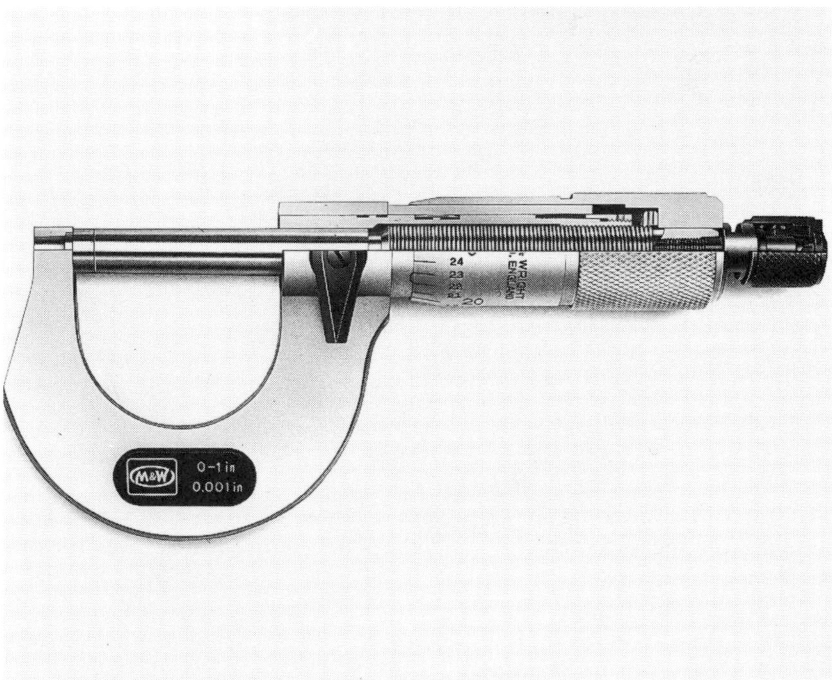

Above far left *A selection of marking out tools. The combination set and engineer's square are in the centre.* (James Neill Ltd)

Fig. 8 **Above left** *A depth gauge and its uses.* (James Neill Ltd)

Above *Spring dividers.* (L.S. Starrett Ltd)

Above right *From top to bottom – outside, inside, and odd-leg calipers.* (James Neill Ltd)

Right *A cutaway view of a micrometer.* (James Neill Ltd)

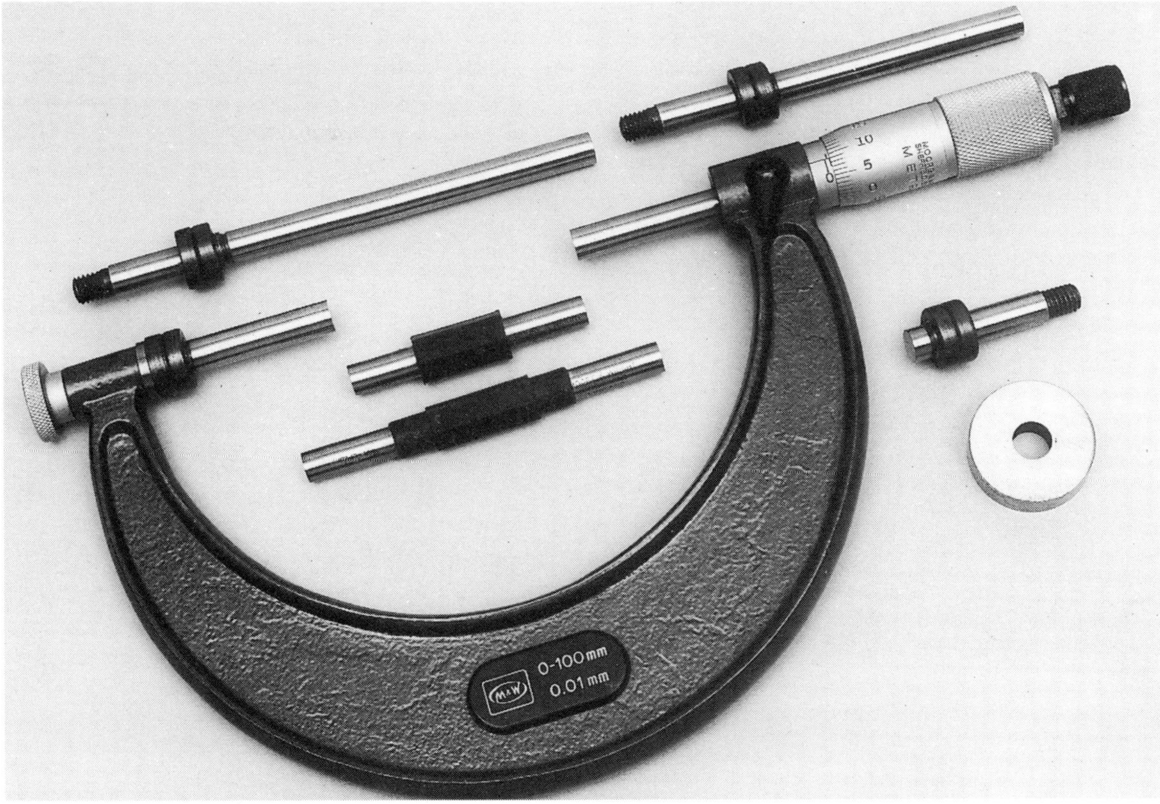

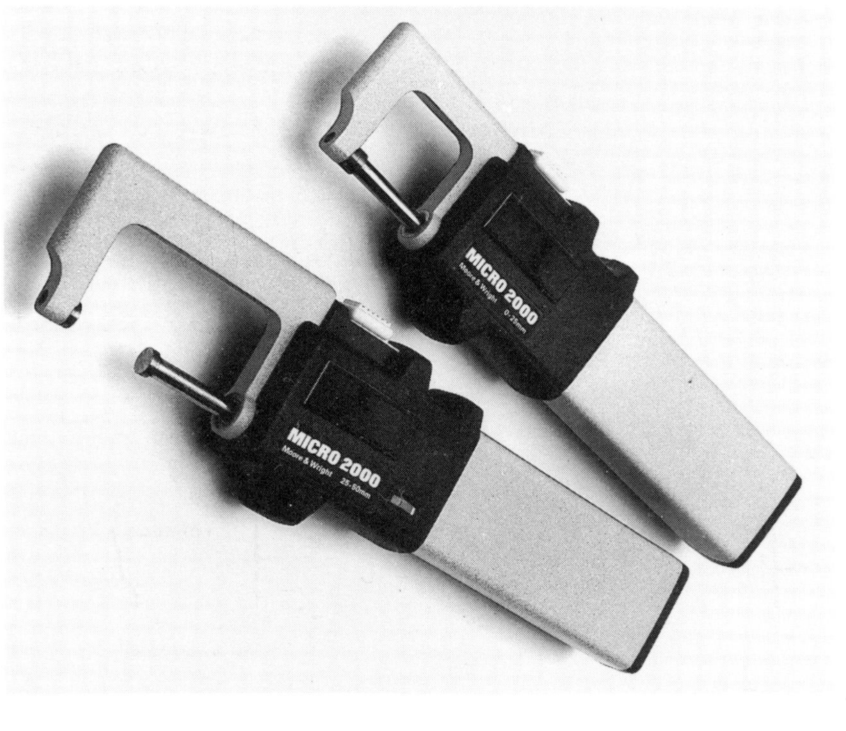

Above *A 0–100 mm micrometer with extension bars.* (James Neill Ltd)

Left *Digital micrometer. This gives a visual display of the reading, which reduces the risk of error.* (James Neill Ltd)

Right *Figs. 9 and 10. The calibration of an imperial and metric micrometer.* (James Neill Ltd)

graduated in either tenths of an inch or millimetres for a length of 1 in or 25 mm. The thimble rotates around the barrel and is divided on its circumference into 25 divisions (imperial) or 50 divisions (metric). Micrometers only measure a total of 1 in (25 mm) so the next size will measure 1in to 2in (25–50 mm). For larger sizes the frame and the barrels, etc, are in two parts and the measuring unit can be clamped into different frame sizes each 1in (25 mm) bigger than the last.

The screw of an imperial micrometer is threaded 40 teeth per inch (40 T.P.I.) So in one revolution of the thimble, the spindle moves ¹⁄₄₀ in or 0.025 in. The thimble is divided on its circumference into 25 parts; if the thimble moves along one of these divisions the spindle will move 1/25 of 0.025 in. or 0.001 in. Therefore each division on the thimble represents 0.001 in.

The barrel carries a datum line with each tenth of an inch divided into four parts, i.e. 0.025. When the micrometer is closed, the 0 of the barrel should coincide with the 0 on the thimble. If it does not, the micrometer should be adjusted so that it does. Alternatively, the discrepancy should be allowed for when calculating the measurement.

Reading the micrometer (imperial)

1. Read the largest number on the sleeve .200
2. Add the number of fortieths visible on the sleeve .075
3. Add the number on the thimble level with the datum line .011

.286

The metric micrometer

The screw has a pitch of 0.5 mm, therefore the spindle moves 0.5 mm for each revolution of the thimble. The thimble is divided into 50 parts, each division representing 0.01 mm movement of the spindle. The barrel is graduated in millimetres and half millimetres.

Reading the metric micrometer

1. Read the largest number on the sleeve. 10.00
2. Add ½ millimetres if necessary. .50
3. Add the number on the thimble level with datum line .16

10.66

Internal micrometers

These are used for measuring internal diameters. The head is similar to the external micrometer but its range of adjustment is only ½ in (13 mm). It's total length is 1 in (25 mm) which means that 1 in (25 mm) is the smallest bore it will enter.

Extension rods of different lengths are available to increase the range of bore sizes and a spacing collar ½ in (12 mm) long can be fitted between the head and the extension rods to give intermediate measurements.

Micrometer depth gauge

This is used for the accurate measuring of holes, shoulders, etc. The range of measurement is usually 0–1 in (0–25 mm) which can be increased by extension rods.

All micrometers should be used with care; the faces of the anvil and spindle should be cleaned prior to use. Never force the barrel into the work as this will give a false reading. If the micrometer is fitted with a ratchet, use it and so apply the same, correct amount of pressure every time.

When not in use, the micrometer should be stored

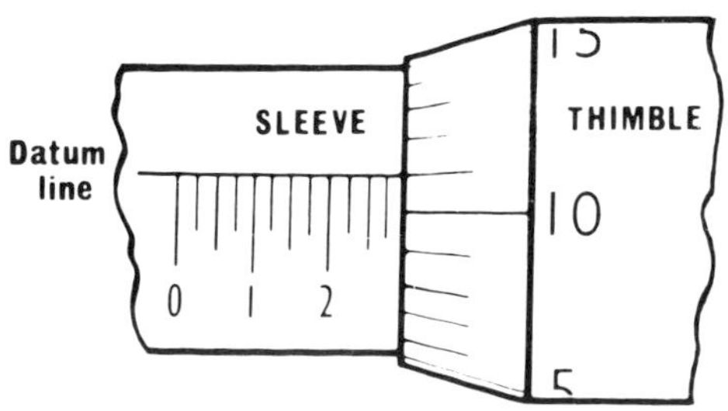

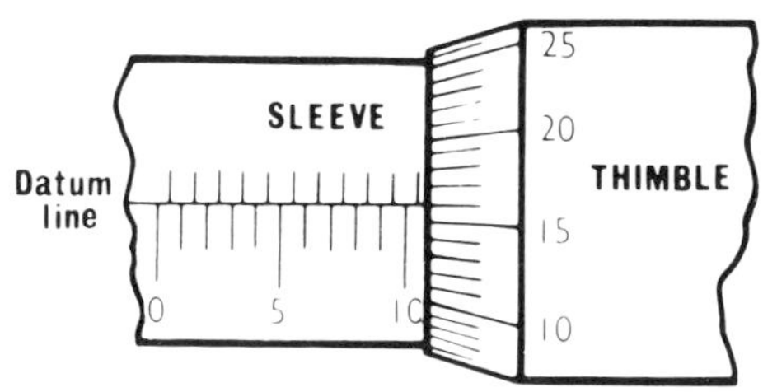

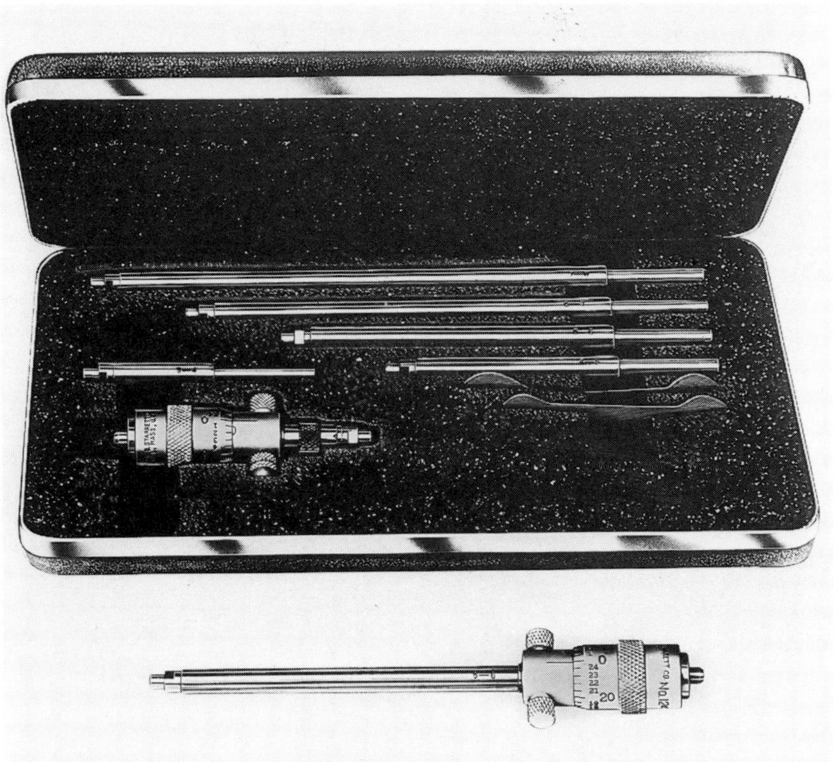

Left *A full set of inside micrometers for measuring cylinder bores, etc. A luxury for the amateur!* (L.S. Starrett & Co)

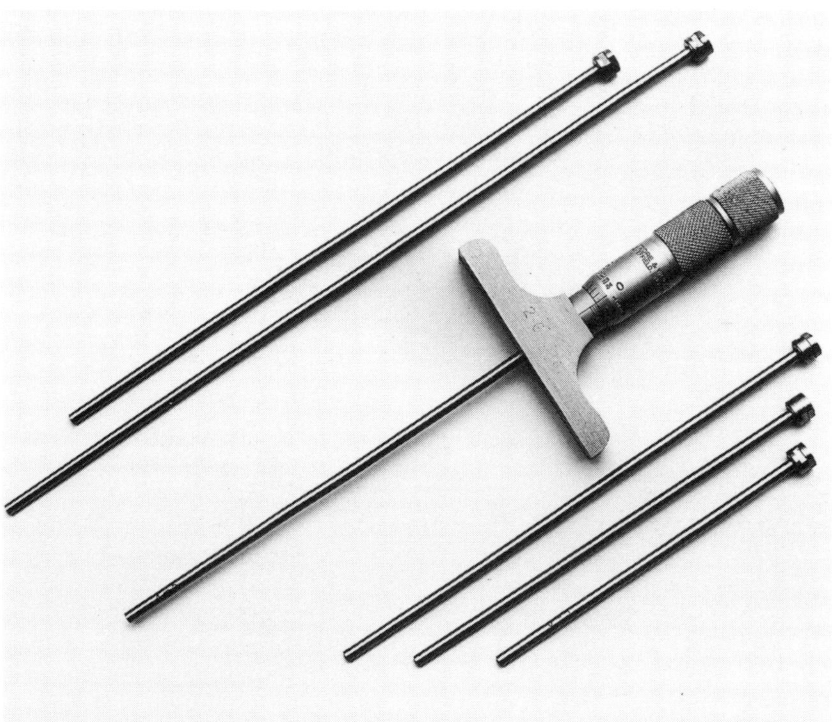

Below left *Micrometer depth gauge with extension bars.* (James Neill Ltd)

Above right *A vernier caliper.* (L.S. Starrett Ltd)

Fig. 11 **Right** *Vernier caliper scale.* (L.S. Starrett Ltd)

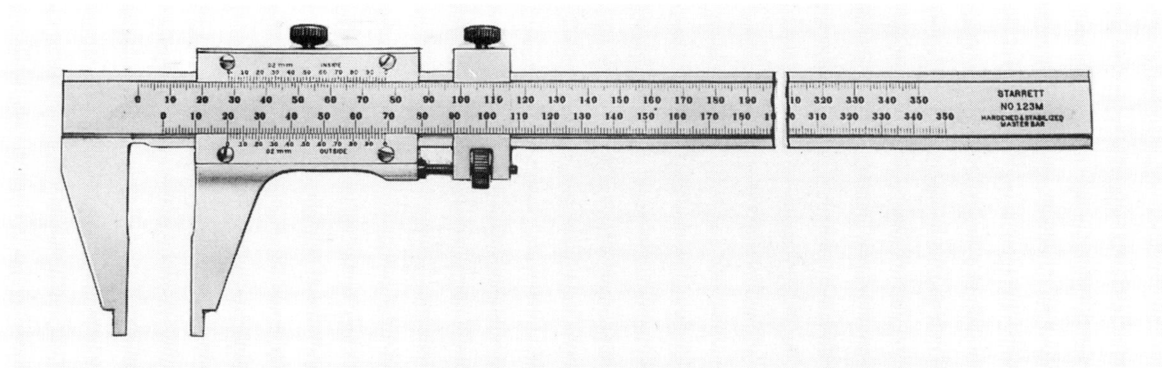

somewhere safe away from any possible damage.

Vernier callipers

This tool is capable of reading accurate measurements over a wider range than a micrometer. It is made in sizes from 6 in (150 mm) upwards and used for measuring internal and external diameters.

Care should be taken when using the callipers to make sure the jaws are not strained in any way, which would make them inaccurate. The fine adjustment screw should always be used to produce an accurate reading.

Reading the Vernier

Vernier scales make use of two scales that are slightly different set alongside each other. They can be used on any scale to enable fine measurements to be made, e.g. micrometer, protractor, etc. The vernier scale (see below) is read in the same way irrespective of the number of divisions on it.

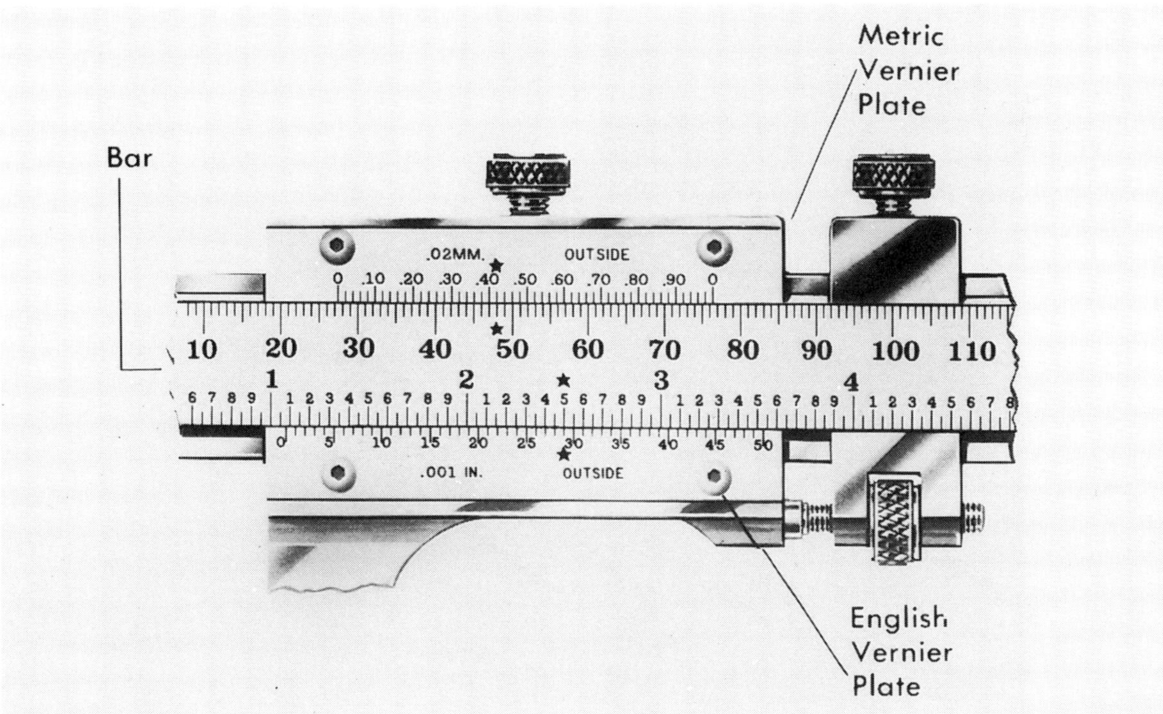

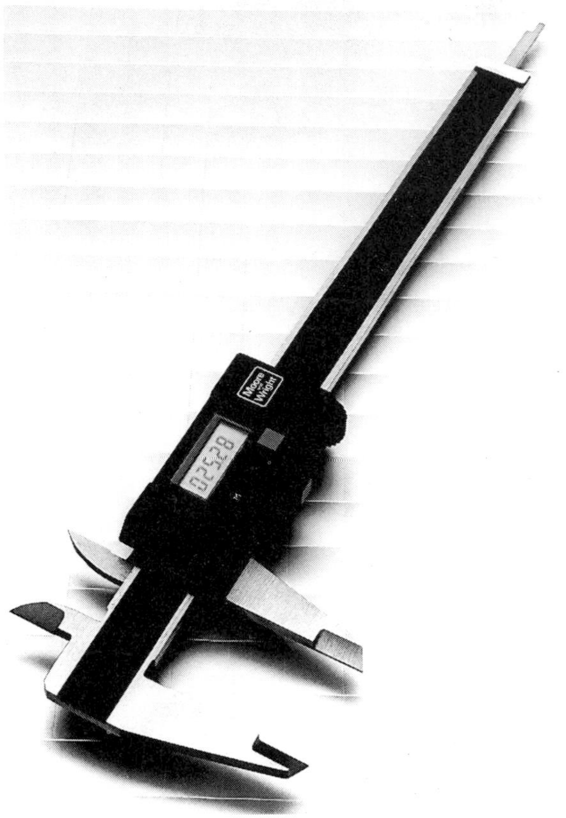

Imperial

1. Read the biggest whole number on the main scale.	1.000
2. Read the number of 1/10ths on the main scale before the 0 on the vernier scale.	0.000
3. Read the number of 1/20ths on the main scale before the 0 on the vernier scale.	0.050
4. Look for a line on the vernier scale that corresponds with any division on the main scale. The number on the vernier scale where this occurs is the 1/1000 ths. Shown by a star on the diagram.	0.029
TOTAL	1.079

Metric

1. Read the number of mm on the main scale before the 0 on the vernier scale.	27.00
2. Look for a line on the vernier scale that corresponds with any division on the main scale. This is the number of 0.2 mm's - 41 x .02 = 0.82 mm.	.82
TOTAL	27.82

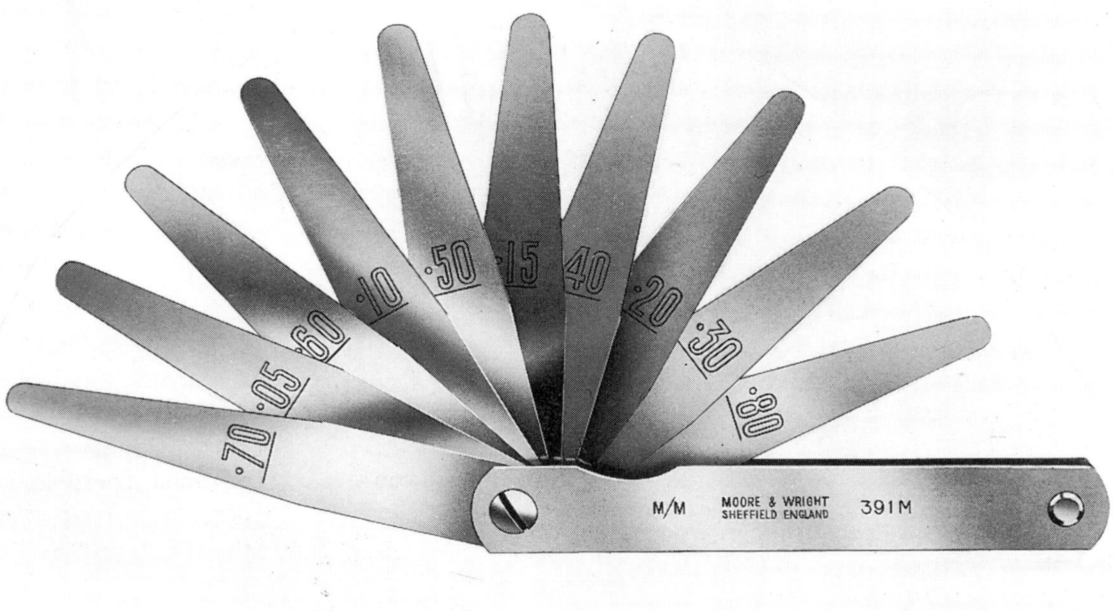

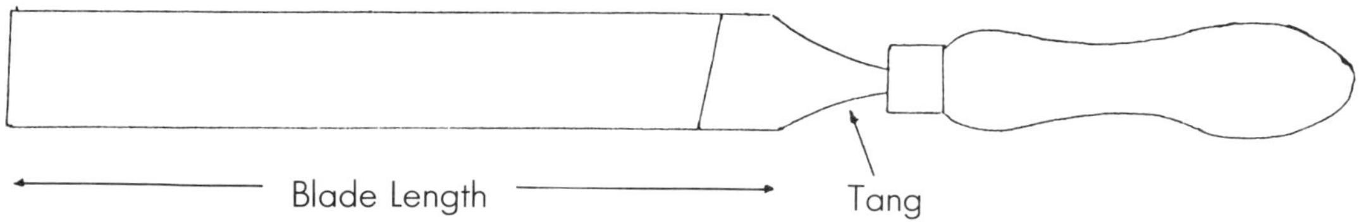

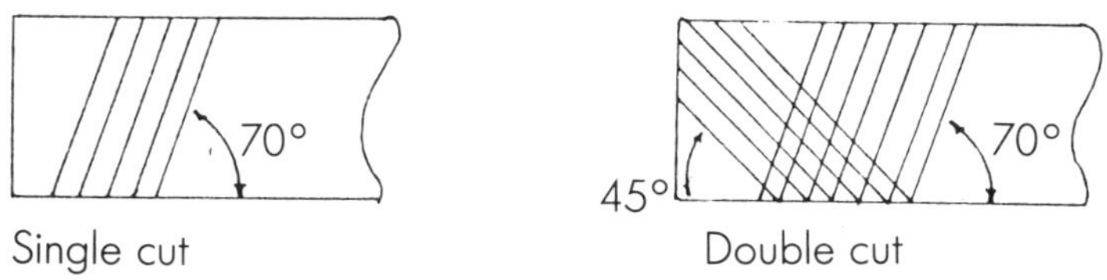

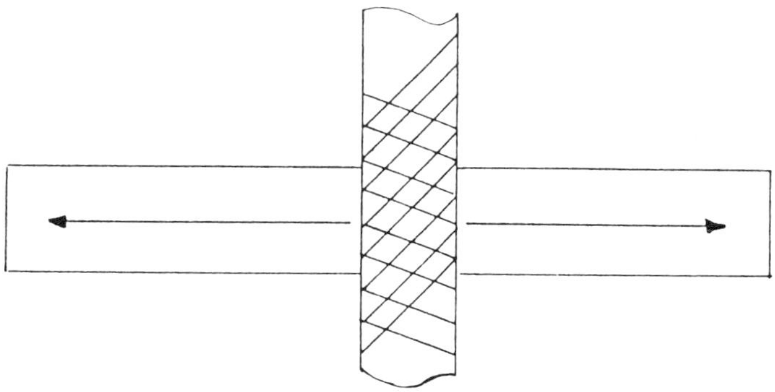

Left *Digital vernier showing the read-out. The 'ears' on the back of the vernier are for measuring internal sizes.* (James Neill Ltd)

Below left *Feeler gauges. These can be used for measuring small gaps, apart from valve adjustments.* (James Neill Ltd)

Fig. 12 **Above** *The basic file.*

Fig. 13 **Middle right** *Single and double cut files.*

Fig. 14 **Right** *Draw filing.*

When measuring internal sizes, the width of the jaws must be added to the measurement shown on the callipers. It is usual to find the dimensions of the jaw marked on them.

Cutting tools

Files

The file is probably the most commonly used cutting tool in any metalworker's workshop and comes in a great variety of shapes and sizes.

Files are made from high carbon steel, the blade is hardened and tempered while the tang is left soft for strength. The handle, usually of wood, should be a tight fit on the tang; split or loose handles should be replaced to prevent accidents.

The teeth on the file blade can be single or double cut. Single cut files have the teeth cut in parallel rows at 70° to one edge. Double cut files have one set of teeth at 70° to one edge and another set running across those at 45° to the other edge.

The grade of the file indicates the coarseness of the teeth, the grades being: rough, bastard, second cut, smooth, dead smooth. The number of teeth per 25 mm (1 in) of the blade varies not only with the grade but also in proportion to the length of the file. A 150 mm (6 in) second cut file will have more teeth per 25 mm than a 250 mm (10 in) second cut file.

Files are specified by length, cut and cross-section. Fig. 15 shows the main types of file and their uses. Riffler files are small double ended files; often the blade is curved for filing in awkward places where little material needs to be removed.

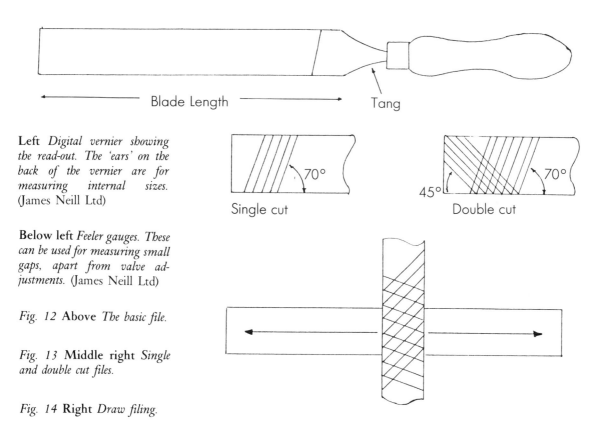

Metal to be filed should be held firmly in a vice with the surface you are filing horizontal, if possible, and as close to the vice jaws as practicable. Your weight should be balanced evenly on both feet, the left foot should be forward of the right if you are holding the handle of the file in the right hand or vice versa if you

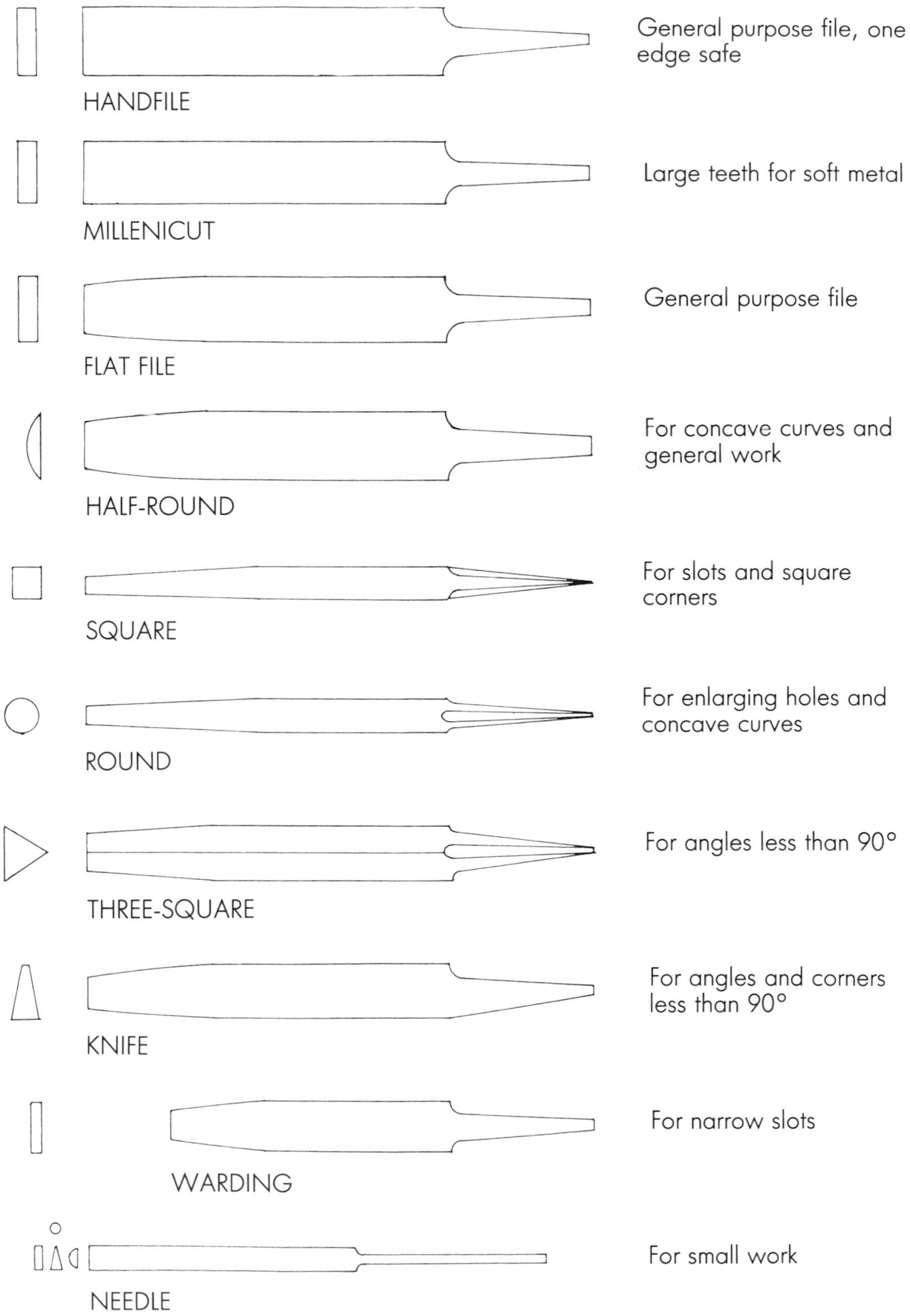
HANDFILE
General purpose file, one edge safe
MILLENICUT
Large teeth for soft metal
FLAT FILE
General purpose file
HALF-ROUND
For concave curves and general work
SQUARE
For slots and square corners
ROUND
For enlarging holes and concave curves
THREE-SQUARE
For angles less than 90°
KNIFE
For angles and corners less than 90°
WARDING
For narrow slots
NEEDLE
For small work

are left handed. The wrist of the hand holding the handle of the file should be kept rigid and the forearm horizontal and level with the work. The other hand should grasp the tip of the file, with the palm resting on top of the blade.

Apply pressure on the forward stroke, relieving it on the backward stroke since files only cut on the forward stroke. To produce a flat surface, the file should be used diagonally across the work, changing direction frequently; always use the full length of the file if possible. Once the surface has been filed to the line by cross-filing, a smooth, fine-grained surface can be produced by draw-filing. A smooth file should be used held at right angles to the length of the metal, the blade should be held with the hands as close together as possible to reduce wobble. The file is then pushed to and fro along the length of the metal until all the cross-filing marks have disappeared.

Files should be looked after carefully; if the teeth become 'pinned' or clogged with pieces of metal they should be cleaned out as the file will not cut efficiently and the work could become scored. File teeth are brittle and easily chipped, so files should be stored carefully and not thrown together in a box.

If you often work on brass, keep a new file to one side for this metal as worn files will not cut very well.

Hammers

Hammer heads are made from high carbon steel with the pein and face hardened and tempered; that is why it is dangerous to hit hammer heads together as the hardened surface can chip and fly anywhere.

Hammers are classified by weight from ¼ lb (0.1 kg) to 3 lb (1.35 kg). For general benchwork a hammer of about 1 lb (0.4 kg) is probably best; a heavy hammer can be unwieldy and tiring to use for any length of time.

Hammers used for beaten metalwork come in a variety of shapes and sizes depending on their purpose. The faces of these hammers should be smooth and polished because any imperfection will be transferred

Fig. 15 **Left** *Files and their uses.*

Right *Ball pein and cross pein hammers.*

Right *A selection of hammers for beaten metalwork. Left to right: combined blocking and planishing hammer, raising hammer, blocking hammer, planishing hammer.*

A selection of mallets. From left to right: tinmans, rawhide, bossing.

to the metal being beaten. For this reason they should never be used for anything other than beaten metalwork.

Mallets and soft faced hammers

Wooden mallets are used for sheet metalwork. Their heads are made of boxwood or Lignum Vitae and the shafts from cane. The tinmans mallet is used for bending sheet metal while the bossing mallet is used for the initial shaping of concave curves.

Rawhide mallets consist of a tightly rolled length of rawhide fixed to a shaft. This mallet gives a softer blow than the boxwood mallet.

Soft-faced hammers are available in a variety of materials: copper, brass, lead, rawhide or plastic. Often the faces are renewable once they become worn or misshapen. They are used where components must not be bruised, such as assembling tight-fitting components.

A useful soft hammer can be made by melting some lead in a suitable container. A steel tube for the handle can be stood in the middle of the container and the lead will set round it. It is important that the tube has holes drilled across the diameter so that the lead can flow into the handle and make a mechanical bond between the two. This will prevent the two parting company, usually at a most inappropriate time.

Metal cutting saws

Hacksaws normally have adjustable frames to accommodate blades of different lengths. The blade holders can be rotated in the frame so that the blade can be held at 90° to it, thus enabling a long cut to be taken or sawing in a confined space.

Hand hacksaw blades are 10 in (250 mm) or 12 in (300 mm) long and ½ in (13 mm) wide. The length is measured by the distance between the centres of the fixing holes. The teeth on the blade are set so that the teeth cut a wider slot than the thickness of the blade to prevent jamming.

Hacksaw blades come in a variety of types and are designated by the material they are made of and the number of teeth per inch (25 mm). This ranges from 18 to 32 teeth per inch (25 mm) and as a basic guide there should always be at least three teeth in contact with the metal. Thin material will therefore need a greater T.P.I. than a thicker one.

Junior hacksaws use blades 6 in (150 mm) long, with pinned ends. The tension on the blade is applied by either the spring of the frame or by tightening the handle. They are used for general purpose work where the standard hacksaw is too large.

Tension files are made from steel wire with spiral teeth which will cut in any direction. They can be used in a special frame or in a standard hacksaw frame, using special links to hold the blades. There are three grades of blade: fine, medium and coarse, each 200 mm long. They should be fitted in the frame with the coloured end of the blade at the handle end of the frame. Piercing saws use a very fine-toothed blade available in different teeth per inch (25 mm) which range from 32 to 80. They are used for cutting thin sheet material, where intricate shapes are needed.

A hacksaw and junior hacksaw.

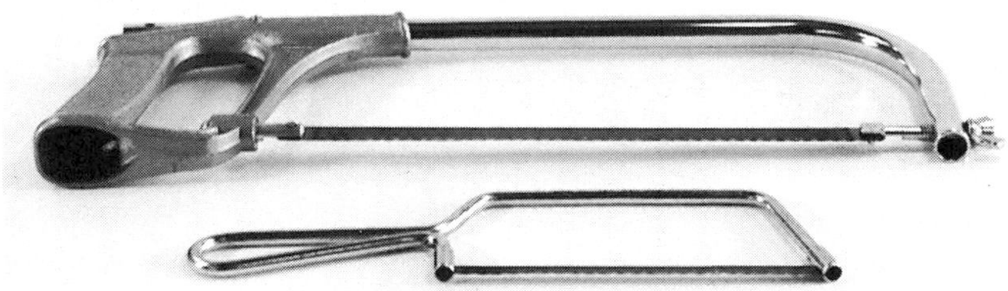

TEETH PER 25 mm	USES
14	LARGE SECTIONS OF SOFT MATERIALS.
18	SMALL SECTIONS OF SOFT MATERIALS, LARGE SECTIONS OF HARD MATERIALS – GENERAL PURPOSE SIZE.
24	SMALL SECTIONS OF HARD MATERIALS, e.g. 3–6 mm TUBE, SHEET AND SECTIONS.
32	VERY SMALL SECTIONS, e.g. LESS THAN 3 mm TUBE, SHEET AND SECTIONS.

Tooth sizes of hand hacksaw blades.

Hand scrapers. From left to right: half-round, flat, triangular.

Scrapers

These tools are made from high carbon steel. They are used where only a very small amount of metal needs to be removed. Normally, scrapers are not used until a surface has first been worked as accurately as possible by other methods.

There are three types of scraper: flat, half round and triangular. The flat scraper is used to make a surface flatter than can be achieved with a file. The half round scraper is for concave surfaces and is ideal for fitting bearings to a shaft. The triangular scraper is used for working into awkward corners where the use of the other shapes would be impossible. Old worn-out files can be converted into useful scrapers. They should be first annealed and ground to the shape required and the blade hardened and tempered to straw colour. The final edge is then achieved by grinding on an oil stone.

Cross-cut and flat chisel.

Cold chisels

Cold chisels are made from high carbon steel; the cutting edge is hardened and tempered, the head is left soft otherwise it would crack or splinter when hit with the hammer. There are four types of cold chisel and the size is denoted by the width of the cutting edge. When the head of the chisel begins to form a mushroom shape after a lot of use, this should be ground off. If it is left, there is the danger that pieces of it will fly off when being hit and cause an injury.

Cold chisels should be kept sharp but care must be taken when grinding not to overheat the cutting edge and draw the temper; this would soften the edge and leave it useless for cutting.

Flat chisels are the most commonly used for general cutting work.

Cross-cut chisels are used for cutting slots or grooves.

The half-round chisel is used for cutting circular grooves and the diamond point chisel for cleaning out corners.

CHAPTER 6

Drills and reamers

Drills are normally made of high speed steel (H.S.S.) and have either a parallel or taper shank. They can also be bought in different lengths: the standard length, known as 'jobbers drills', for general purpose work; long series drills, for deeper hole drilling; and stub drills, which are much shorter than jobbers drills, making them more robust.

One of the most important aspects of drilling is to ensure that the drill is sharpened correctly and is revolving at the right speed. A small bench grinder is essential for sharpening drills properly. The drill must be presented to the grinding wheel at the correct angle of 59° and then rotated so that the tip clearance is produced at the right angle. The diagrams in Fig. 17 show the effect of incorrect grinding.

A drill grinding attachment can be bought to fit on the grinding machine; this will give quick and accurate results. Attempting to drill holes with a blunt drill will normally result in an inaccurate hole, with the possibility of the drill overheating, losing its hardness and becoming useless for further work.

Before drilling a hole, the position should be carefully marked with a centre punch; this will locate the point of the drill and prevent it skidding over the surface of the metal. The work piece should be securely fixed to prevent vibration producing an irregular shaped hole. When drilling large diameter holes, it is best to use a small drill first to act as a pilot otherwise the chisel point of the large drill will have difficulty in penetrating the surface of the metal. The pilot drill should be just bigger than the chisel point of the large drill. Drilling small pieces of sheet metal calls for some care. It is essential to hold the work firmly with a hand vice or mole grips onto a piece of wood; if practicable, a G-cramp could be used instead. This is because there is always the possibility that the drill will 'catch' as it breaks through the underside of the sheet; this would be sufficient to pull the sheet from the grasp of bare hands and spin it round on the drill point to the obvious detriment of your hands. The drill catches because the point breaks through the metal before the full diameter of the drill has entered the sheet, a possibility that increases with the size of the drill.

If a lot of drilling in sheet metal is contemplated, the point angle of the drill should be modified to 140° as shown in Fig. 18.

To protect painted or polished surfaces it is a good idea to use a wide strip or strips of clear sticky tape to prevent the swarf from the drill scratching the surface.

When drilling plastic it is usual to use a slow helix drill for thermosetting plastic (a plastic that has been hardened by heat during manufacture) and a quick helix drill for a thermoplastic one (that softens when heated), but a normal one can be used with care. The work should be firmly clamped and the position of the hole carefully marked. The drill should not be forced through; thermo setts tend to chip and thermo plastics will soften and tend to grip the drill. Soluble oil or even plain water can help prevent this happening, while thermo setts are drilled dry.

Counterbores are used to make a recess for the head of a cheese head screw. The pilot which fits down the hole for the screw ensures that the two holes are concentric. They can also be used for spot facing, which is the machining of the rough surface of a casting to provide a flat seating for a washer.

If a counterbore is not available, then the end of a normal drill can be ground flat and used for the

Fig. 16 Twist drill nomenclature. (S.K.F. Dormer Ltd)

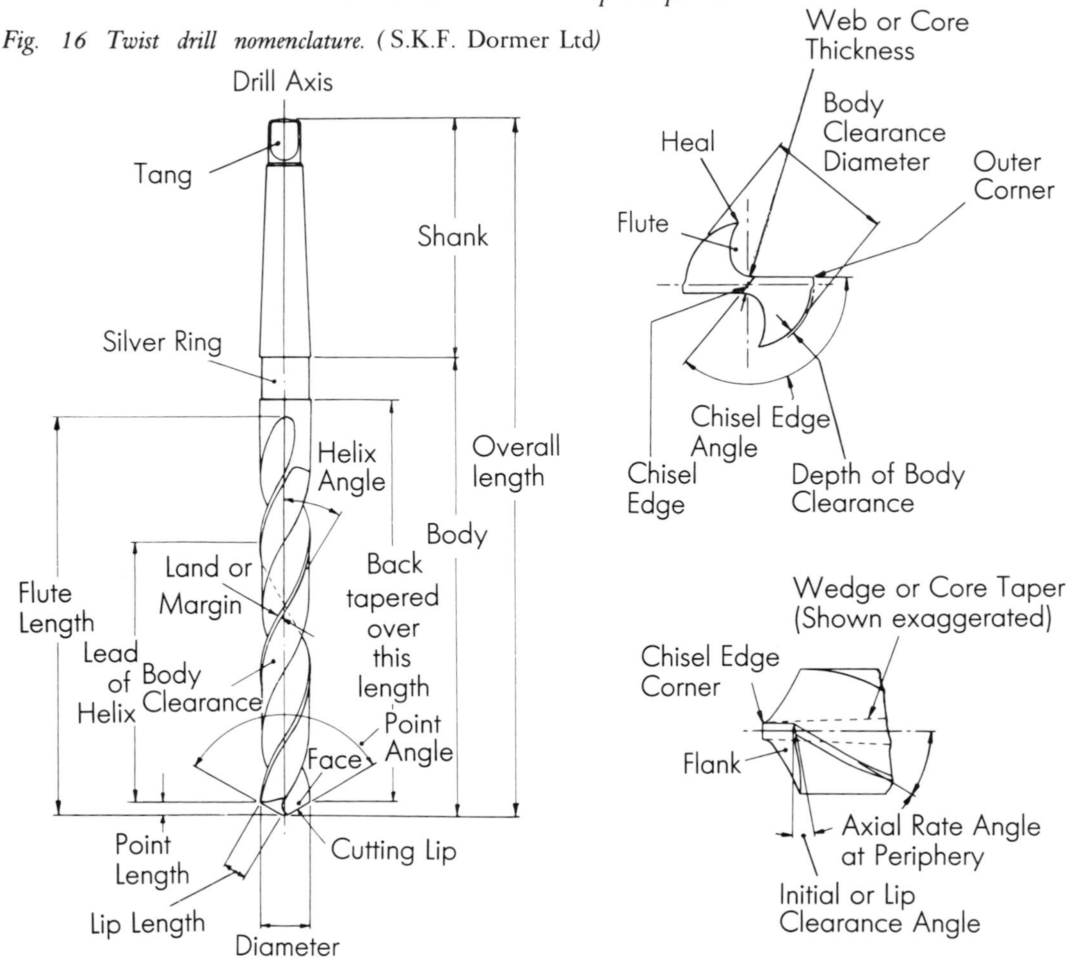

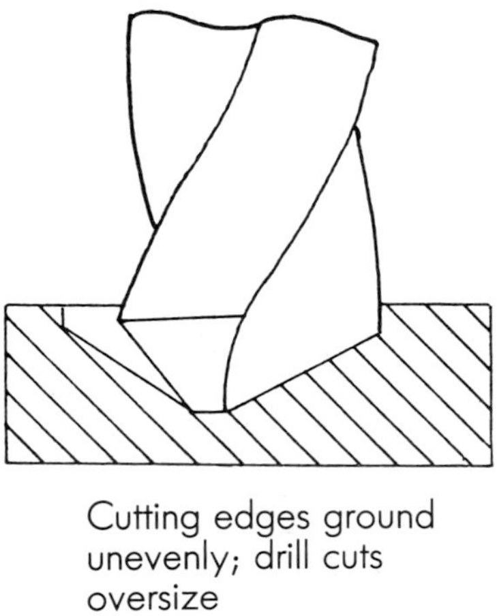

Fig. 17 The effects of incorrect grinding.

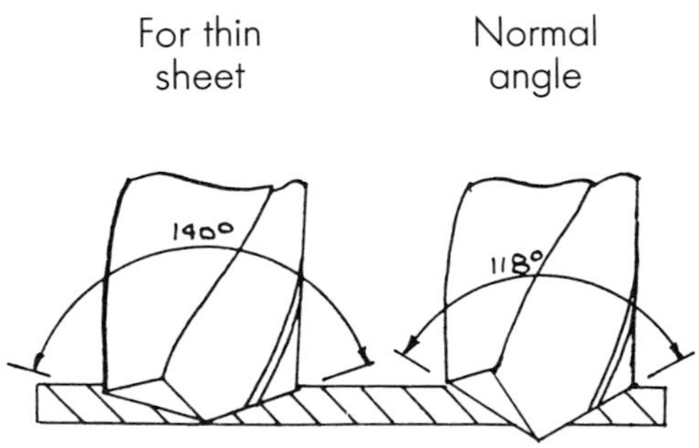

Fig. 18 Drill point modified for sheet metal.

Fig. 19 A flat drill.

operation. The main difficulty here is ensuring that the two holes are concentric.

Countersink drills are used to enlarge the beginning of a hole to take the head of a countersunk screw, and for countersinking prior to riveting. They are made with an included angle of 60° or 90°, the second being used for setting in screw heads. The rose countersink is usually made of high carbon steel and is used for soft materials such as wood. It is made with a square or round shank.

The machine countersink is made from high speed steel and will withstand use on harder materials. Care is needed in the use of both types because they cannot normally be sharpened. A centre drill is a twist drill and countersink combined. It is also known as a combination drill or slocombe drill. Its main use is for spotting the centre of a hole prior to drilling in the lathe or preparing the work for mounting on a centre. These drills range in size from 3 mm diameter upwards, and the angle of their cutting edges is 60° to correspond with the 60° angle of lathe centre. While they are mainly used for lathe work they can be used to start off a small diameter hole as their sturdy construction prevents the point wandering, which is always a possibility with small drills.

Tank cutters and hole saws are used for cutting out large washers or large holes in thin plate. The tank cutter is adjustable for size, the cutter being locked in position by means of a wing nut. Hole saws are not adjustable and, unlike the tank cutter, can be used

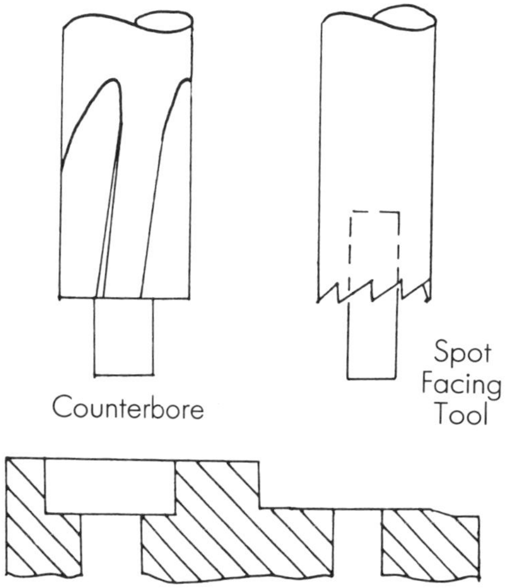

Fig. 20 A counterbore and spot facer.

in a power drill. Plenty of coolant is required when cutting through metal, though hole saws will cut through wood with ease. The more expensive types of hole saw will have blades of H.S.S. while the cheaper variety usually have low carbon steel blades which will dull quickly on hard material.

It is possible to make a flat drill as shown in Fig. 19 for one-off or awkward sizes. The drill should be made from silver steel and the end heated and forged

Taper shank and straight shank drills.

Left *Large drills with reduced shanks for use in ½" (13 mm) chucks.*

Below left *Machine vice for use with a drill stand or machine.*

Below *Hand vice for holding sheet metal while drilling*

Bottom left *Tank cutter. Held in a hand brace and used to cut holes in sheet metal.*

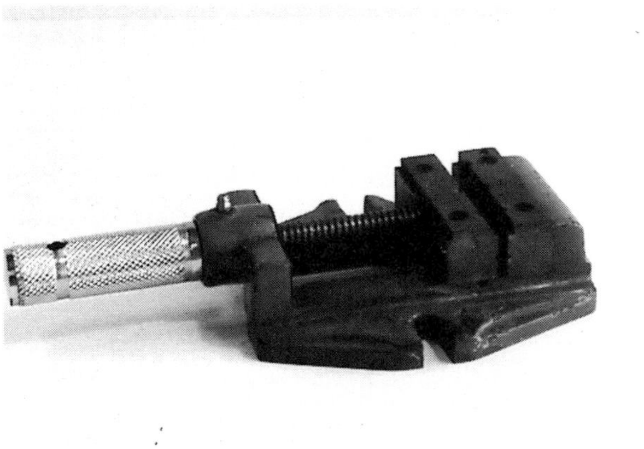

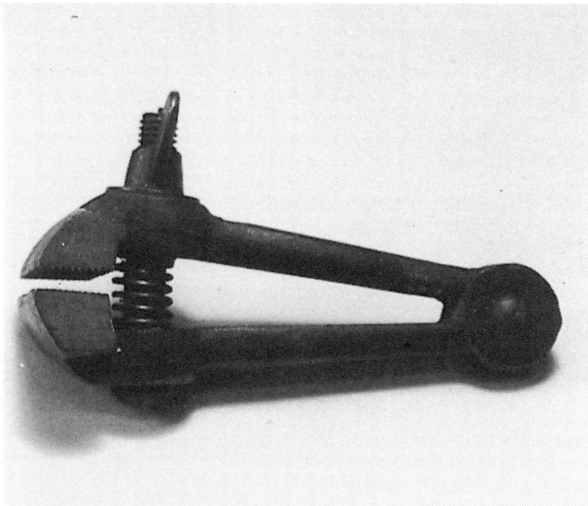

to shape. After filing or grinding to size, it should be hardened and then tempered to dark straw. This type of drill does have the disadvantage of scraping rather than cutting and has a greater tendency to wander, but it is better than none at all.

Flat bottomed drills and peg drills for counter boring can also be made from silver steel, hardened and tempered in the same way as the flat drill.

Reamers and reaming

Reamers are used to produce a smooth, true to size hole; they are made from high speed steel and should be looked after with care.

Right *Hole punch. Available in a variety of sizes. Square punches can be obtained.*

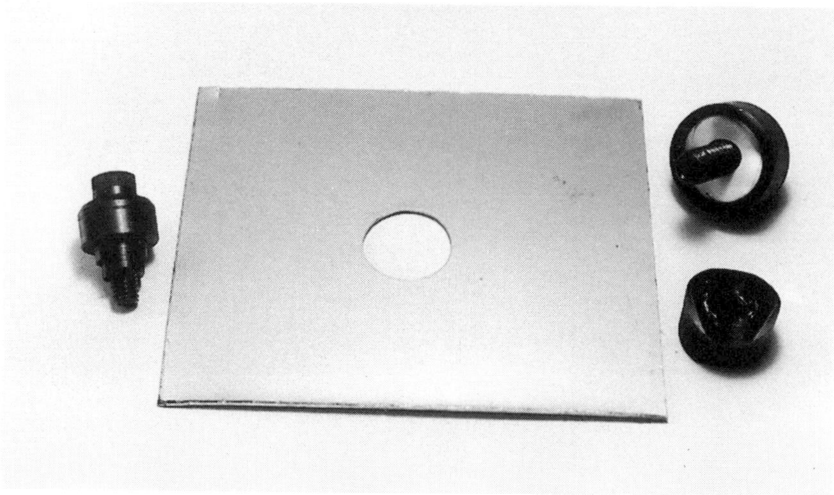

Below *Reamer nomenclature.* (S.K.F. Dormer Ltd)

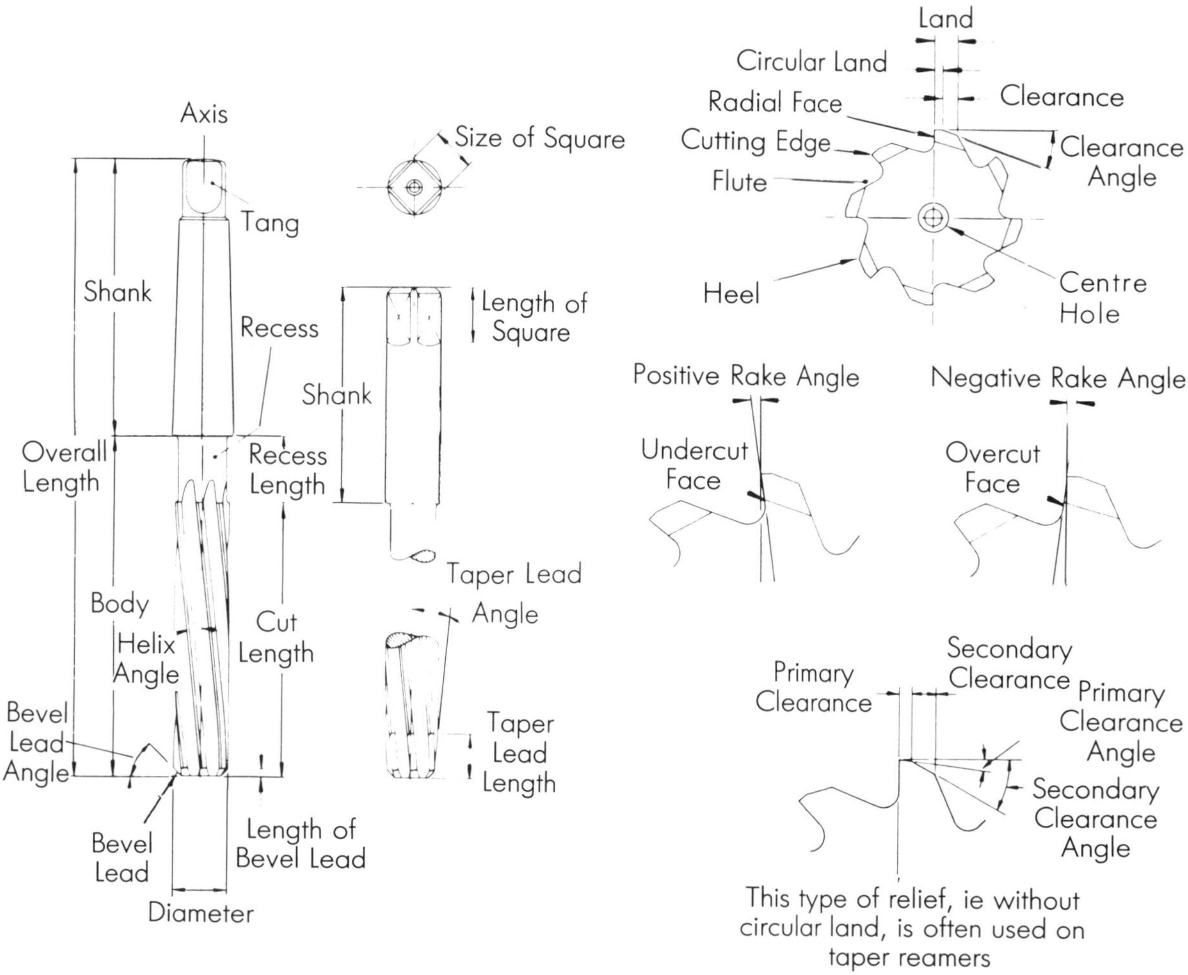

Taper shank reamers for use in a machine.

Parallel shank reamers for use by hand or in a machine.

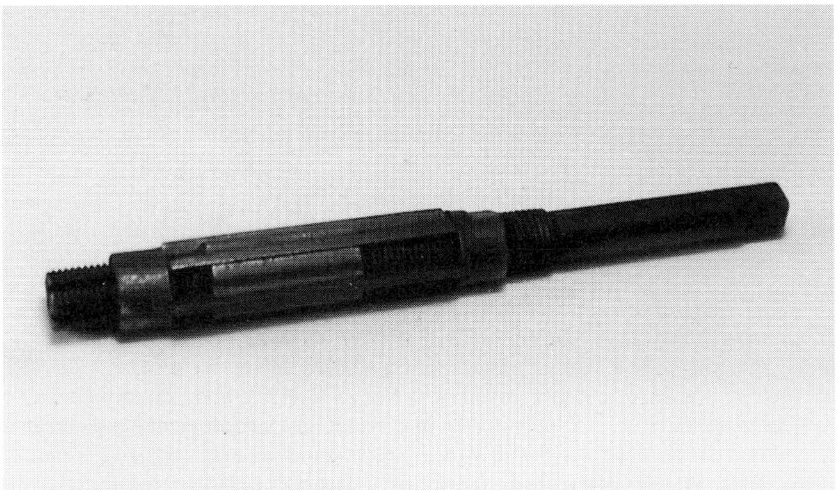

An adjustable reamer.

The drill used before reaming should be sharpened correctly to produce as smooth a hole as possible and the hole should be drilled carefully. A reamer will follow the drilled hole so it must be as accurate as possible. The size of the hole is important; the amount of metal left to be removed must not be too much or the reamer will have great difficulty in cutting. Too little metal left to remove will cause the reamer to rub rather than cut. Fig. 21 gives the amount of metal to be left for the reamer to cut.

Hand reamers are held in a tap wrench and should be used with some cutting lubricant such as 'Trefolex'. It is essential that the reamer is turned clockwise when cutting and while removing the tool from the hole. This prevents the cutting edges being dulled as they rub against the metal.

Machine and hand reamers can be used in a drilling machine providing the speed can be reduced to less than half that recommended for drilling.

Adjustable hand reamers have a two-fold advantage over normal reamers in that they can be adjusted slightly to match the hole being reamed to the shaft to give a perfect fit. They can also be dismantled and the blades sharpened easily.

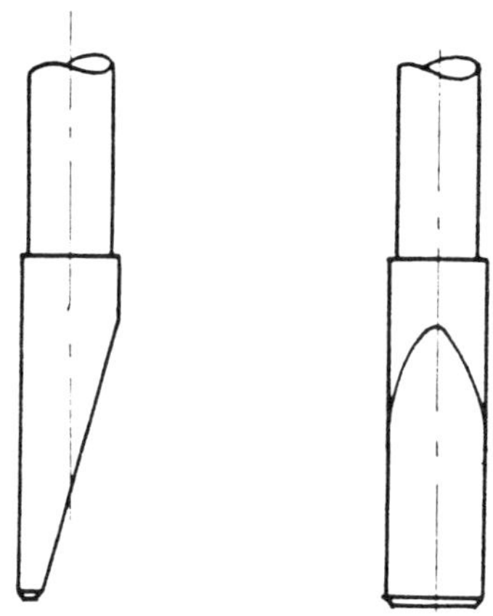

Fig. 22 Hand-made reamer.

If you have no reamer, then a usable one can be made from a piece of silver steel of the correct diameter. The cutting portion should be filed or machined to exactly half the diameter of the rod, angled at the end and a slight lead filed on. The tools should then be hardened and tempered to straw, see Fig. 22. Another name for this tool is a D-bit.

Fig. 21 Stock removal.

SIZE OF REAMED HOLE:	WHEN PRE-DRILLED	WHEN PRE-CORE DRILLED
UP TO 10 INCLUSIVE	0.30	0.20
OVER 10 TO 14 INCLUSIVE	0.40	0.25
OVER 14 TO 18 INCLUSIVE	0.50	0.25
OVER 18 TO 30 INCLUSIVE	0.50	0.30
OVER 30 TO 50 INCLUSIVE	1.00	0.40

SIZE OF REAMED HOLE:	WHEN PRE-DRILLED	WHEN PRE-CORE DRILLED
UP TO $\frac{3}{8}$″ INCLUSIVE	.010	.007
OVER $\frac{3}{8}$″ TO $\frac{3}{4}$″ INCLUSIVE	$\frac{1}{64}$	.010
OVER $\frac{3}{4}$″ TO $1\frac{1}{4}$″ INCLUSIVE	.020	.012
OVER $1\frac{1}{4}$″ TO 2″ INCLUSIVE	$\frac{1}{32}$	$\frac{1}{64}$

Overleaf *Imperial and metric equivalents. These tables include the old gauge or number drills and letter drills.* (S.K.F. Dormer Ltd)

Above are listed general approximations of the amount of stock to be removed by a reamer. The second column shows stock removal when a two flute drill only has been used. The third, when a core drill has been used as a pre-finishing tool. Figures are in millimetres, except those shown in inches, and the derived drill diameters are all stocked sizes for whole millimetre reamers. It is essential to understand that parallel machine reamers only cut on the bevel lead, that parallel hand reamers which have both bevel and taper leads, may cut on both, but in neither case do the lands on the body do any cutting. Generally standard reamers are made right hand cutting with left hand spiral flutes, the spiral angle and number of flutes being at the manufacturer's discretion.

Frac.	mm	Gauge	Inch
	.30		.0118
	.32		.0126
	.343	80	.0135
	.35		.0138
	.368	79	.0145
	.38		.0150
1/64	.397		.0156
	.40		.0157
	.406	78	.0160
	.42		.0165
	.45		.0177
	.457	77	.0180
	.48		.0189
	.50		.0197
	.508	76	.0200
	.52		.0205
	.533	75	.0210
	.55		.0217
	.572	74	.0225
	.58		.0228
	.60		.0236
	.610	73	.0240
	.62		.0244
	.635	72	.0250
	.65		.0256
	.660	71	.0260
	.68		.0268
	.70		.0276
	.711	70	.0280
	.72		.0283
	.742	69	.0292
	.75		.0295
	.78		.0307
	.787	68	.0310
1/32	.794		.0312
	.80		.0315
	.813	67	.0320
	.82		.0323
	.838	66	.0330
	.85		0335
	.88		.0346
	.889	65	.0350
	.90		.0354
	.914	64	.0360
	.92		.0362
	.940	63	.0370
	.95		.0374
	.965	62	.0380
	.98		.0386
	.991	61	.0390
	1.00		.0394
	1.016	60	.0400
	1.041	59	.0410
	1.05		.0413
	1.067	58	.0420
	1.092	57	.0430
	1.10		.0433
	1.15		.0453
	1.181	56	.0465
3/64	1.191		.0469
	1.20		.0472
	1.25		.0492
	1.30		.0512
	1.321	55	.0520
	1.35		.0531
	1.397	54	.0550
	1.40		.0551

Frac.	mm	Gauge	Inch
	1.45		.0571
	1.50		.0591
	1.511	53	.0595
	1.55		.0610
1/16	1.588		.0625
	1.60		.0630
	1.613	52	.0635
	1.65		.0650
	1.70		.0669
	1.702	51	.0670
	1.75		.0689
	1.778	50	.0700
	1.80		.0709
	1.85		.0728
	1.854	49	.0730
	1.90		.0748
	1.930	48	.0760
	1.95		.0768
5/64	1.984		.0781
	1.994	47	.0785
	2.00		.0787
	2.05		.0807
	2.057	46	.0810
	2.083	45	.0820
	2.10		.0827
	2.15		.0846
	2.184	44	.0860
	2.20		.0866
	2.25		.0886
	2.261	43	.0890
	2.30		.0906
	2.35		.0925
	2.375	42	.0935
3/32	2.381		.0938
	2.40		.0945
	2.438	41	.0960
	2.45		.0965
	2.489	40	.0980
	2.50		.0984
	2.527	39	.0995
	2.55		.1004
	2.578	38	.1015
	2.60		.1024
	2.642	37	.1040
	2.65		.1043
	2.70		.1063
	2.705	36	.1065
	2.75		.1083
7/64	2.778		.1094
	2.794	35	.1100
	2.80		.1102
	2.819	34	.1110
	2.85		.1122
	2.870	33	.1130
	2.90		.1142
	2.946	32	.1160
	2.95		.1161
	3.00		.1181
	3.048	31	.1200
	3.10		.1220
1/8	3.175		.1250
	3.20		.1260
	3.25		.1280
	3.264	30	.1285
	3.30		.1299
	3.40		.1339

Frac.	mm	Gauge	Inch
	3.454	29	.1360
	3.50		.1378
	3.569	28	.1405
9/64	3.572		.1406
	3.60		.1417
	3.658	27	1440
	3.70		.1457
	3.734	26	.1470
	3.75		.1476
	3.797	25	.1495
	3.80		.1496
	3.861	24	.1520
	3.90		.1535
	3.912	23	.1540
5/32	3.969		.1562
	3.988	22	.1570
	4.00		.1575
	4.039	21	.1590
	4.089	20	.1610
	4.10		.1614
	4.20		.1654
	4.216	19	.1660
	4.25		.1673
	4.30		.1693
	4.305	18	.1695
11/64	4.366		.1719
	4.394	17	.1730
	4.40		.1732
	4.496	16	.1770
	4.50		.1772
	4.572	15	.1800
	4.60		.1811
	4.623	14	.1820
	4.70	13	.1850
	4.75		.1870
3/16	4.762		.1875
	4.80	12	.1890
	4.851	11	.1910
	4.90		.1929
	4.915	10	.1935
	4.978	9	.1960
	5.00		.1969
	5.055	8	.1990
	5.10		.2008
	5.105	7	.2010
13/64	5.159		.2031
	5.182	6	.2040
	5.20		.2047
	5.220	5	.2055
	5.25		.2067
	5.30		.2087
	5.309	4	.2090
	5.40		.2126
	5.410	3	.2130
	5.50		.2165
7/32	5.556		.2188
	5.60		.2205
	5.613	2	.2210
	5.70		.2244
	5.75		.2264
	5.791	1	.2280
	5.80		.2283
	5.90		.2323
	5.944	A	.2340
15/64	5.953		.2344
	6.00		.2362

Frac.	mm	Letter	Inch
	6.045	B	.2380
	6.10		.2402
	6.147	C	.2420
	6.20		.2441
	6.248	D	2460
	6.25		.2461
	6.30		.2480
1/4	6.350	E	.2500
	6.40		.2520
	6.50		.2559
	6.528	F	.2570
	6.60		.2598
	6.629	G	.2610
	6.70		.2638
17/64	6.747		.2656
	6.75		.2657
	6.756	H	.2660
	6.80		.2677
	6.90		.2717
	6.909	I	.2720
	7.00		.2756
	7.036	J	.2770
	7.10		.2795
	7.137	K	.2810
9/32	7.144		.2812
	7.20		.2835
	7.25		.2854
	7.30		.2874
	7.366	L	.2900
	7.40		.2913
	7.493	M	.2950
	7.50		.2953
19/64	7.541		.2969
	7.60		.2992
	7.671	N	.3020
	7.70		.3031
	7.75		.3051
	7.80		.3071
	7.90		.3110
5/16	7.938		.3125
	8.00		.3150
	8.026	O	.3160
	8.10		.3189
	8.20		.3228
	8.204	P	.3230
	8.25		.3248
	8.30		.3268
21/64	8.334		.3281
	8.40		.3307
	8.433	Q	.3320
	8.50		.3346
	8.60		.3386
	8.611	R	.3390
	8.70		.3425
11/32	8.731		.3438
	8.75		.3445
	8.80		.3465
	8.839	S	.3480
	8.90		.3504
	9.00		.3543
	9.093	T	.3580
	9.10		.3583
23/64	9.128		.3594
	9.20		.3622
	9.25		.3642
	9.30		.3661

Frac.	mm	Letter	Inch	Frac.	mm	Inch
	9.347	U	.3680		13.70	.5394
	9.40		.3701		13.75	.5413
	9.50		.3740		13.80	.5433
3/8	9.525		.3750	35/64	13.891	.5469
	9.576	V	.3770		13.90	.5472
	9.60		.3780		14.00	.5512
	9.70		.3819		14.25	.5610
	9.75		.3839	9/16	14.288	.5625
	9.80		.3858		14.50	.5709
	9.804	W	.3860	37/64	14.684	5781
	9.90		.3898		14.75	.5807
25/64	9.922		.3906		15.00	.5906
	10.00		.3937	19/32	15.081	.5938
	10.084	X	.3970		15.25	.6004
	10.10		.3976	39/64	15.478	.6094
	10.20		.4016		15.50	.6120
	10.25		.4035		15.75	.6201
	10.262	Y	.4040	5/8	15.875	.6250
	10.30		.4055		16.00	.6299
13/32	10.319		.4062		16.25	.6398
	10.40		.4094	41/64	16.272	,6406
	10.490	Z	.4130		16.50	.6496
	10.50		.4134	21/32	16.669	.6562
	10.60		.4173		16.75	.6594
	10.70		.4213		17.00	.6693
27/64	10.716		.4219	43/64	17.066	.6719
	10.75		.4232		17.25	.6791
	10.80		.4252	11/16	17.462	.6875
	10.90		.4291		17.50	.6890
	11.00		.4331		17.75	.6988
	11.10		.4370	45/64	17.859	.7031
7/16	11.112		.4375		18.00	.7087
	11.20		.4409		18.25	.7185
	11.25		.4429	23/32	18.256	.7188
	11.30		.4449		18.50	.7283
	11.40		.4488	47/64	18.653	.7344
	11.50		.4528		18.75	.7382
20/64	11.509		.4531		19.00	.7480
	11.60		.4567	3/4	19.050	.7500
	11.70		.4606		19.25	.7579
	11.75		.4626	49/64	19.447	.7656
	11.80		.4646		19.50	.7677
	11.90		.4685		19.75	.7776
15/32	11.906		.4688	25/32	19.844	.7812
	12.00		.4724		20.00	.7874
	12.10		.4764	51/64	20.241	.7969
	12.20		.4803		20.25	.7972
	12.25		.4823		20.422	.8040
	12.30		.4843		20.50	.8071
31/64	12.303		.4844	13/16	20.638	.8125
	12.40		.4882		20.75	.8619
	12.50		.4921		21.00	.8268
	12.60		.4961	53/64	21.034	.8281
1/2	12.70		.5000		21.25	.8366
	12.75		.5020	27/32	21.431	.8438
	12.80		.5039		21.50	.3465
	12.90		.5079		21.75	.8563
	13.00		.5118	55/64	21.828	.8594
33/64	13.097		.5156		22.00	.8661
	13.10		.5157	7/8	22.225	.8750
	13.20		.5197		22.25	.8760
	13.25		.5217		22.50	.8858
	13.30		.5236	57/64	22.622	.8906
	13.40		.5276		22.75	.8957
17/32	13.494		.5312		23.00	.9055
	13.50		.5315	29/32	23.019	.9062
	13.60		.5354		23.25	.9154

Frac.	mm	Inch	Frac.	mm	Inch
59/64	23.416	.9219		34.50	1.3583
	23.50	.9252	1, 23/64	34.528	1.3594
	23.75	.9350	1, 3/8	34.925	1.3750
15/16	23.812	.9375		35.00	1.3780
	24.00	.9449	1,25/64	35.322	1.3906
61/64	24.209	.9531		35.50	1.3976
	24.25	.9547	1,13/32	35.719	1.4062
	24.50	.9646		36.00	1.4173
31/32	24.606	.9688	1,27/64	36.116	1.4219
	24.75	.9744		36.50	1.4370
	25.00	.9843	1, 7/16	36.512	1.4375
63/64	25.003	.9844	1,29/64	36.909	1.4531
	25.25	.9941		37.00	1.4567
1	25.400	1.0000	1,15/32	37.306	1.4688
	25.50	1.0039		37.50	1.4764
	25.75	1.0138	1,31/64	37.703	1.4844
1, 1/64	25.797	1.0156		38.00	1.4961
	26.00	1.0236	1, 1/2	38.100	1.5000
1, 1/32	26.194	1.0312	1,33/64	38.497	1.5156
	26.25	1.0335		38.50	1.5157
	26.50	1.0433	1,17/32	38.894	1.5312
1, 3/64	26.591	1.0469		39.00	1.5354
	26.75	1.0531	1,35/64	39.291	1.5469
1, 1/16	26.988	1.0625		39.50	1.5551
	27.00	1.0630	1, 9/16	39.688	1.5625
	27.25	1.0728		40.00	1.5748
1, 5/64	27.384	1.0781	1,37/64	40.084	1.5781
	27.50	1.0827	1,19/32	40.481	1.5938
	27.75	1.0925		40.50	1.5945
1, 3/32	27.781	1.0938	1,39/64	40.878	1.6094
	28.00	1.1024		41.00	1.6142
1, 7/64	28.178	1.1094	1, 5/8	41.275	1.6250
	28.25	1.1122		41.50	1.6339
	28.50	1.1220	1,41/64	41.672	1.6406
1, 1/8	28.575	1.1250		42.00	1.6535
	28.75	1.1319	1,21/32	42.069	1.6562
1, 9/64	28.972	1.1406	1,43/64	42.466	1.6719
	29.00	1.1417		42.50	1.6732
	29.25	1.1516	1,11/16	42.862	1.6875
1, 5/32	29.369	1.1562		43.00	1.6929
	29.50	1.1614	1,45/64	43.259	1.7031
	29.75	1.1713		43.50	1.7126
1,11/64	29.766	1.1719	1,23/32	43.656	1.7188
	30.00	1.1811		44.00	1.7323
1, 3/16	30.162	1.1875	1,47/64	44.053	1.7344
	30.25	1.1909	1, 3/4	44.450	1.7500
	30.50	1.2008		44.50	1.7520
1,13/64	30.559	1.2031	1,49/64	44.847	1.7656
	30.75	1.2106		45.00	1.7717
1, 7/32	30.956	1.2188	1,25/32	45.244	1.7812
	31.00	1.2205		45.50	1.7913
	31.25	1.2303	1,51/64	45.641	1.7969
1,15/64	31.353	1.2344		46.00	1.8110
	31.50	1.2402	1,13/16	46.038	1.8125
1, 1/4	31.75	1.2500	1,53/64	46.434	1.8281
	32.00	1.2598		46.50	1.8307
1,17/64	32.147	1.2656	1,27/32	46.831	1.8438
	32.50	1.2795		47.00	1.8504
1, 9/32	32.544	1.2812	1,55/64	47.228	1.8594
	32.766	1.2900		47.50	1.8701
1,19/64	32.941	1.2969	1, 7/8	47.625	1.8750
	33.00	1.2992		48.00	1.8898
1.5/16	33.338	1.3125	1,57/64	48.022	1.8906
	33.50	1.3189	1,29/32	48.419	1.9062
1,21/64	33.734	1.3281		48.50	1.9094
	34.00	1.3386	1,59/64	48.816	1.9219
1, 11/32	34.131	1.3438		49.00	1.9291

Frac.	mm	Inch	Frac.	mm	Inch
1,15/16	49.212	1.9375	2, 3/8	60.325	2.3750
	49.50	1.9488		61.00	2.4016
1,61/64	49.609	1.9531	2,13/32	61.119	2.4062
	50.00	1.9685	2, 7/16	61.912	2.4375
1,31/32	50.006	1.9688		62.00	2.4409
1,63/64	50.403	1.9844	2,15/32	62.706	2.4688
	50.50	1.9882		63.00	2.4803
2	50.800	2.0000	2, 1/2	63.500	2.5000
	51.000	2.0079		64.00	2.5197
2, 1/32	51.594	2.0312	2,17/32	64.294	2.5312
	52.00	2.0472		65.00	2.5591
2, 1/16	52.388	2.0625	2, 9/16	65.088	2.5625
	53.00	2.0866	2,19/32	65.881	2.5938
2, 3/32	53.181	2.0938		66.00	2.5984
2, 1/8	53.975	2.1250	2, 5/8	66.675	2.6250
	54.00	2.1260		67.00	2.6378
2, 5/32	54.769	2.1562	2,21/32	67.469	2.6562
	55.00	2.1654		68.00	2.6772
2, 3/16	55.562	2.1875	2,11/16	68.262	2.6875
	56.000	2.2047		69.00	2.7165
2, 7/32	56.356	2.2188	2,23/32	69.056	2.7188
	57.00	2.2441	2, 3/4	69.850	2.7500
2, 1/4	57.150	2.2500		70.00	2.7559
2, 9/32	57.944	2.2812	2,25/32	70.644	2.7812
	58.00	2.2835		71.00	·2.7953
2, 5/16	58.738	2.3125	2,13/16	71.438	2.8125
	59.00	2.3228		72.00	2.8346
2, 11/32	59.531	2.3438	2,27/32	72.231	2.8438
	60.00	2.3622		73.00	2.8740

Frac.	mm	Inch	Frac.	mm	Inch
2, 7/8	73.025	2.8750	3, 3/8	85.725	3.3750
2,29/32	73.819	2.9062		86.00	3.3858
	74.00	2.9134	3,13/32	86.519	3.4062
2,15/16	74.612	2.9375		87.00	3.4252
	75.00	2.9528	3, 7/16	87.312	3.4375
2,31/32	75.406	2.9688		88.00	3.4646
	76.00	2.9921	3,15/32	88.106	3.4688
3	76.200	3.0000	3, 1/2	88.900	3.5000
3, 1/32	76.994	3.0312		89.00	3.5039
	77.00	3.0315		90.00	3.5433
3, 1/16	77.788	3.0625	3, 9/16	90.488	3.5625
	78.00	3.0709		91.00	3.5827
3, 3/32	78.581	3.0938		92.00	3.6220
	79.00	3.1102	3, 5/8	92.075	3.6250
3, 1/8	79.375	3.1250		93.00	3.6614
	80.00	3.1496	3,11/16	93.662	3.6875
3, 5/32	80.169	3.1562		94.00	3.7008
3, 3/16	80.962	3.1875		95.00	3.7402
	81.00	3.1890	3, 3/4	95.250	3.7500
3, 7/32	81.756	3.2188		96.00	3.7795
	82.00	3.2283	3,13/16	96.838	3.8125
3, 1/4	82.550	3.2500		97.00	3.8189
	83.00	3.2677		98.00	3.8583
3, 9/32	83.344	3.2812	3, 7/8	98.425	3.8750
	84.00	3.3071		99.00	3.8976
3, 5/16	84.138	3.3125		100.00	3.9370
3,11/32	84.931	3.3438	3,15/16	100.012	3.9375
	85.00	3.3465	4	101.600	4.0000

CHAPTER 7

Screw threads and screwcutting

The type of screwthreads fitted to your vehicle will depend on its age and nationality. Most British cars produced between the wars and for a few years after were fitted with British Standard Fine (B.S.F.) or British Standard Whitworth (B.S.W.). The B.S.F. thread was used where vibration was likely to occur; the B.S.W. thread was used in aluminium or cast iron where its coarser pitch provided greater strength.

Continental cars used the metric system as did some British cars, notably the Bullnose Morris, M.G. engines (up to 1955) and vintage Sunbeams.

After the Second World War, the United Kingdom, Canada, and the United States agreed on a common thread called the Unified thread, divided into Unified National Fine (U.N.F.) and Unified National Coarse (U.N.C.). More recently the I.S.O. metric thread has been introduced into some British cars, mainly by manufacturers who have production centres in both Britain and Europe producing models with many identical components.

If you are at all unsure what threads are fitted to your car or on parts that may have been replaced by non-standard items, you will need a micrometer or vernier callipers and a screw pitch gauge, see illustration. First measure the outside diameter of the

Screw pitch gauge for checking screw threads. (James Neill Ltd)

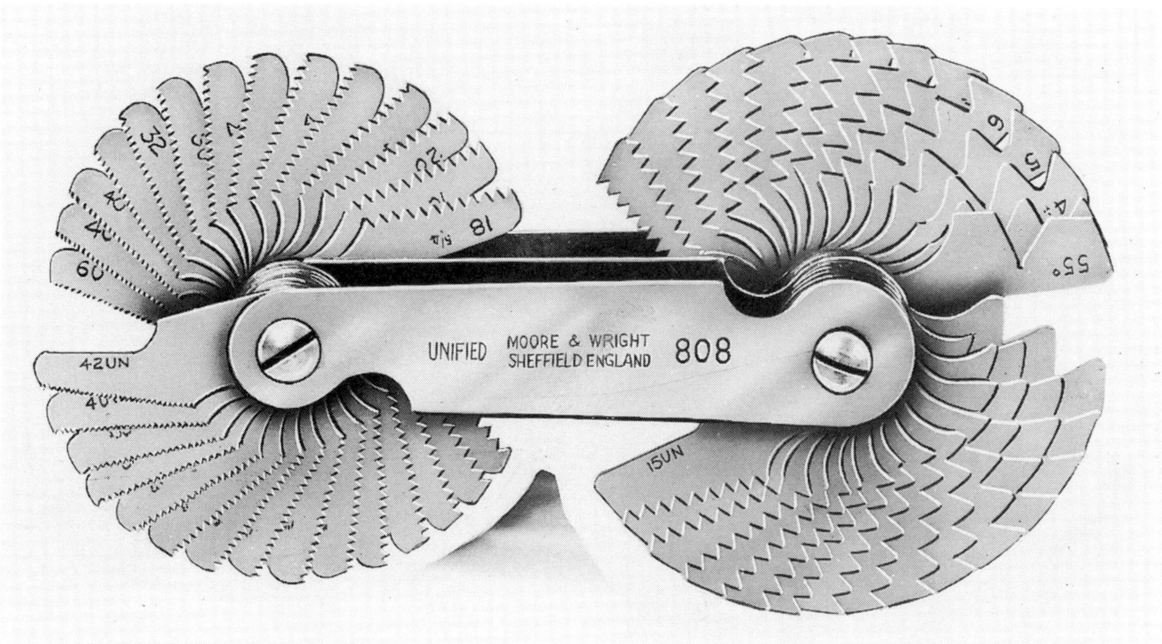

thread; this will tell you whether it is an imperial size ¼ in, ⅜ in, etc, or metric size 6 mm, 8 mm, etc. Then select the blade from the screw pitch gauge which corresponds with this.

If, for example, the outside diameter was ¼ in (.250) it could be ¼ in B.S.F. ¼ in B.S.W. ¼ in U.N.F. or ¼ in U.N.C. Each of these threads has a different pitch, and also B.S.F. and B.S.W. have a 55° thread form while U.N.F. and U.N.C. have a 60° thread form. Try each of the blades in turn until one matches exactly with the thread form of the bolt. Though this sounds complicated it is surprising how quickly you will be able to distinguish visually the different pitches, which will cut down on the amount of checking needed.

Always take great care that the nuts and bolts you use match each other, a 10 mm nut will turn onto a ⅜ B.S.W. bolt easily and will tighten fairly well, but the difference in size and the angles of the thread, 55° for the B.S.W. and 60° for the metric, will mean that the strength of the resulting combination will be far less than if the correct nut had been used and the threads could fail with possibly disastrous results. Metric nuts and bolts can be identified by two circles stamped into the face of the nut and the head of the bolt. Fig.23; shows a diagram of a thread and the names of the various parts.

To cut an internal thread the first thing to do is to drill a hole slightly larger than the core diameter of the thread. The correct size can be found by referring to the tables at the end of this chapter; this will give the correct depth of thread.

If the correct size of drill is not available, it is possible to use one very slightly larger, up to 0.1 mm or 0.004 on sizes between ¼ in (6 mm) and ½ in (12 mm) diameter. Any larger will reduce the strength of the thread considerably. On no account should a smaller size drill be used; this will make the thread difficult to cut and may cause the tap to bind and perhaps break off in the hole.

The tool used to cut an internal thread is called a tap. There are three of each size in a set: they are the taper tap, which is used first, the second or intermediate tap, used as its name implies second, and the plug or bottoming tap which is used last, mainly in blind holes where the thread must reach to the bottom of the hole (see Fig.24). They are made of either high speed or carbon steel. The taper tap should be held in the tap wrench and a small amount of lubricant applied to the cutting edges. There are special cutting compounds that can be bought but any oil or grease will be better than none for steel. Paraffin

Fig. 23 Thread details.

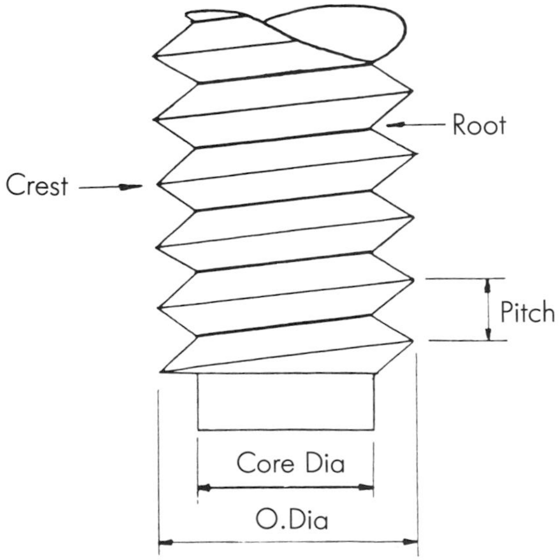

Fig. 24 Cross sectional view of a set of taps.

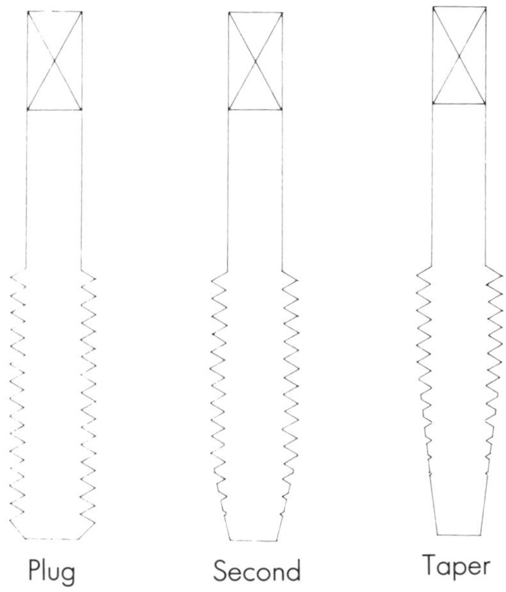

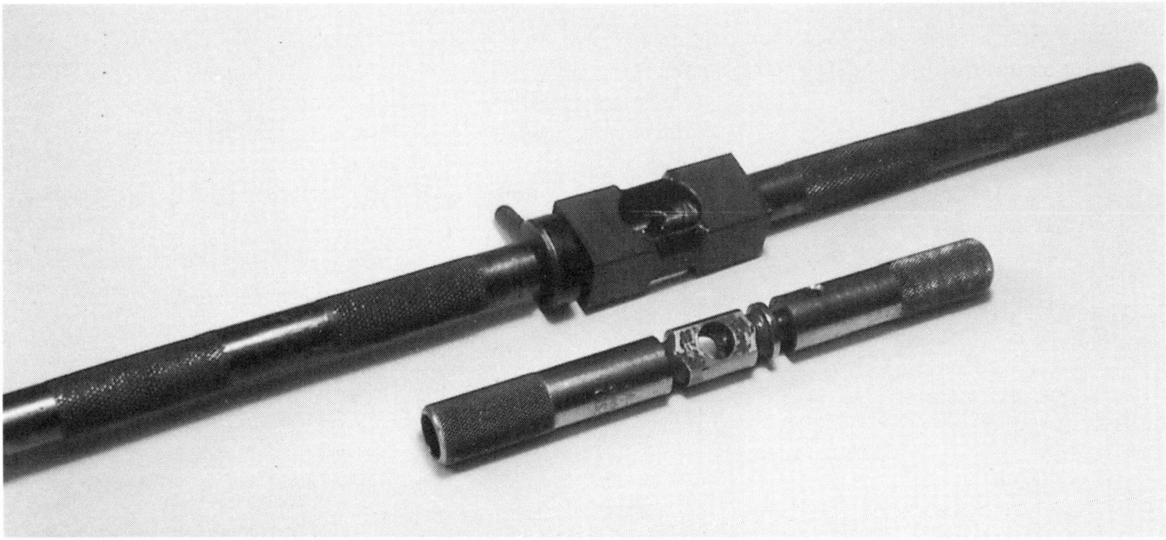

is best for aluminium and brass, while cast iron should be cut dry.

It is very important for the tap to enter the hole true, otherwise a drunken thread will result. The tap should be started in the hole turning clockwise for a right-hand thread; as soon as the tap begins to bite into the metal, it should be checked for square in two directions with an engineers square; if it is out of square, this can easily be seen as one handle of the tap wrench will be higher than the other.

As soon as the tap is started square, the thread can be cut, turning the wrench one full turn forward followed by half a turn back. This turning back is important as it breaks off the chip of metal being formed by the cutting edge of the tap. Failure to turn the tap backwards will result in the swarf collecting in the flutes of the tap and finally jamming the whole thing solid. The usual consequence of this is the tap breaking. While the tap is cutting the thread, it will not need any downward pressure on the tap wrench; the shape of the teeth on the tap will pull it down into the hole; indeed, any pressure that is applied is

Above *Tap wrenches.*

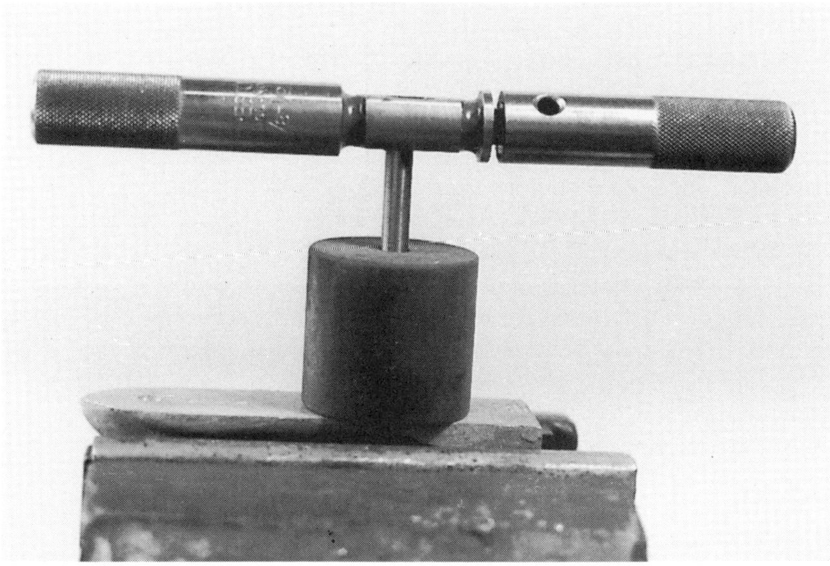

Right *Tap guide for starting taps at 90°.*

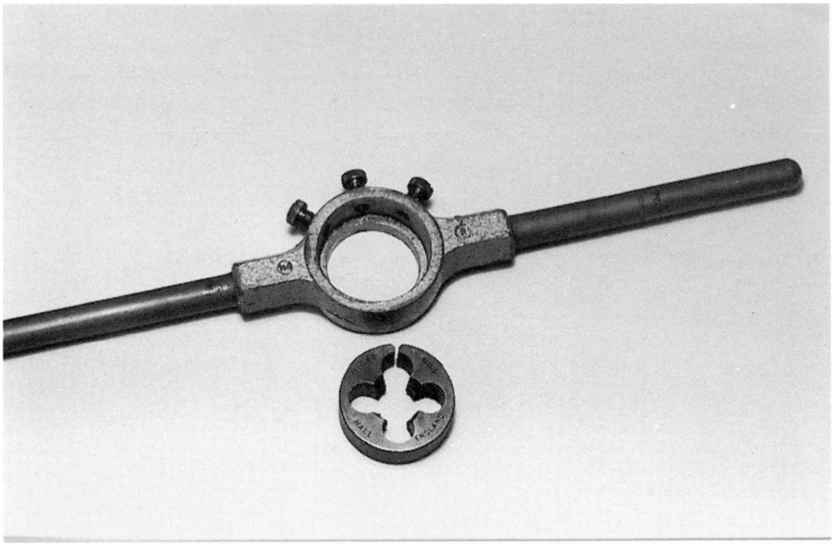

Left *Circular split die and die stock.*

Below right *Die nuts for cleaning up damaged threads.*

Bottom right *A rethreading file for use on damaged threads.*

likely to produce a drunken thread.

If your taps are of the type where the shank is the same diameter or larger than the T, then a simple guide (see illustration) can be made to help achieve a square start to the thread. This should preferably be made of metal though a good hard wood will suffice. Obviously the top and bottom surfaces must be parallel to each other and at right angles to the hole and the hole should be the same size as the shank of the tap. The thickness of the block should allow the tap to reach the metal and be supported by the shank, but leaving enough clearance at the top to enable the tap to cut several threads into the metal.

The guide is held in one hand and the tap started with the other. This cannot be used in all circumstances but it will help in many situations.

If the metal you are tapping is not too thick, it is possible to cut a full thread with the taper tap, but where a blind hole is being tapped the second and plug taps will have to be used. As soon as the tap reaches the bottom of the hole, stop turning as the tap can easily break or the bottom teeth chip. Before using the second tap and also between using the second and plug taps, any swarf that has collected at the bottom of the hole must be removed, otherwise it will be impossible to thread the hole to the bottom. Should you have the misfortune to break off a tap inside the hole you have problems. If the tap has broken leaving some of the shank above the surface, it may be possible to use a pair of mole grips or a similar tool to turn the tap out, having removed as much swarf as possible from the hole. If the tap remains below the surface your options are limited; it is impossible to drill out the tap as it is harder than the drill.

One method of removing a broken tap is to use a tap extractor. This tool has three fingers which fit down the flutes of the tap once the swarf has been removed. The extractor is then turned, unscrewing the tap from the hole.

If this method does not work, then spark erosion is the only suitable method open to you. This involves using an electric spark to burn out, or erode, the tap, turning it into a powder. Obviously this requires specialized equipment which may be available at your local engineering works or from other engineers who work with special steels and die-making.

External threads are cut with a tool called a die, which is held in a die stock. The type of die most commonly used is called a circular split die, see illustration. The die should be placed into the die stock with the engraved side showing; this is because this side of the die has a slight taper on the teeth to help the die to start cutting. The centre screw of the die stock should be tightened into the split first, to expand the die — again this will help the die to start cutting — and the two outer screws need to be 'nipped' in to hold the die firm.

The end of the metal bar should be chamfered

to ease the work of the die and a small amount of lubricant applied to it. The die and die stock should now be placed on the work with the writing on the die downwards. The die should be held square to the work, pressure applied, and the die stock turned clockwise.

When it has started cutting it should be checked to see if it is square to the bar; if it is, turn the stock through 90° and check again. If it is still square, start cutting the thread. Should the die stock be out of true, which will be seen as one handle of the stock will be higher than the other, pressure should be applied to the handle that is higher and the die stock turned through 90° and checked again; this should be done until both handles are level.

The cutting operation is the same as for the internal thread: one full turn forward, followed by a half turn backwards, to break off the swarf. Again it is important that, once the die is cutting a true thread, no pressure is applied to the diestock as this will almost certainly produce a drunken thread.

Having cut the thread to the correct length, the die and die stock should be removed, and the thread tested with a nut or in the hole into which it is going to be fitted. Should the thread feel tight it can be eased by running the die down it again. This time the centre screw of the die stock should be loosened slightly and the outer screws tightened, squeezing the die closer. It can then be run down the thread again to remove a small amount of metal and the fit of the thread tested again. When cutting both parts of a thread, the internal one should be cut first, then the external one cut to suit with the adjustable die.

Die nuts (see illustration) are similar in appearance to a normal nut, though larger for any given size and with teeth like a die inside. They are not designed to cut threads but to clean up damaged ones. Their hexagonal shape enables them to be turned with a spanner or socket in a confined space.

Rethreading files (illustrated) are also used for repairing damaged or rusty threads; they are double-ended, and each face has teeth cut to suit a thread of different teeth per inch or pitch. This means that one file has the capacity for cleaning up eight different threads.

To remove a stud from its hole, a stud remover can be used; if not, two nuts should be run onto the thread, then tightened together so that they are locked onto the stud. The lower nut should then be turned and if all goes well the stud will unscrew from its hole. Should the stud refuse to move, easing oil left to soak in may do the trick. If the stud is in aluminium, heat may be the answer, as the aluminium will expand quicker than the steel stud, but be careful with the amount of heat you apply.

If the stud has broken flush with the surface, a stud extractor will have to be used. Firstly, the broken end of the stud should be filed flat; the centre of the stud should then be centre punched and the correct size hole drilled into the stud. The extractor is then

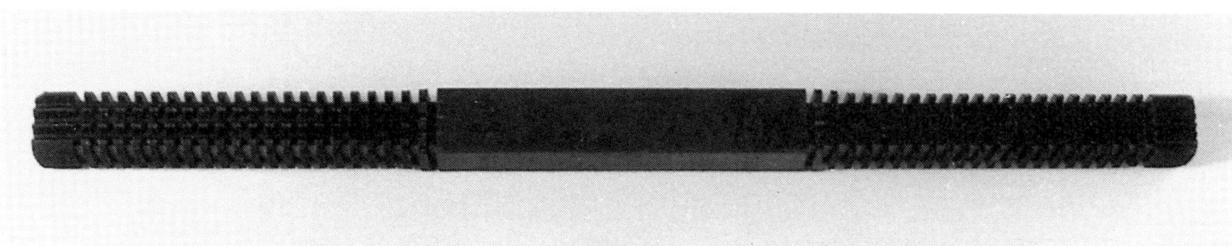

Fig. 25 Self-tapping screws, suggested hole and drill sizes in thermopliable plastics.
Note: Because of the vast difference in these plastics, this table is intended only as a guide. It may be necessary to increase or decrease the recommended hole size to obtain optimum fastening conditions.

SCREW SIZE NO. AND NOMINAL DIAMETER	NORMAL PENETRATION HOLE DIAMETER REQUIRED IN.	DRILL SIZE MM	ALTERNATIVES	MINIMUM PENETRATION IN BLIND HOLES
2 (0.086″)	0.070	1.80	50	1/4″
4 (0.112″)	0.093	2.35	42	1/4″
6 (0.138″)	0.114	2.90	32	1/4″
8 (0.164″)	0.135	3.40	29	5/16″
10 (0.186″)	0.154	3.90	23	5/16″
12 (0.212″)	0.180	4.60	15	3/8″
14 (0.242″)	0.210	5.30	4	3/8″

screwed into the hole anticlockwise and as it tightens it should unscrew the stud.

Should it prove necessary to drill out the whole of the stud, great care must be taken in accurately centre punching the centre of the stud and drilling carefully with a pilot drill first. Do not let the drill wander away from the centre of the stud, especially if the stud is in aluminium. The drill will find the aluminium much easier to cut than the stud, and will be forced into the aluminium by the steel of the stud even if the work is clamped down.

If the broken stud is one of a set, e.g. a manifold stud, it will help to centre punch the broken stud accurately if the manifold is bolted up and a transfer centre punch used. Alternatively, a punch made from a piece of silver steel of the right diameter can be used.

Self-tapping screws

Another type of screw is the self-tapping screw, made of hardened steel, which is able to cut its own thread in metal or plastics. They are available in the following head shapes, which have either a plain or cross slot for a screwdriver: pan, hexagonal, countersunk or raised countersunk. For best results it is important that the correct size hole is drilled to match the size of the screw and the thickness and type of material. The tables at the end of this chapter give an accurate guide for the majority of installations.

Heli-coil inserts

Where a thread has stripped inside a hole, it is not always possible to retap the hole to a larger size; in this instance a heli-coil insert may be the answer.

The damaged hole should first be drilled out to the correct oversize, and a special tap used to cut a thread inside the hole. The insert, which is a coil of diamond section steel wire, should be screwed into the thread that has been cut, using a special tool. When it is fully home, the tool is removed and the insert is ready to accept the original bolt or stud.

Fig. 27 Self-tapping screws.

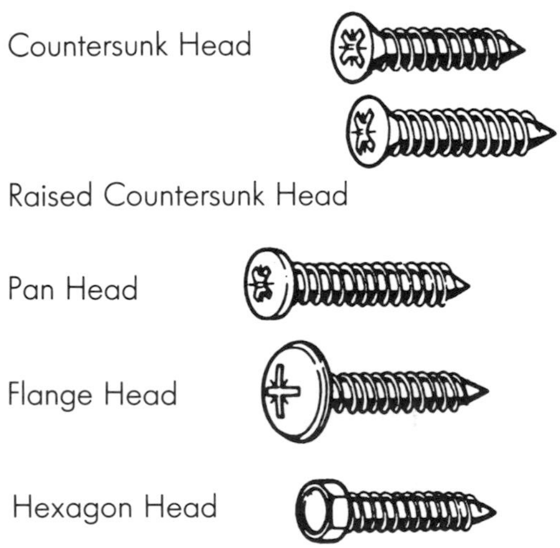

Fig. 26 Self-tapping screws, suggested hole and drill sizes in mild steel, brass, aluminium alloy, stainless steel and monel metal sheet.

Note: It is important that the correct hole size is used and the recommendations below should be followed, but a slightly larger hole may have to be used in very hard material, and a smaller one in very soft material.

SCREW SIZE	MATERIAL THICKNESS			PIERCED OR EXTRUDED	DRILLED OR CLEAN-PUNCHED HOLES		
NO. AND NOMINAL DIA.	IN.	MM	SWG OR FRACTION	HOLE DIA IN.	HOLE DIA. REQUIRED IN.	DRILL SIZE MM	ALTERNATIVES
2	0.018	0.45	26	–	0.063	1.60	52
(0.086″)	0.036	0.91	20	–	0.073	1.85	49
	0.064	1.62	16	–	0.077	1.95	48
4	0.018	0.45	26	–	0.081	2.05	46
(0.112″)	0.036	0.91	20	0.098	0.091	2.30	42
	0.064	1.62	16	–	0.095	2.40	41
	0.080	2.03	14	–	0.102	2.60	38
6	0.018	0.45	26	–	0.092	2.35	42
(0.138″)	0.036	0.91	20	0.111	0.110	2.80	35
	0.064	1.62	16	–	0.116	2.95	32
	0.080	2.03	14	–	0.122	3.10	31
	0.104	2.64	12	–	0.126	3.20	30
8	0.028	0.71	22	–	0.114	2.90	33
(0.164″)	0.036	0.91	20	0.136	0.122	3.10	$\frac{1}{8}$″
	0.048	1.22	18	–	0.126	3.20	30
	0.064	1.62	16	–	0.134	3.40	29
	0.104	2.64	12	–	0.146	3.70	26
	0.125	3.18	$\frac{1}{8}$″	–	0.150	3.80	25
10	0.028	0.71	22	–	0.134	3.40	29
(0.186″)	0.048	1.22	18	–	0.142	3.60	28
	0.064	1.62	16	–	0.150	3.80	25
	0.104	2.64	12	–	0.161	4.10	20
	0.125	3.18	$\frac{1}{8}$″	–	0.169	4.30	18
	0.187	4.75	$\frac{3}{16}$″	–	0.177	4.50	16
12	0.028	0.71	22	–	0.161	4.10	20
(0.212″)	0.048	1.22	18	–	0.169	4.30	18
	0.064	1.62	16	–	0.177	4.50	16
	0.104	2.64	12	–	0.189	4.80	12
	0.125	3.18	$\frac{1}{8}$″	–	0.193	4.90	10
	0.187	4.75	$\frac{3}{16}$″	–	0.201	5.10	7
14	0.048	1.22	18	–	0.189	4.80	12
(0.242″)	0.064	1.62	16	–	0.205	5.20	6
	0.080	2.03	14	–	0.213	5.40	3
	0.125	3.18	$\frac{1}{8}$″	–	0.224	5.70	1
	0.187	4.75	$\frac{3}{16}$″	–	0.232	5.90	A
	0.250	6.35	$\frac{1}{4}$″	–	0.236	6.00	B

Thread information tables. (S.K.F. Dormer Ltd)

I.S.O. METRIC COARSE

THREAD FORM

r = Basic Radius = ·1443 p

hn = Basic Height of Internal Thread & Depth of Thread Engagement = ·54127 p

hs = Basic Height of External Thread = **·61344** p

p = Pitch

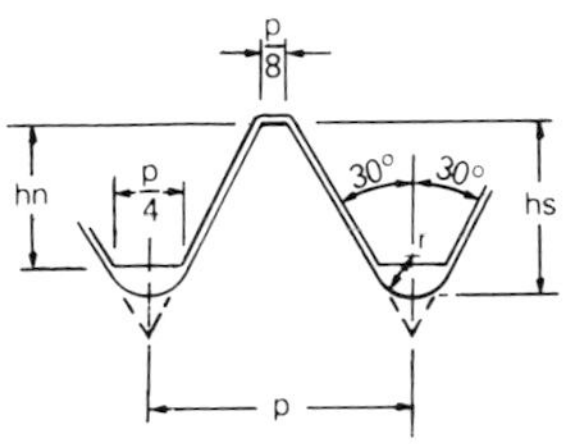

nom. dia. mm	pitch mm	basic major diameter mm	basic effective diameter mm	basic minor diameter of external threads mm	basic minor diameter of internal threads mm	recom-mended tapping drill size mm	clearance drill size mm
1	0.25	1.000	0.838	0.693	0.729	0.75	1.05
1.1	0.25	1.100	0.938	0.793	0.829	0.85	1.15
1.2	0.25	1.200	1.038	0.893	0.929	0.95	1.25
1.4	0.30	1.400	1.205	1.032	1.075	1.10	1.45
1.6	0.35	1.600	1.373	1.170	1.221	1.25	1.65
1.8	0.35	1.800	1.573	1.370	1.421	1.45	1.85
2	0.40	2.000	1.740	1.509	1.567	1.60	2.05
2.2	0.45	2.200	1.908	1.648	1.713	1.75	2.25
2.5	0.45	2.500	2.208	1.948	2.013	2.05	2.60
3	0.50	3.000	2.675	2.387	2.459	2.50	3.10
3.5	0.60	3.500	3.110	2.764	2.850	2.90	3.60
4	0.70	4.000	3.545	3.141	3.242	3.30	4.10
4.5	0.75	4.500	4.013	3.580	3.688	3.70	4.60
5	0.80	5.000	4.480	4.019	4.134	4.20	5.10
6	1.00	6.000	5.350	4.773	4.917	5.00	6.10
7	1.00	7.000	6.350	5.773	5.917	6.00	7.20
8	1.25	8.000	7.188	6.466	6.647	6.80	8.20
9	1.25	9.000	8.188	7.466	7.647	7.80	9.20
10	1.50	10.000	9.026	8.160	8.376	8.50	10.20
11	1.50	11.000	10.026	9.160	9.376	9.50	11.20
12	1.75	12.000	10.863	9.853	10.106	10.20	12.20
14	2.00	14.000	12.701	11.546	11.835	12.00	14.25
16	2.00	16.000	14.701	13.546	13.835	14.00	16.25
18	2.50	18.000	16.376	14.933	15.294	15.50	18.25
20	2.50	20.000	18.376	16.933	17.294	17.50	20.25
22	2.50	22.000	20.376	18.933	19.294	19.50	22.25
24	3.00	24.000	22.051	20.319	20.752	21.00	24.25
27	3.00	27.000	25.051	23.319	23.752	24.00	27.25
30	3.50	30.000	27.727	25.706	26.211	26.50	30.50
33	3.50	33.000	30.727	28.706	29.211	29.50	33.50
36	4.00	36.000	33.402	31.093	31.670	32.00	36.50
39	4.00	39.000	36.402	34.093	34.670	35.00	39.50
42	4.50	42.000	39.077	36.479	37.129	37.50	42.50
45	4.50	45.000	42.077	39.479	40.129	40.50	45.50
48	5.00	48.000	44.752	41.866	42.587	43.00	48.50
52	5.00	52.000	48.752	45.866	46.587	47.00	53.00
56	5.50	56.000	52.428	49.252	50.046	50.50	57.00

I.S.O. METRIC SPECIAL PITCHES

THREAD FORM

r = Basic Radius = ·1443 p

hn = Basic Height of Internal Thread & Depth of Thread Engagement = ·54127 p

hs = Basic Height of External Thread = **·61344** p

p = Pitch

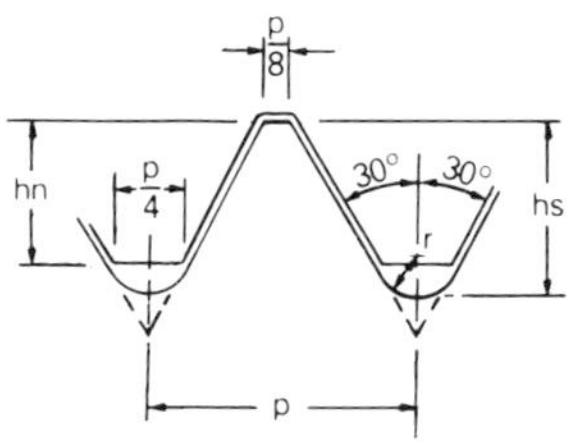

nom. dia. mm	pitch mm	basic major diameter mm	basic effective diameter mm	basic minor diameter of external threads mm	basic minor diameter of internal threads mm	recommended tapping drill size mm	clearance drill size mm
1.7	0.35	1.700	1.473	1.270	1.321	1.35	1.80
2.0	0.45	2.000	1.708	1.448	1.513	1.55	2.10
2.3	0.40	2.300	2.040	1.809	1.867	1.90	2.40
2.6	0.45	2.600	2.308	2.048	2.113	2.15	2.70
3.0	0.60	3.000	2.610	2.264	2.350	2.40	3.10
4.0	0.75	4.000	3.513	3.080	3.188	3.20	4.10
5.0	0.90	5.000	4.415	3.896	4.026	4.10	5.10
5.5	0.90	5.500	4.915	4.396	4.526	4.60	5.60
8.0	0.75	8.000	7.513	7.080	7.188	7.20	8.20
9.0	1.00	9.000	8.350	7.773	7.917	8.00	9.20
10.0	0.75	10.000	9.513	9.080	9.188	9.20	10.20
10.0	1.00†	10.000	9.350	8.773	8.917	9.00	10.20
12.0	1.00	12.000	11.350	10.773	10.917	11.00	12.20
12.0	1.50	12.000	11.026	10.160	10.376	10.50	12.20
14.0	1.50	14.000	13.026	12.160	12.376	12.50	14.25
16.0	1.00	16.000	15.350	14.773	14.917	15.00	16.25
20.0	1.00	20.000	19.350	18.773	18.917	19.00	20.25
20.0	2.00	20.000	10.701	17.546	17.835	18.00	20.25
24.0	1.00	24.000	23.350	22.773	22.917	23.00	24.25
24.0	1.50	24.000	23.026	22.160	22.376	22.50	24.25
25.0	1.50*	25.000	24.026	23.160	23.376	23.50	25.25
32.0	1.50*	32.000	31.026	30.160	30.376	30.50	32.50

I.S.O. METRIC FINE

THREAD FORM

r = Basic Radius = ·1443 p

hn = Basic Height of Internal Thread & Depth of Thread Engagement = ·54127 p

hs = Basic Height of External Thread = **·61344** p

p = Pitch

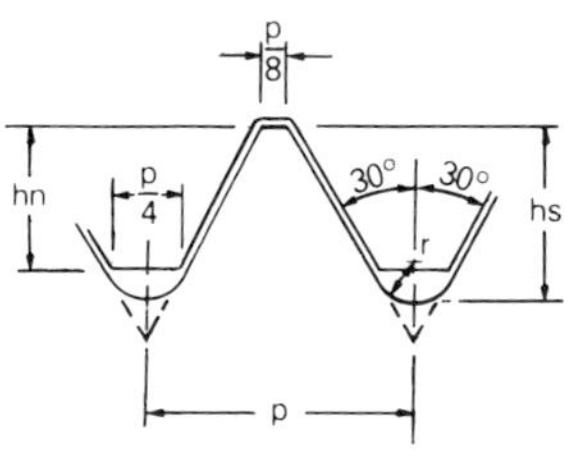

nom. dia. mm	pitch mm	basic major diameter mm	basic effective diameter mm	basic minor diameter of external threads mm	basic minor diameter of internal threads mm	recommended tapping drill size mm	clearance drill size mm
3.0	0.35	3.000	2.773	2.570	2.621	2.65	3.10
4.0	0.50	4.000	3.675	3.387	3.459	3.50	4.10
5.0	0.50	5.000	4.675	4.387	4.459	4.50	5.10
6.0	0.75	6.000	5.513	5.080	5.188	5.20	6.10
7.0	0.75	7.000	6.513	6.080	6.188	6.20	7.20
8.0	1.00	8.000	7.350	6.773	6.917	7.00	8.20
10.0	1.25	10.000	9.188	8.466	8.647	8.80	10.20
12.0	1.25†	12.000	11.188	10.466	10.647	10.80	12.20
14.0	1.25†	14.000	13.188	12.466	12.647	12.80	14.25
16.0	1.50*	16.000	15.026	14.160	14.376	14.50	16.25
18.0	1.50†	18.000	17.026	16.160	16.376	16.50	18.25
20.0	1.50*	20.000	19.026	18.160	18.376	18.50	20.25
22.0	1.50	22.000	21.026	20.160	20.376	20.50	22.25
24.0	2.00	24.000	22.701	21.546	21.835	22.00	24.25
27.0	2.00	27.000	25.701	24.546	24.835	25.00	27.25
30.0	2.00	30.000	28.701	27.546	27.835	28.00	30.50

NOTES: Pitch/Diameter combinations marked thus(*) are Metric Spark Plug.
Pitch/Diameter combinations marked thus (†) are Metric Conduit.

UNIFIED COARSE

(U.N.C.)

THREAD FORM

r = Basic Radius = ·1443 p

hn = Basic Height of Internal Thread & Depth of Thread Engagement = ·54127 p

hs = Basic Height of External Thread = **·61344** p

p = Pitch = $\frac{1}{\text{t.p.i.}}$

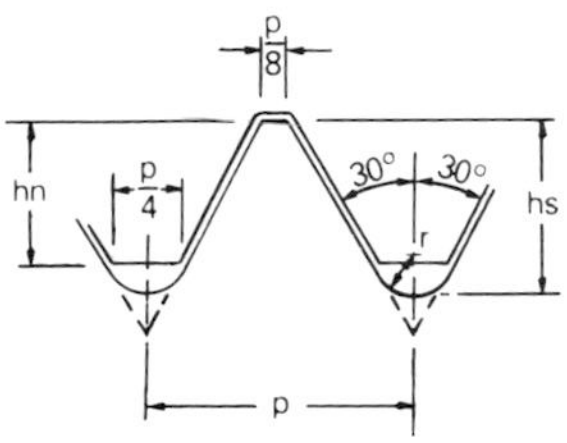

nom. size	t.p.i.	basic major diameter inches	basic effective diameter inches	basic minor dia. of ext. threads inches	basic minor dia. of int. threads inches	recommend-ed tapping drill size mm	clearance drill size mm
No. 1	64	0.0730	0.0629	0.0538	0.0561	1.55	1.95
No. 2	56	0.0860	0.0744	0.0641	0.0667	1.85	2.30
No. 3	48	0.0990	0.0855	0.0734	0.0764	2.10	2.65
No. 4	40	0.1120	0.0958	0.0813	0.0849	2.35	2.95
No. 5	40	0.1250	0.1088	0.0943	0.0979	2.65	3.30
No. 6	32	0.1380	0.1177	0.0997	0.1042	2.85	3.60
No. 8	32	0.1640	0.1437	0.1257	0.1302	3.50	4.30
No. 10	24	0.1900	0.1629	0.1389	0.1449	3.90	4.90
No. 12	24	0.2160	0.1889	0.1649	0.1709	4.50	5.60
1/4	20	0.2500	0.2175	0.1887	0.1959	5.10	6.50
5/16	18	0.3125	0.2764	0.2443	0.2524	6.60	8.10
3/8	16	0.3750	0.3344	0.2983	0.3073	8.00	9.70
7/16	14	0.4375	0.3911	0.3499	0.3602	9.40	11.30
1/2	13	0.5000	0.4500	0.4056	0.4167	10.80	13.00
9/16	12	0.5625	0.5084	0.4603	0.4723	12.20	14.50
5/8	11	0.6250	0.5660	0.5135	0.5266	13.50	16.25
3/4	10	0.7500	0.6850	0.6273	0.6417	16.50	19.25
7/8	9	0.8750	0.8028	0.7387	0.7547	19.50	22.50
1	8	1.0000	0.9188	0.8466	0.8647	22.25	25.75
1, 1/8	7	1.1250	1.0322	0.9497	0.9704	25.00	29.00
1, 1/4	7	1.2500	1.1572	1.0747	1.0954	28.00	32.00
1, 3/8	6	1.3750	1.2667	1.1705	1.1946	30.75	35.50
1, 1/2	6	1.5000	1.3917	1.2955	1.3196	34.00	38.50
1, 3/4	5	1.7500	1.6201	1.5046	1.5335	39.50	45.00
2	4, 1/2	2.0000	1.8557	1.7274	1.7594	45.00	51.00
2, 1/4	4, 1/2	2.2500	2.1057	1.9774	2.0094	52.00	58.00

UNIFIED FINE

(U.N.F.)

THREAD FORM

r = Basic Radius = ·1443 p

hn = Basic Height of Internal Thread & Depth of Thread Engagement = ·54127 p

hs = Basic Height of External Thread = ·**61344** p

p = Pitch = $\frac{1}{\text{t.p.i.}}$

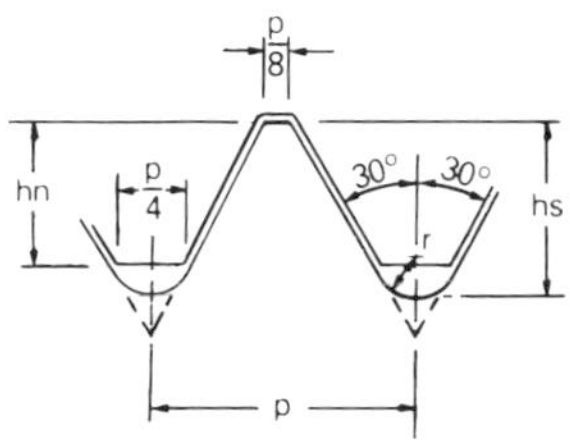

nom. size	t.p.i.	basic major diameter inches	basic effective diameter inches	basic minor dia. of ext. threads inches	basic minor dia. of int. threads inches	recommended tapping drill size mm	clearance drill size mm
No. 0	80	0.0600	0.0519	0.0447	0.0465	1.25	1.60
No. 1	72	0.0730	0.0640	0.0560	0.0580	1.55	1.95
No. 2	64	0.0860	0.0759	0.0668	0.0691	1.90	2.30
No. 3	56	0.0990	0.0874	0.0771	0.0797	2.15	2.65
No. 4	48	0.1120	0.0985	0.0864	0.0894	2.40	2.95
No. 5	44	0.1250	0.1102	0.0971	0.1004	2.70	3.30
No. 6	40	0.1380	0.1218	0.1073	0.1109	2.95	3.60
No. 8	36	0.1640	0.1460	0.1299	0.1339	3.50	4.30
No. 10	32	0.1900	0.1697	0.1517	0.1562	4.10	4.90
No. 12	28	0.2160	0.1928	0.1722	0.1773	4.70	5.60
1/4	28	0.2500	0.2268	0.2062	0.2113	5.50	6.50
5/16	24	0.3125	0.2854	0.2614	0.2674	6.90	8.10
3/8	24	0.3750	0.3479	0.3239	0.3299	8.50	9.70
7/16	20	0.4375	0.4050	0.3762	0.3834	9.90	11.30
1/2	20	0.5000	0.4675	0.4387	0.4459	11.50	13.00
9/16	18	0.5625	0.5264	0.4943	0.5024	12.90	14.50
5/8	18	0.6250	0.5889	0.5568	0.5649	14.50	16.25
3/4	16	0.7500	0.7094	0.6733	0.6823	17.50	19.25
7/8	14	0.8750	0.8286	0.7874	0.7977	20.40	22.50
1	12	1.0000	0.9459	0.8978	0.9098	23.25	25.75
1, 1/8	12	1.1250	1.0709	1.0228	1.0348	26.50	29.00
1, 1/4	12	1.2500	1.1959	1.1478	1.1598	29.50	32.00
1, 3/8	12	1.3750	1.3209	1.2728	1.2848	32.75	35.50
1, 1/2	12	1.5000	1.4459	1.3978	1.4098	36.00	38.50

BRITISH ASSOCIATION

(B.A.)

THREAD FORM

r = Basic Radius = ·1808346 p

h = Basic Depth of Thread = ·6 p

p = Pitch

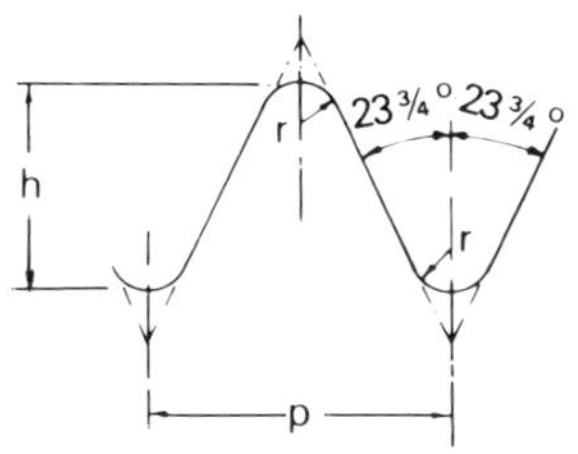

NON-PREFERRED THREAD SERIES

B.A. no.	pitch inches	basic depth of thread inches	basic major diameter inches	basic effective diameter inches	basic minor diameter inches	recommended tapping drill size mm	clearance drill size mm
0	0.0394	0.0236	0.2362	0.2126	0.1890	5.10	6.10
1	0.0354	0.0213	0.2087	0.1874	0.1661	4.50	5.40
2	0.0319	0.0191	0.1850	0.1659	0.1468	4.00	4.80
3	0.0287	0.0172	0.1614	0.1441	0.1268	3.40	4.20
4	0.0260	0.0156	0.1417	0.1262	0.1106	3.00	3.70
5	0.0232	0.0139	0.1260	0.1120	0.0980	2.65	3.30
6	0.0209	0.0125	0.1102	0.0976	0.0850	2.30	2.90
7	0.0189	0.0113	0.0984	0.0870	0.0756	2.05	2.60
8	0.0169	0.0102	0.0866	0.0764	0.0661	1.80	2.25
9	0.0154	0.0092	0.0748	0.0656	0.0563	1.55	1.95
10	0.0138	0.0083	0.0669	0.0587	0.0504	1.40	1.75
11	0.0122	0.0073	0.0591	0.0518	0.0445	1.20	1.60
12	0.0110	0.0066	0.0512	0.0445	0.0378	1.05	1.40
13	0.0098	0.0059	0.0472	0.0413	0.0354	0.98	1.30
14	0.0091	0.0054	0.0394	0.0339	0.0283	0.80	1.10
15	0.0083	0.0050	0.0354	0.0305	0.0256	0.70	0.98
16	0.0075	0.0045	0.0311	0.0266	0.0220	0.60	0.88

BRITISH STANDARD WHITWORTH

(B.S.W.)

THREAD FORM

r = Basic Radius = ·137329 p

h = Basic Depth of Thread = ·640327 p

p = Pitch = $\frac{1}{\text{t.p.i.}}$

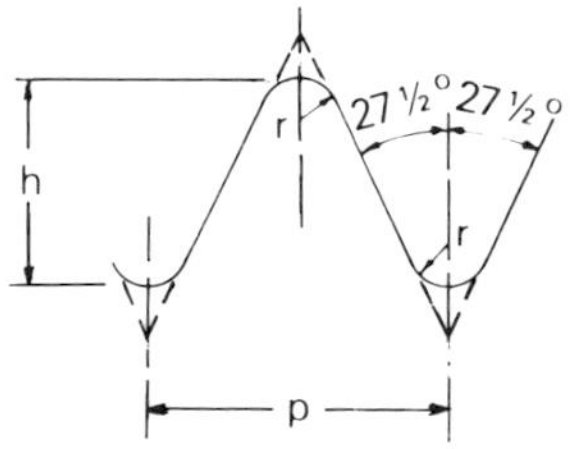

NON-PREFERRED THREAD SERIES

nom. dia. inches	t.p.i.	basic depth of thread inches	basic major diameter inches	basic effective diameter inches	basic minor diameter inches	recommended tapping drill size mm	clearance drill size mm
1/16	60	0.0107	0.0625	0.0518	0.0411	1.20	1.65
3/32	48	0.0133	0.0938	0.0805	0.0672	1.85	2.50
1/8	40	0.0160	0.1250	0.1090	0.0930	2.55	3.30
5/32	32	0.0200	0.1562	0.1362	0.1162	3.20	4.10
3/16	24	0.0267	0.1875	0.1608	0.1341	3.70	4.90
7/32	24	0.0267	0.2188	0.1921	0.1654	4.50	5.70
1/4	20	0.0320	0.2500	0.2180	0.1860	5.10	6.50
5/16	18	0.0356	0.3125	0.2769	0.2413	6.50	8.10
3/8	16	0.0400	0.3750	0.3350	0.2950	7.90	9.70
7/16	14	0.0457	0.4375	0.3918	0.3461	9.30	11.30
1/2	12	0.0534	0.5000	0.4466	0.3932	10.50	13.00
9/16	12	0.0534	0.5625	0.5091	0.4557	12.10	14.50
5/8	11	0.0582	0.6250	0.5668	0.5086	13.50	16.25
11/16	11	0.0582	0.6875	0.6293	0.5711	15.00	17.75
3/4	10	0.0640	0.7500	0.6860	0.6220	16.25	19.25
13/16	10	0.0640	0.8125	0.7485	0.6845	18.00	21.00
7/8	9	0.0711	0.8750	0.8039	0.7328	19.25	22.50
15/16	9	0.0711	0.9375	0.8664	0.7953	20.75	24.00
1	8	0.0800	1.0000	0.9200	0.8400	22.00	25.75
1, 1/8	7	0.0915	1.1250	1.0335	0.9420	24.75	29.00
1, 1/4	7	0.0915	1.2500	1.1585	1.0670	28.00	32.00
1, 3/8	6	0.1067	1.3750	1.2683	1.1616	30.25	35.50
1, 1/2	6	0.1067	1.5000	1.3933	1.2866	33.50	38.50
1, 5/8	5	0.1281	1.6250	1.4969	1.3688	35.50	41.50
1, 3/4	5	0.1281	1.7500	1.6219	1.4938	39.00	45.00
1, 7/8	4, 1/2	0.1423	1.8750	1.7327	1.5904	41.50	48.00
2	4, 1/2	0.1423	2.0000	1.8577	1.7154	44.50	51.00
2, 1/4	4	0.1601	2.2500	2.0899	1.9298	51.00	58.00
2, 1/2	4	0.1601	2.5000	2.3399	2.1798	57.00	64.00

BRITISH STANDARD TAPER PIPE

(Rc Series)

THREAD FORM

r = Basic Radius = ·137278 p

h = Basic Depth of Thread = ·640327 p

p = Pitch = $\frac{1}{\text{t.p.i.}}$

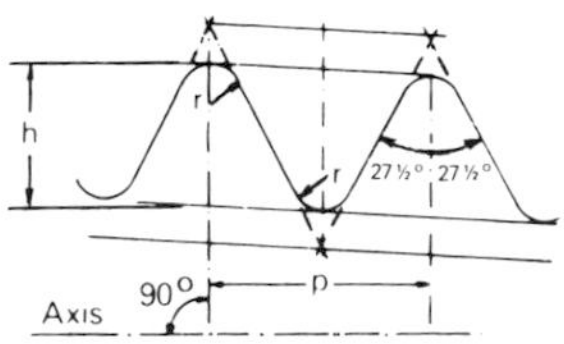

Taper 1 in 16 on dia. (shown exaggerated in diagram)

nom. size inches	t.p.i.	basic depth of thread inches	basic diameters at gauge plane*			recommended tapping drill size mm
			major diameter inches	effective diameter inches	minor diameter inches	
1/16	28	0.0229	0.304	0.2812	0.2583	6.40
1/8	28	0.0229	0.383	0.3601	0.3372	8.40
1/4	19	0.0337	0.518	0.4843	0.4506	11.20
3/8	19	0.0337	0.656	0.6223	0.5886	14.75
1/2	14	0.0457	0.825	0.7793	0.7336	18.25
3/4	14	0.0457	1.041	0.9953	0.9496	23.75
1	11	0.0582	1.309	1.2508	1.1926	30.00
1, 1/4	11	0.0582	1.650	1.5918	1.5336	38.50
1, 1/2	11	0.0582	1.882	1.8238	1.7656	44.50
2	11	0.0582	2.347	2.2888	2.2306	56.00
2, 1/2	11	0.0582	2.960	2.9018	2.8436	71.00

*'Gauge plane' – The plane, perpendicular to the axis, at which the major cone has the gauge diameter.

NOTE: The gauge plane is theoretically located at the face of the internal thread or at a distance equal to the basic gauge length from the small end of the external thread.

BRITISH STANDARD FINE

(B.S.F.)

THREAD FORM

r = Basic Radius = ·137329 p

h = Basic Depth of Thread = ·640327 p

p = Pitch = $\frac{1}{\text{t.p.i.}}$

NON-PREFERRED THREAD SERIES

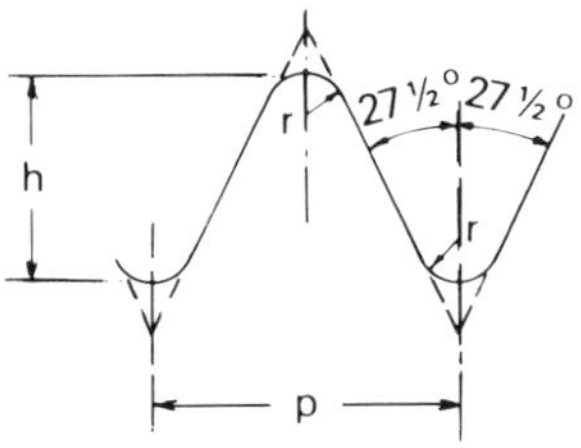

nom. dia. inches	t.p.i.	basic depth of thread inches	basic major diameter inches	basic effective diameter inches	basic minor diameter inches	recommended tapping drill size mm	clearance drill size mm
3/16	32	0.0200	0.1875	0.1675	0.1475	4.00	4.90
7/32	28	0.0229	0.2188	0.1959	0.1730	4.60	5.70
1/4	26	0.0246	0.2500	0.2254	0.2008	5.30	6.50
5/16	22	0.0291	0.3125	0.2834	0.2543	6.80	8.10
3/8	20	0.0320	0.3750	0.3430	0.3110	8.30	9.70
7/16	18	0.0356	0.4375	0.4019	0.3663	9.70	11.30
1/2	16	0.0400	0.5000	0.4600	0.4200	11.10	13.00
9/16	16	0.0400	0.5625	0.5225	0.4825	12.70	14.50
5/8	14	0.0457	0.6250	0.5793	0.5336	14.00	16.25
11/16	14	0.0457	0.6875	0.6418	0.5961	15.50	17.75
3/4	12	0.0534	0.7500	0.6966	0.6432	16.75	19.25
7/8	11	0.0582	0.8750	0.8168	0.7586	19.75	22.50
1	10	0.0640	1.0000	0.9360	0.8720	22.75	25.75
1, 1/8	9	0.0711	1.1250	1.0539	0.9828	25.50	29.00
1, 1/4	9	0.0711	1.2500	1.1789	1.1078	28.50	32.00
1, 3/8	8	0.0800	1.3750	1.2950	1.2150	31.50	35.50
1, 1/2	8	0.0800	1.5000	1.4200	1.3400	34.50	38.50
1, 3/4	7	0.0915	1.7500	1.6585	1.5670	41.00	45.00
2	7	0.0915	2.0000	1.9085	1.8170	47.00	52.00
2, 1/4	6	0.1067	2.2500	2.1433	2.0366	53.00	58.00
2, 1/2	6	0.1067	2.5000	2.3933	2.2866	58.00	64.00

BRITISH STANDARD PIPE

THREAD FORM

r = Basic Radius = ·137329 p

h = Basic Depth of Thread = ·640327 p

p = Pitch = $\frac{1}{\text{t.p.i.}}$

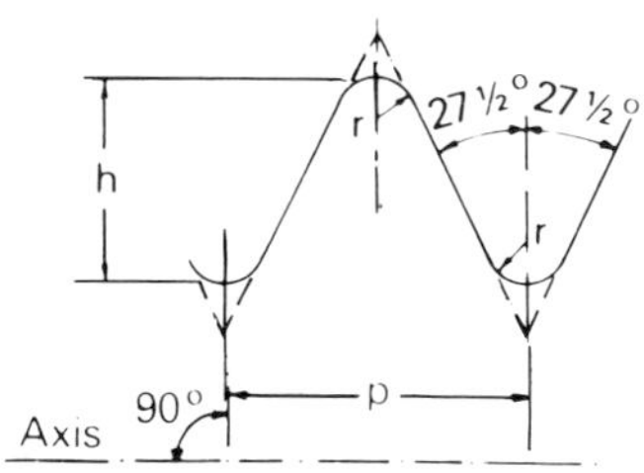

nom. size inches	t.p.i.	basic depth of thread inches	basic major diameter inches	basic effective diameter inches	basic minor diameter inches	recommended tapping drill size	
						Rp mm	G mm
1/16	28	0.0229	0.304	0.2812	0.2583.	6.60	6.80
1/8	28	0.0229	0.383	0.3601	0.3372	8.60	8.80
1/4	19	0.0337	0.518	0.4843	0.4506	11.50	11.80
3/8	19	0.0337	0.656	0.6223	0.5886	15.00	15.25
1/2	14	0.0457	0.825	0.7793	0.7336	18.50	19.00
5/8	14	0.0457	0.902	0.8563	0.8106		21.00
3/4	14	0.0457	1.041	0.9953	0.9496	24.00	24.50
7/8	14	0.0457	1.189	1.1433	1.0976		28.25
1	11	0.0582	1.309	1.2508	1.1926	30.25	30.75
1, 1/4	11	0.0582	1.650	1.5918	1.5336	39.00	39.50
1, 1/2	11	0.0582	1.882	1.8238	1.7656	45.00	45.00
1, 3/4	11	0.0582	2.116	2.0578	1.9996		51.00
2	11	0.0582	2.347	2.2888	2.2306	56.50	57.00
2, 1/4	11	0.0582	2.587	2.5288	2.4706		
2, 1/2	11	0.0582	2.960	2.9018	2.8436		
2, 3/4	11	0.0582	3.210	3.1518	3.0936		
3	11	0.0582	3.460	3.4018	3.3436		
3, 1/4	11	0.0582	3.700	3.6418	3.5836		
3, 1/2	11	0.0582	3.950	3.8918	3.8336		
3, 3/4	11	0.0582	4.200	4.1418	4.0836		
4	11	0.0582	4.450	4.3918	4.3336		

NO SIZES OF B.S. DRILLS ARE RECOMMENDED IN B.S. 1157:1975 FOR THIS RANGE

Fig. 28 Nuts, bolts, washers.

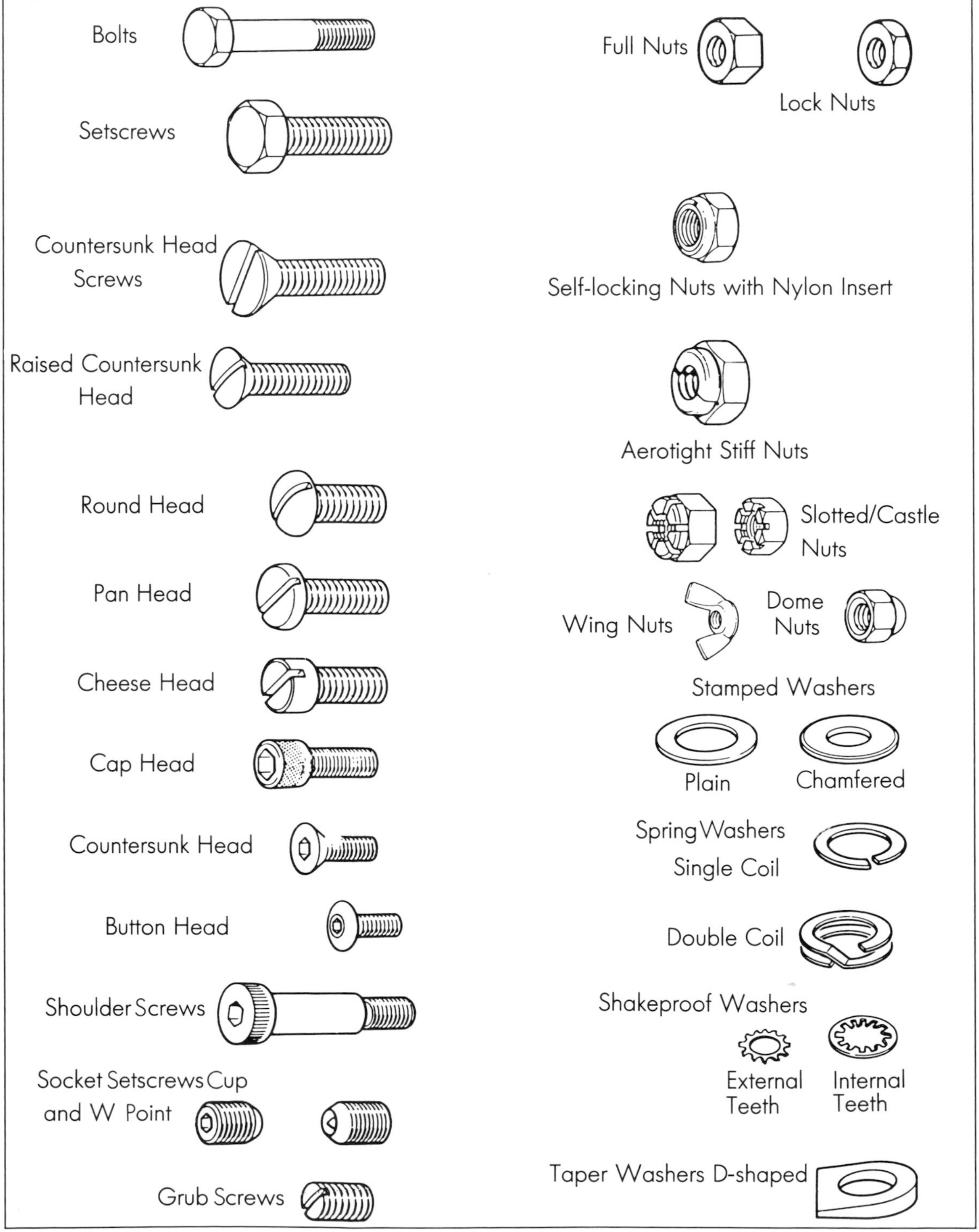
Bolts
Setscrews
Countersunk Head Screws
Raised Countersunk Head
Round Head
Pan Head
Cheese Head
Cap Head
Countersunk Head
Button Head
Shoulder Screws
Socket Setscrews Cup and W Point
Grub Screws
Full Nuts
Lock Nuts
Self-locking Nuts with Nylon Insert
Aerotight Stiff Nuts
Slotted/Castle Nuts
Wing Nuts
Dome Nuts
Stamped Washers
Plain
Chamfered
Spring Washers Single Coil
Double Coil
Shakeproof Washers
External Teeth
Internal Teeth
Taper Washers D-shaped

Fig. 29 Other fixings.

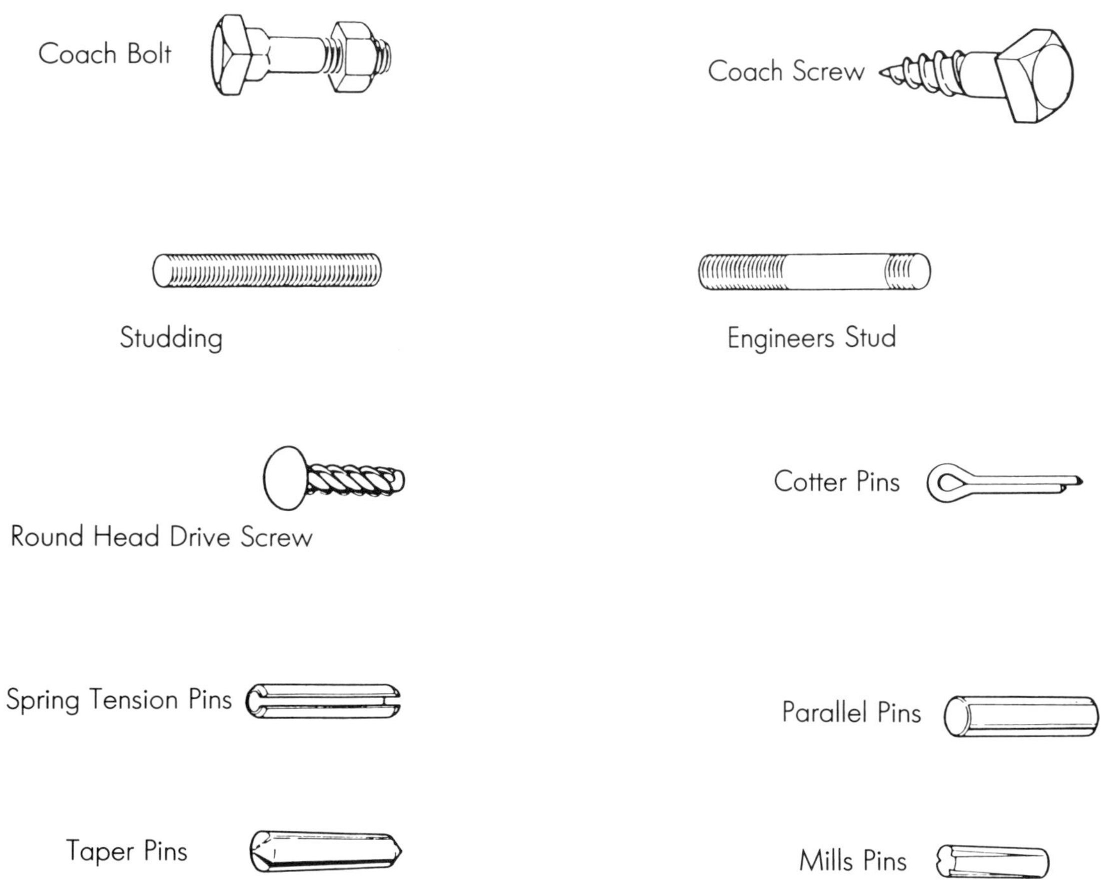

Fig. 30 Riveting.

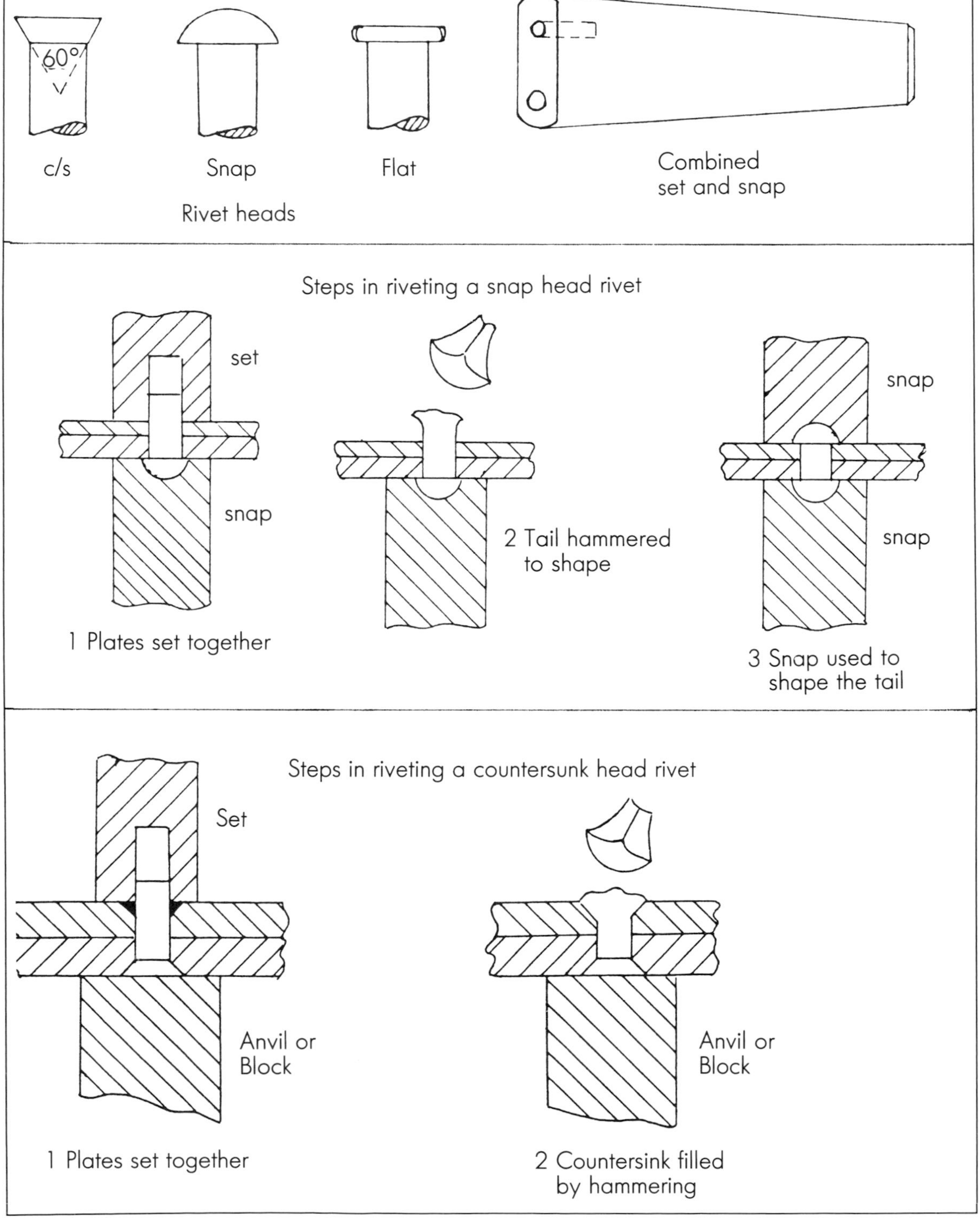
60°
c/s
Snap
Flat
Rivet heads
Combined
set and snap
Steps in riveting a snap head rivet
set
snap
1 Plates set together
2 Tail hammered
to shape
snap
snap
3 Snap used to
shape the tail
Steps in riveting a countersunk head rivet
Set
Anvil or
Block
1 Plates set together
Anvil or
Block
2 Countersink filled
by hammering

CHAPTER 8

Riveting

Riveting is a means of joining metals together in a permanent fashion. Rivets fall into two main groups: solid rivets and blind or 'pop' rivets. Solid are stronger and have to be worked from both sides and closed by hand; 'Pop', on the other hand, can be worked from one side using special riveting pliers.

Solid rivets are normally made from mild steel, aluminium, copper or brass, and should be used in similar metal to prevent problems of electrolytic corrosion, particularly between steel and aluminium. They are available with the shaped heads shown in Fig. 30.

Before starting to rivet metal together it should be decided what head shape is going to be used and the diameter of the shank. For the best results, the diameter of the shank should not exceed three times the thickness of the plates being joined and should not be less than the thickness of the plates.

When riveting two pieces together, the position of the holes should be marked and centre punched on one piece of metal. If possible, clamp the pieces together and drill *one* hole through the pieces. It is important that the drill is the correct size; if it is too large, the rivet will not grip the sides of the hole but bend it in. Where it is not possible to drill through the pieces together, the first hole in each piece should be drilled, any burrs removed and the hole countersunk, if necessary. The size of the countersink should be twice the diameter of the rivet; any larger and it would be difficult to fill; much smaller and it would remove some of the strength of the rivet.

The first rivet should be placed through the hole and the plates closed together with the rivet set. With a snap head rivet, the head should be supported with the rivet snap while the tail is formed with the ball pein head of the hammer to either a round head, finished with a rivet snap, or the countersink filled.

The head of a countersunk rivet should be supported on a flat surface — an anvil or heavy block of metal is best. Do not use the vice for hammering on; the casting may crack unless the vice has been designed for this purpose. Once the rivet is closed, do not continue to hammer the rivet because it may work harden and crack. Before clenching a rivet, the tail should be cut to the right length. If a countersunk rivet is being formed, three-quarters of the diameter of the shank should be left; for a snap head rivet, the allowance is one and a half times the diameter of the shank.

Once the first rivet has been clenched, the remaining holes can be drilled. Do not attempt to drill more than one hole in each piece of metal while they are separated because the holes will not line up accurately enough, no matter how carefully you mark out and drill. When riveting thin sheets to thicker material it is better not to countersink the thin material as this would weaken it, but to countersink the thicker material so that the thin sheet is forced into the countersink by the rivet.

Loose rivets for hood frames and other movable parts should be assembled with a washer between the two parts, preferably of brass, to prevent rusting. The rivet should be greased lightly and then clenched until the joint is firm.

To remove a snap head rivet, the head should be ground or filed off. If you intend using a cold chisel to remove the head, cut across the centre of the head in two directions so that it looks like a hot cross bun. It will then chisel away more easily. Do not attempt to drill right through the rivet as it is almost impossible to ensure that the drill will line up perfectly with the original hole and this will only cause more problems. Once the head has been removed, the shank of the rivet can be driven out with a pin punch. Do not use a sharp punch as this will merely swell the end of the shank into the hole.

Countersunk rivets should be carefully centre punched and the countersunk portion of the rivet drilled out. The rest of the rivet can then be driven out.

Where rivets have been used to join chassis frames or other items that are under stress, and it is found that one or more are showing signs of becoming loose, do not try to tighten them. It is much better to remove them all, even those that may appear sound, and use high tensile bolts instead. The holes must be a good fit on the bolts and it may be necessary to enlarge the holes to the next size up. Self-locking nuts should be used, or plain nuts with the end of the bolts peened over to lock the nut on the thread.

Ensure that the joint is clean and rust-free before bolting up. It is not advisable to paint the joint, because the layer of paint could flake away, leaving the joint slightly loose, which will lead to further trouble. This also applies to riveted joints.

The advantage of 'pop' or blind rivets is that they can be used when access is restricted to one side of the work. Their main disadvantage is that they are not as strong as solid rivets. There are two head shapes, pan and countersunk, which are available in steel, monel, aluminium and in certain applications, copper, cupro-nickel and stainless steel. The rivets are normally available in three diameters, with each size having three different lengths, though aluminium rivets are available in a longer size. Retail outlets usually sell the three sizes as short, medium and long, and it is important that the rivets are matched to the correct thickness of material being riveted. If the rivet is too short it will 'pop' before it has gripped the work sufficiently; too long and it will also 'pop' before it has begun to compress the work. Rivets that are too long can have washers put under the head or on the tail to increase the thickness of the material being riveted. Washers can also be used to spread the clamping pressure when riveting soft or brittle material such as plastics, leather, hardboard, etc.

The 'King Klik' Metro Range of aluminium alloy rivets are available in three different diameters that have a much wider range of lengths, giving a grip range from 0.5 mm (0.020 in) to 36 mm ($1^1/_7$ in). Tables showing the complete range of these and standard blind rivets are shown on pages 65–67.

For marking out and drilling the holes for the rivets, the procedure for 'pop' riveting is the same as that for solid rivets. Once the first pair of holes has been drilled, the rivet is placed through the hole. The riveting tool should now be placed over the mandrel of the rivet, after checking that the nozzle of the tool is the correct size for the rivet. The handles of the tool must be held apart so that the tail of the rivet will pass through the gripping jaws of the riveting tool. When the nozzle is in contact with the head of the rivet, the handles of the riveting tool must be squeezed together while applying pressure to the head of the rivet to keep it in place. The mandrel will be pulled through the tail of the rivet, compressing the end of it and expanding that part of the tail inside the work. When the tail has been compressed, the mandrel will break with a 'pop' and the rivet will be fixed in place.

Until recently, sheet metal that had to be bolted together, where one side was inaccessible, meant the use of captive nuts resistance-welded to the underside of the sheet. If these became loose or broken off, or the sheet they were attached to had to be replaced, the amateur restorer was in difficulties with their replacement. Now there is a system of rivet nuts that can be used for a wide range of applications where access to a loose nut is impossible or time consuming. These rivet nuts — there are three basic types, — T, X and J, can be installed with the same riveting tool as used for 'pop' rivets. The correct size hole is drilled and the rivet nut placed into the hole. A Threaded mandrel is screwed into the rivet nut and this mandrel is then pulled by the riveting tool until the rivet nut is firmly anchored to the sheet. The mandrel is then unscrewed and the rivet nut is ready to accept a screw. The charts on pages 69–71 show a cross-sectional view of each type of rivet nut together with a table of sizes and data.

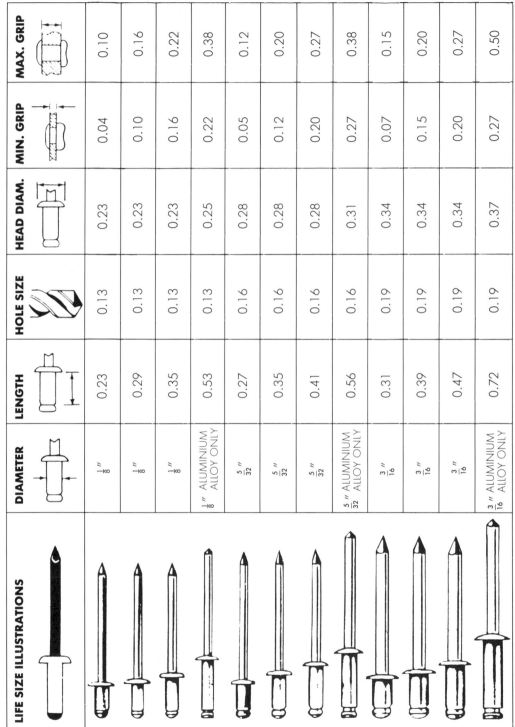

Fig. 31 Standard pop rivets. (Riveting Systems Ltd)

DOME HEAD RIVETS OF ALUMINIUM ALLOY, STEEL OR MONEL. ALL MANDRELS ARE STEEL. RIVET DIAMETERS ARE FRACTIONAL INCH. OTHER DIMENSIONS ARE DECIMAL INCH.

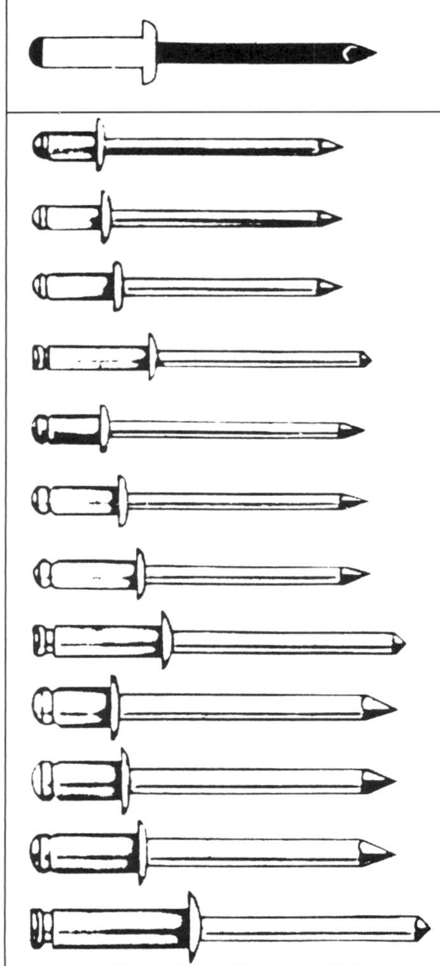

LIFE SIZE ILLUSTRATIONS	DIAMETER	LENGTH	HOLE SIZE	HEAD DIAM.	MIN. GRIP	MAX. GRIP
	$\frac{1}{8}''$	0.23	0.13	0.23	0.04	0.10
	$\frac{1}{8}''$	0.29	0.13	0.23	0.10	0.16
	$\frac{1}{8}''$	0.35	0.13	0.23	0.16	0.22
	$\frac{1}{8}''$ ALUMINIUM ALLOY ONLY	0.53	0.13	0.25	0.22	0.38
	$\frac{5}{32}''$	0.27	0.16	0.28	0.05	0.12
	$\frac{5}{32}''$	0.35	0.16	0.28	0.12	0.20
	$\frac{5}{32}''$	0.41	0.16	0.28	0.20	0.27
	$\frac{5}{32}''$ ALUMINIUM ALLOY ONLY	0.56	0.16	0.31	0.27	0.38
	$\frac{3}{16}''$	0.31	0.19	0.34	0.07	0.15
	$\frac{3}{16}''$	0.39	0.19	0.34	0.15	0.20
	$\frac{3}{16}''$	0.47	0.19	0.34	0.20	0.27
	$\frac{3}{16}''$ ALUMINIUM ALLOY ONLY	0.72	0.19	0.37	0.27	0.50

Fig. 32 Pages 66–67: King Klick Metro Range of blind rivets. (Riveting Systems Ltd.)

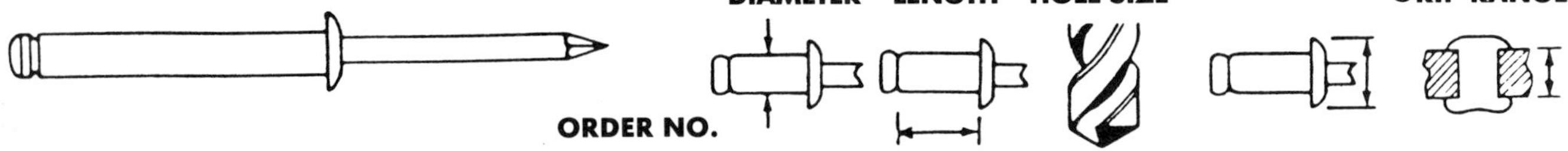

ALLUMINIUM ALLOY — **DIMENSIONS IN MILLIMETRES** — **DOME HEAD**

ORDER NO.	DIAMETER	LENGTH	HOLE SIZE		GRIP RANGE
TA2904	2.9	4	3	5.9	0.5–2.5
TA2906	2.9	6	3	5.9	2.6–4.0
TA2908	2.9	8	3	5.9	4.1–6.0
TA2910	2.9	10	3	5.9	6.1–8.0
TA2912	2.9	12	3	5.9	8.1–10.0
TA2915	2.9	15	3	5.9	10.1–12.0
TA2918	2.9	18	3	5.9	12.1–15.0
TA3906	3.9	6	4	7.5	1.5–3.5
TA3907	3.9	7	4	7.5	3.6–4.5
TA3908	3.9	8	4	7.5	4.6–6.5
TA3910	3.9	10	4	7.5	6.6–7.5
TA3912	3.9	12	4	7.5	7.6–9.5
TA3915	3.9	15	4	7.5	9.6–12.0
TA3918	3.9	18	4	7.5	12.1–15.0

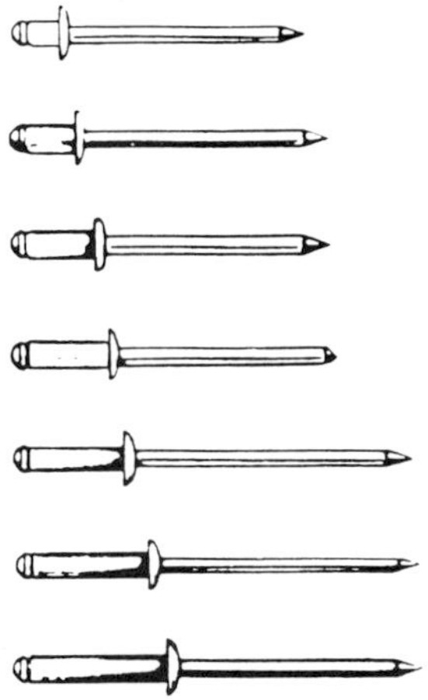

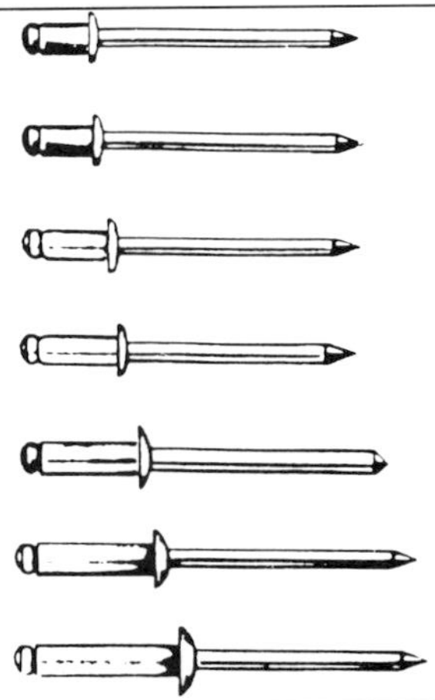

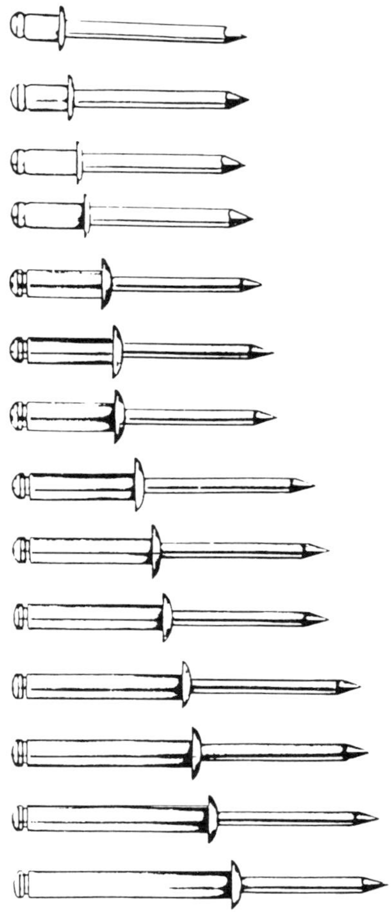

TA4906	4.9	6	5	9.5	1.5–3.5
TA4908	4.9	8	5	9.5	3.6–5.0
TA4910	4.9	10	5	9.5	5.1–7.0
TA4912	4.9	12	5	9.5	7.1–9.5
TA4914	4.9	14	5	9.5	9.6–11.5
TA4916	4.9	16	5	9.5	11.6–13.0
TA4918	4.9	18	5	9.5	13.1–15.0
TA4921	4.9	21	5	9.5	15.1–18.0
TA4924	4.9	24	5	9.5	18.1–21.0
TA4927	4.9	27	5	9.5	21.1–24.0
TA4930	4.9	30	5	9.5	24.1–27.0
TA4932	4.9	32	5	9.5	27.1–29.0
TA4935	4.9	35	5	9.5	29.1–31.0
TA4940	4.9	40	5	9.5	31.1–36.0

STEEL WASHERS–To spread the clamping force when rivets are used in soft materials.
Finish–Bright Zinc Plated.

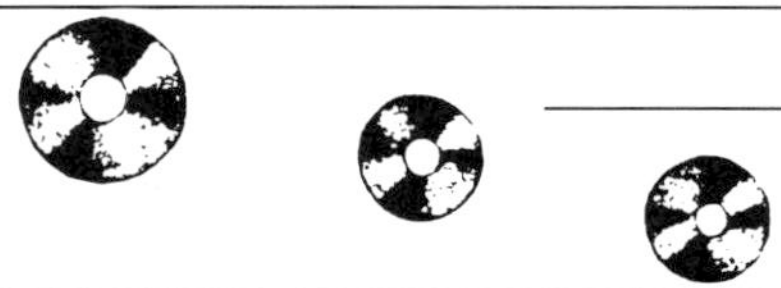

W2.9	WASHERS FOR 2.9 MM RIVETS
W3.9	WASHERS FOR 3.9 MM RIVETS
W4.9	WASHERS FOR 4.9 MM RIVETS

SYSTEM T

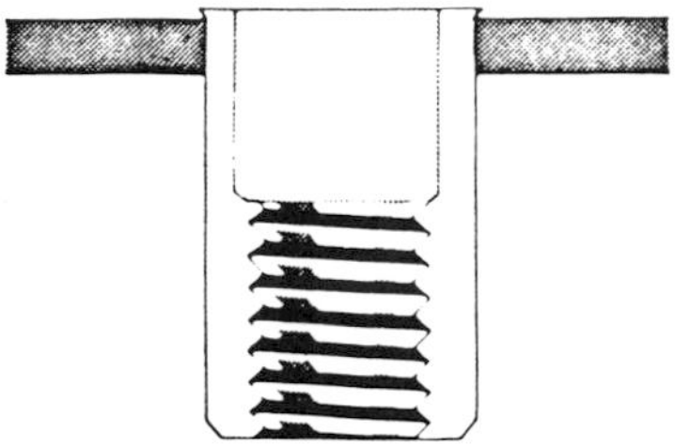

1 The rivet nut is placed into the hole drilled in the workpiece.

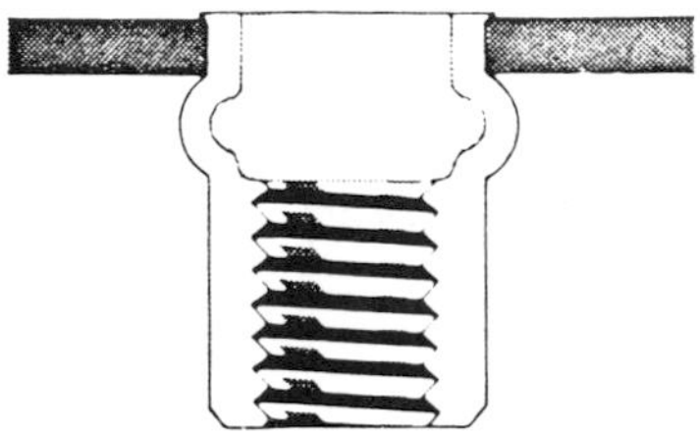

2 The installation tool pulls the threaded part of the rivet nut shank upwards. The plain, unthreaded part of the shank is compressed and bulges outwards. The flange is forced against the surface of the work.

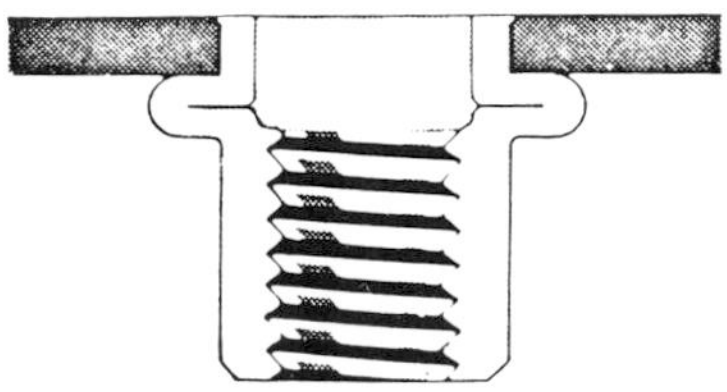

3 The bulge is completely expanded. The flange has buried itself into the work along the hole edge. The rivet nut is securely anchored and presents a flush surface.

SYSTEM X

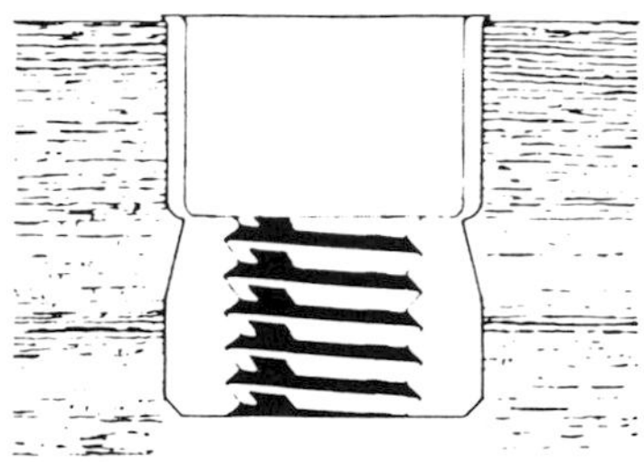

1 The rivet nut is placed into the hole. The shell of the fastener is connected by a thin wall of material to the internally threaded core.

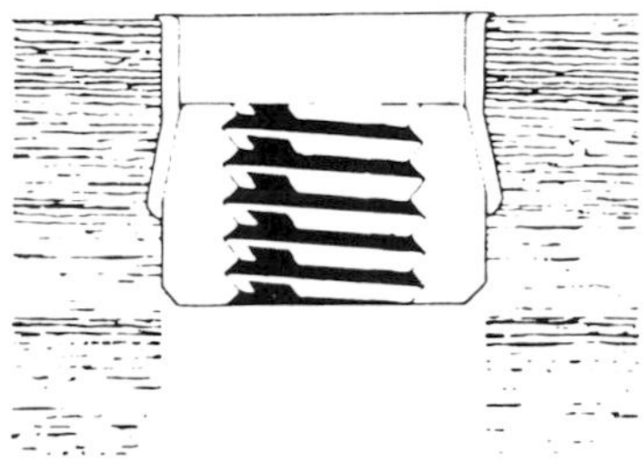

2 The installation tool pulls the core upwards, breaking the thin wall between core and shell. The core enters the shell which starts to expand outwards into the work.

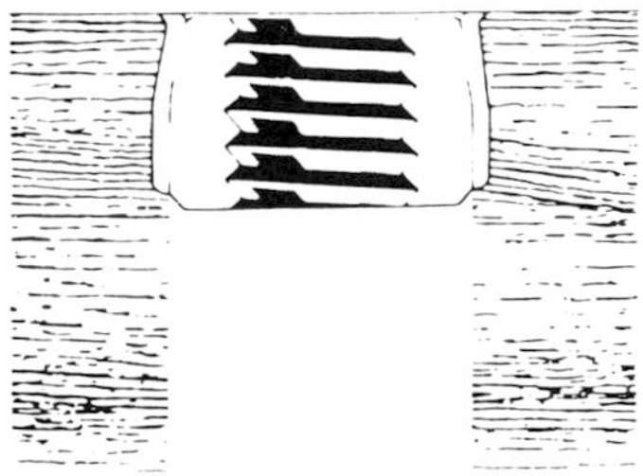

3 The shell is expanded into the work. In work thicknesses less than the depth of the shell, the shell is also bulged at the back of the work. The flange is seated in the work surface.

SYSTEM J

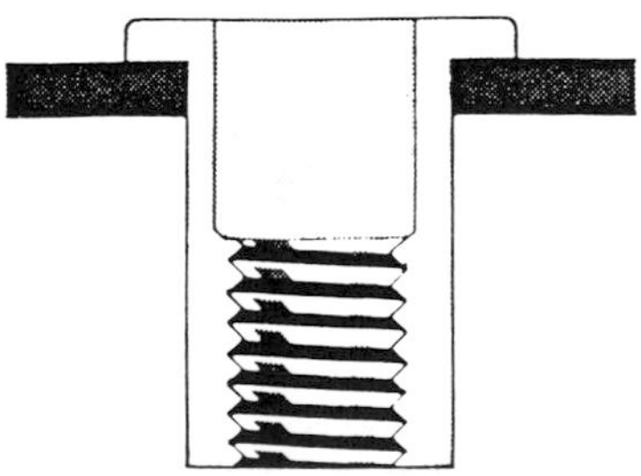

1 The rivet nut is placed into the hole drilled in the workpiece.

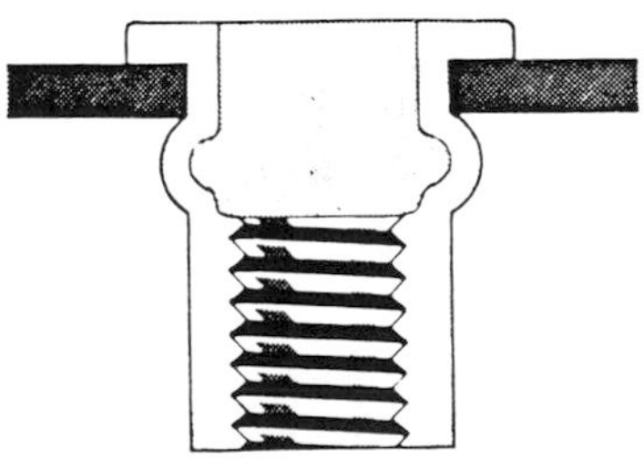

2 The installation tool pulls the threaded part of the rivet nut shank upwards. The plain part is compressed and bulges outwards. The flange is forced against the surface of the work.

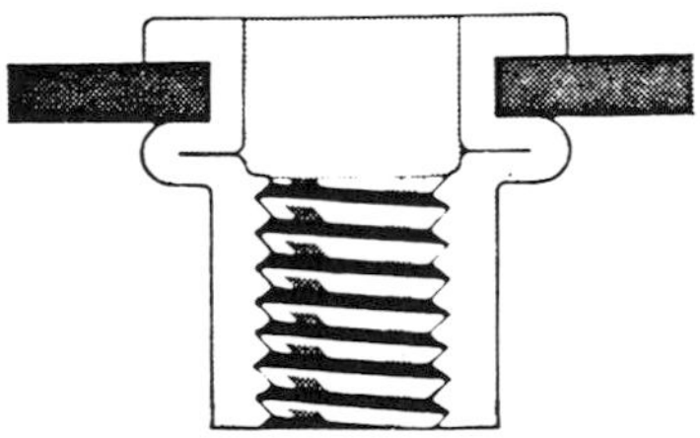

3 The fully expanded bulge and the flange securely clamp the rivet nut to the work, ready to take a screw.

Fig. 33 The T-rivet nut. (Riveting Systems Ltd).

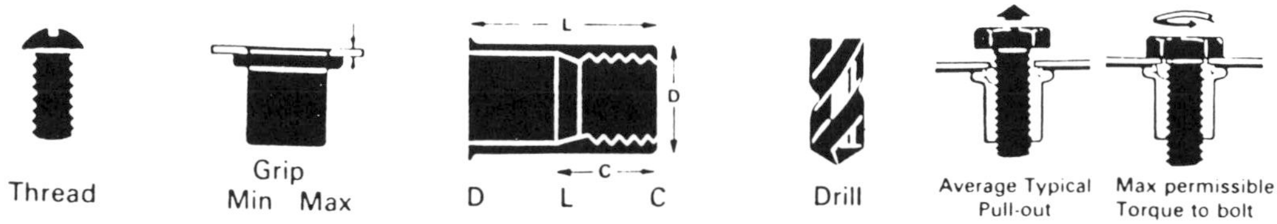

STEEL ZINC PLATED (EXCEPT M3 WHICH IS BRASS, ZINC PLATED)		**METRIC**			**DIMENSIONS IN MILLIMETRES**		
Thread	Grip Min–Max	D	L	C	Drill	Average Typical Pull-out	Max permissible Torque to bolt
M3†	0.51–1.27	4.72	9.02	5.21	4.8	–	13 lbf
M4	0.51–1.27	6.32	10.41	6.35	6.4	920 lbf	45
M5	0.51–1.27	7.11	11.81	6.10	7.2	1,280	70
M6	0.76–3.25	9.5	15.5	8.51	9.6	1,520	110
M8	0.91–3.25	10.57	16.0	9.27	10.6	–	145
STEEL ZINC PLATED		**IMPERIAL, UNIFIED, B.A.**			**DIMENSIONS IN INCHES**		
6 UNC 6 UNF 4 BA	.020–.050	.249	.410	.250	$\frac{1}{4}$	920 lbf	45 lbf
8 UNC 8 UNF	.020–.050	.249	.410	.250	$\frac{1}{4}$	920	45
10 UNC 10 UNF $\frac{3}{16}$ BSW 2 BA	.020–.050	.280	.465	.240	$\frac{9}{32}$	1,280	70
$\frac{1}{4}$ UNC $\frac{1}{4}$ UNF $\frac{1}{4}$ BSW 0 BA	.030–.128	.374	.610	.335	$\frac{3}{8}$	1,520	110

† Except M3 which is brass, zinc plated.
Hole dimensions may have to be varied according to hardness, brittleness and thickness. Generally, holes in hard or thick materials should be larger than in soft or thin. The T system can be used in thicker material if installation and function are proved suitable.

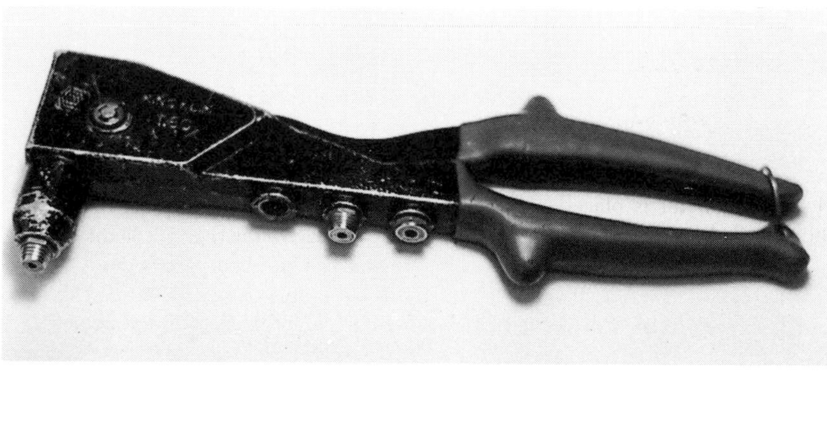

Pop rivet gun.

Fig. 34 The X-rivet nut. (Riveting Systems Ltd).

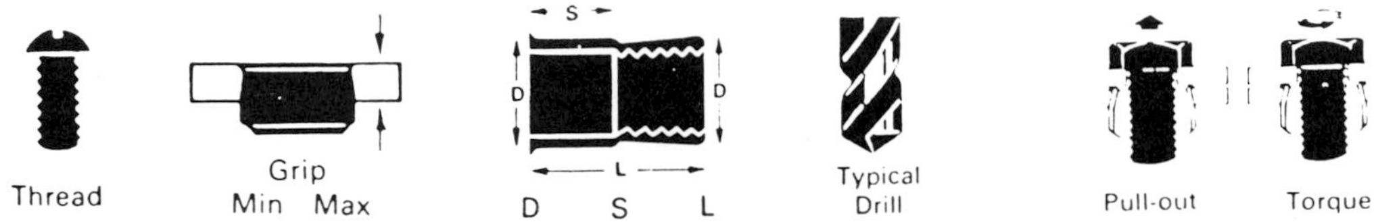

Thread	Grip Min	Grip Max	D	S	L	Typical Drill	
STEEL, ZINC PLATED			**METRIC**			**DIMENSIONS IN MILLIMETRES**	
M3			4.74	4.91	9.66	4.8	
M4			6.33	4.91	6.4		
M5	0.85	NO MAX	7.12	4.91	9.66	7.2	SEE TABLE BELOW
M6			9.50	6.69	13.21	9.6	
M8			12.68	7.96	15.75	12.7	
M10			14.27	9.48	18.80	14.3	
STEEL, ZINC PLATED			**IMPERIAL, UNIFIED, BA**			**DIMENSIONS IN INCHES**	
4 UNC	0.034	NO MAX	.186	.193	.380	$\frac{3}{16}$	
6 UNC 6 UNF 4 BA	0.034	NO MAX	.218	.193	.380	$\frac{7}{32}$	The pull-out and torque of the X-rivet system depend very much on the nature and thickness of the work material and on the hole size.
8 UNC 8 UNF	0.034	NO MAX	.249	.193	.380	$\frac{1}{4}$	
10 UNC 10 UNF $\frac{3}{16}$ BSW 2 BA	0.034	NO MAX.	.280	.193	.380	$\frac{9}{32}$	
$\frac{1}{4}$ UNF $\frac{1}{4}$ UNC $\frac{1}{4}$ BSW $\frac{1}{4}$ BSF 0 BA	0.034	NO MAX	.374	.263	.520	$\frac{3}{8}$	Pull out (tensile) strength is very high. The average test force to pull a 10 mm ⅜″ rivet nut out of 6 mm steel was 4,480 lbf, 2,032 Kp.
$\frac{5}{16}$ UNC $\frac{5}{16}$ UNF $\frac{5}{16}$ BSW $\frac{5}{16}$ BSF	0.034	NO MAX.	.499	.313	.620	$\frac{1}{2}$	
$\frac{3}{8}$ UNC $\frac{3}{8}$ UNF $\frac{3}{8}$ BSW $\frac{3}{8}$ BSF	0.034	NO MAX.	.562	.373	.740	$\frac{9}{16}$	

Hole dimensions given in the table are typical for general, non-critical sheet metal applications. Generally, holes in hard or thick material should be larger than in soft or thin materials.

Fig. 35 The J-rivet nut. Riveting Systems Ltd).

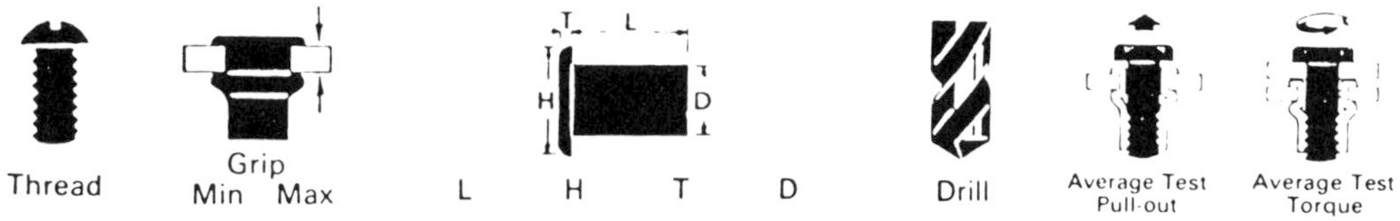

Hole sizes in the table for the J-rivet system below apply to drilling or piercing. The general oversize tolerance is +0,10mm, +0.004". Stricter tolerances are needed for high stress situations.
The table is continued over the page.

ALUMINIUM ALLOY			IMPERIAL, UNIFIED, BA					DIMENSIONS IN INCHES	
Thread	Grip Min	Grip Max	L	H	T	D	Drill	Average Test Pull-out	Average Test Torque
	.076	.100	.375						
4 BA	.141	.160	.437	.320	.035	.187	.190	770 lbf	23 lbf in
	.181	.200	.500						
	.076	.100	.438						
6-32 UNC	.141	.160	.500	.330	.035	.187	.190	770	23
	.181	.200	.562						
	.076	.100	.438						
8-32 UNC	.141	.160	.500	.362	.035	.219	.220	900	32
	.181	.200	.625						
	.076	.120	.500						
10-32 UNF	.121	.160	.500	.382	.035	.250	.252	1130	45
3/16 BSW	.161	.200	.562						
2 BA	.201	.240	.625						
1/4 UNC									
1/4 UNF	.010	.100	.562						
1/4 BSW	.101	.160	.625	.520	.063	.344	.347	2400	150
1/4 BSF	.161	.220	.687						
0 BA									
5/16 UNC	.010	.100	.625						
5/16 UNF	.101	.160	.687	.615	.063	.406	.409	3100	220
5/16" BSW	.161	.220	.750						
5/16 BSF									
3/8 UNC									
3/8 UNF	.010	.100	.625						
3/8 BSW	.101	.160	.687	.692	.063	.469	.472	3700	320
3/8 BSF	.161	.220	.750						

The J-rivet nut continued.

ALUMINIUM ALLOY				METRIC			DIMENSIONS IN MILLIMETRES		
M3	1.0 3.0 5.0	2.0 4.0 6.0	8.5 10.5 12.5	6.8	0.9	4.5	4.55	350 kp	2.6Nm
M4	1.0 3.0 5.0	2.0 4.0 6.0	12.0 14.0 16.0	8.3	0.9	5.5	5.55	400	3.6
M5	0.25 3.0 5.0	2.0 4.0 6.0	13.0 15.0 17.0	9.8	0.9	6.5	6.55	500	5.0
M6	0.25 1.5 4.5	1.5 3.0 6.0	15.0 16.5 19.5	12.5	1.5	8.5	8.6	1100	17.0
M8	0.25 4.0 5.5	2.5 5.5 7.0	16.5 19.5 21.0	15.6	1.5	10.5	10.6	1400	23.0
M10	0.25 4.0 5.5	2.5 5.5 7.0	18.5 21.5 23.0	18.5	1.5	12.5	12.6	1700	36.0
STEEL AND BRASS				**METRIC**			**DIMENSIONS IN MILLIMETRES**		
M3	1.0 3.0 5.0	2.0 4.0 6.0	8.5 10.5 12.5	8.00	0.75	5.0	5.1	550 kp	5.3 Nm
M4	1.0 3.0 5.0	2.0 4.0 6.0	9.75 11.75 13.75	10.00	0.75	6.0	6.1	1000	7.4
M5	1.0 3.0 5.0	2.0 4.0 6.0	11.00 13.00 16.00	11.00	1.0	7.0	7.1	1500	10.5
M6	0.25 3.0 4.5	1.5 4.5 6.0	13.00 16.00 17.50	13.00	1.5	9.0	9.1	2000	35.0
M8	0.25 3.0 4.5	1.5 4.5 6.0	14.50 17.50 19.00	16.00	1.5	11.0	11.1	3200	48.0
M10	0.25 3.0 4.5	1.5 4.5 6.0	15.00 18.00 19.50	18.00	1.5	12.0	12.1	4000	75.0

CHAPTER 9

Joining metals with heat

Soft soldering

Soft soldering is a low temperature method of joining metal together using a suitable alloy. Soft solder is an alloy of tin and lead with a small addition of antimony or bismuth to improve its properties.

The table shows the four main types of soft solder available. Of these, the tinman's and the plumber's solders will serve all the common needs of the car restorer.

There are two basic types of flux used in soft soldering — passive and active. Passive fluxes are usually supplied in paste form and are resin or tallow-based. These fluxes will protect the cleaned surface of the joint from oxidation. However, they will not remove any grease or dirt, even that from apparently clean hands. Active fluxes are usually liquid, 'Bakers Fluid' perhaps being one of the best known. These fluxes will remove a limited amount of grease and will corrode the metal if left for any length of time. For this reason, they should not be used for electrical wiring work as some of the flux will be drawn up under the insulation of the wire and resist all attempts at removal. It will then gradually eat through the wire.

Soft solders.

COMPOSITION OF SOFT SOLDERS						
SOLDER						**USES**
BLOW PIPE OR FINE	345	65		0.5	183°C	COMPONENTS NEEDING A FREE RUNNING SOLDER
TINMAN'S	48	50		2	205°C	GENERAL PURPOSE WORK
PLUMBER'S	66	34			250°C	WIPED JOINTS LEAD LOADING
PEWTERER'S	25	25	50		96°C	SOLDER FOR TIN AND LEAD ALLOYS

Wherever active fluxes are used they should be thoroughly washed off afterwards.

Soldering irons come in different shapes and sizes; they can be heated either by gas stove or electrically.

How to solder.

Clean the joint thoroughly and ensure that it is close fitting as solder should not be used to fill gaps, and if it does the joint will be weak. Apply the flux to the joint.

Heat the soldering iron; one with a copper bit heated in a flame will reach the correct temperature when the flame turns green.

The iron should be dipped quickly into the flux to clean it and then held onto, or rubbed with, the stick of solder, until the bit is covered.

The iron is held onto the joint until the metal has reached the same temperature as the solder; the iron is then drawn slowly along the joint. As soon as the iron begins to cool it should be reheated.

Solder can be applied direct to the work using a gas blowtorch to heat the work and rubbing the solder along the joint. Care must be taken to ensure that the work is not overheated, so forming oxides on the surface which will prevent the solder adhering to the joint.

Sweating is a method of soldering where the two parts are coated with solder before they are put together. They are then placed together and heat applied until the solder melts and joins the parts together. A good example of this is the soldering of a pipe inside a fitting; if the parts were assembled first, only a ring of solder would be holding the parts together at the top of the fitting. Coating the end of the pipe with solder before assembly and then heating the joint results in a much stronger join. Solder paint, which is a mixture of powdered solder and flux, can be painted onto the parts before assembly and then the work heated.

Rules for successful soldering

1. The joint must be clean.
2. The joint must be close fitting.
3. The correct flux must be used.
4. The soldering iron must be in good condition and properly tinned.
5. The work must be heated to the temperature of the molten solder. On small work or thin sheet, the heat of the iron is sufficient to do this. On thicker work it is sometimes necessary to heat the whole job; this can be done by placing the work into a domestic oven or by use of a blowlamp or gas torch. It is important not to overheat the work.
6. The work should be cleaned after soldering to remove any residue of flux.

Leading, or body solder, is used to fill dents or gaps in panel joins on steel bodywork. The solder used has a high lead content and because of its composition it becomes pasty before it finally melts to a liquid. This property enables it to be spread over the surface of the metal providing the heat is carefully controlled.

Solder with a high lead content does not adhere easily to steel and the panel must first be tinned with normal soft solder. Naturally the area must be cleaned to bare rust-free metal and the tinning kept as thin as possible. The body solder is applied by heating the end of the solder stick with a blowtorch and as it becomes pasty pressing it onto the panel and twisting a small piece off. This is done over the area to be filled. Next the solder is carefully heated until it becomes pasty, to be spread with a spatula made from either stainless steel or a hardwood such as beech. It is important that the tinning on the panel is melted as the lead is spread, otherwise it will not adhere properly to the panel. The spatula should be rubbed in resin flux or tallow occasionally to help produce a smooth surface on the solder. The advantage of a wooden spatula, or 'bat' as it is sometimes called, over a stainless steel one is that it can be easily shaped to suit the area being filled, particularly the concave join between wing and body side.

It is important to make sure the area is properly filled before using a 'Surform' or millenicut file to shape the lead. If, after shaping the lead, there are some small pin holes in the surface and you are loathe to use the blow torch and perhaps ruin the shape you have achieved, they can be filled with tinmans or fine solder and a soldering iron, though this is tricky on a vertical panel. Perhaps it would be best to stop while you are ahead and use body filler for the final touch.

Silver soldering

Where a stronger joint is required than can be obtained with soft solder, silver or hard solder can provide the answer; in some cases the only answer. As its name suggests, it contains a percentage of silver which accounts for its high price.

The table on page 75 shows the range of silver solders and their melting points. The reason for having a range of solders is quite simple. Where an article has to be built up of several different pieces — e.g. a coffee pot with soldered-on base, handle, spout and lid hinge — it would be very difficult, if not impossible, to do this with one type of solder. However, the silversmith can start with the highest melting point solder and work down the range without disturbing the pieces already fixed in position.

Silver solder is ideal for copper and copper alloys since brazing uses a brass filler rod which melts at the same temperature as these alloys, causing great difficulty in joining them together without reducing the parts being joined to a molten blob, especially if they are small and a blowtorch is used as the heat source. Because of the extra heat required for silver soldering and brazing, a small hearth built up from fire bricks can be very useful. Old electric night storage heaters provide a good source of firebricks.

Silver solders.

TYPE	COMPOSITION	FLUX	MELTING POINT
ENAMELLING	81% SILVER PLUS COPPER & ZINC	BORAX	800°C
HARD	78% SILVER	BORAX	775°C
MEDIUM	74% SILVER	BORAX	750°C
EASY	67% SILVER	BORAX	720°C
EASY-FLO	50% SILVER	EASY-FLO	625°C

How to silver solder

1. The joint must be clean and close fitting, wired together if necessary.
2. Mix the flux to a smooth paste with water and apply to the joint.
3. Heat the joint; the flux will first dry and then be seen to melt. At this point the joint is near the correct temperature.
4. Apply the solder. When it melts capillary action should make it flow along the joint. It is important that the solder is melted by the heat of the metal rather than the flame.
5. Remove the heat and allow the work to cool before moving.
   Sometimes it is easier or more convenient to cut small pieces of solder and lay them in the joint prior to heating. This will avoid overheating the joint, which will lead to the formation of scale, preventing the solder from joining the parts together.

Brazing

Next up the temperature scale is brazing or bronze welding, depending on the filler rod used. This process requires a temperature of 950°C – 1,000°C to achieve a good joint so a powerful blowtorch, an oxy-acetylene or oxy-propane set or a carbon arc torch fitted to an arc welder, is needed.

Where heavy sections are involved or fine control is needed, an oxy-acetylene set will prove the most versatile.

The actual process of brazing is very similar to hard soldering: the joint should be prepared in the same way. Although brazing flux is capable of cleaning a certain amount of rust from the joint, it is easier if you can make it as clean as possible. The flux should be mixed with water and applied to the joint, which should then be heated to bright cherry red. The end of the brazing rod, or spelter, as it is correctly named, should be heated, dipped into the dry powder flux and held onto the joint. It is important that the spelter is melted by the heat of the metal rather than that of the torch, otherwise the spelter may well sit on the join and prevent the work from heating up. Once the spelter has melted and run into the join, the work should be left to cool before moving. It is not advisable to quench the joint in water as this can lead to the joint becoming brittle and cracking under load.

A simple brazing hearth can be made using refractory bricks on an angle iron stand.

Welding

Welding is a method of joining metals together by heat where the metals being joined are actually melted at the joint face. In most cases, a filler rod of similar metal is melted into the joint to complete the weld.

The source of heat can either be electricity or a combustible gas mixed with oxygen. Electric welding can be one of several types:

Manual Metallic Arc (M.M.A.) This is perhaps the most common form of arc welding used in home workshops: it consists of a transformer with an adjustable output of amperes. One of the leads from the transformer should be clamped to the work piece and is called the earth lead. The other lead has an insulated clamp for holding the consumable electrode. When the electrode is brought into contact with the work piece, the circuit is completed and an arc is formed between the electrode and the work, the heat generated being sufficient to melt both the work and electrode.

Because the welding current is induced by magnetic action between the windings, there is no direct connection between the mains supply and the output cables. Should the circuit be completed by a person touching both the electrode and the earthed workpiece, only a very small current will flow. The degree to which this may be felt will depend on the individual and the prevailing conditions. For instance dampness will always increase conductivity but the current can never reach above a level of complete safety on the output side of the transformer.

Correct protection for the eyes is also essential — a heat resisting face mask fitted with the correct grade of darkened glass must be used. Sunglasses or gas welding goggles are not good enough and their use could result in serious eye damage. It is also important for people or pets in the vicinity not to look at the arc since they will also be affected.

The amperage setting on the welder must be altered to suit both the thickness of the work and the diameter of the electrode. The thicker the work, the higher the setting must be to produce sufficient heat to melt the metal of the work and the electrode. The table shows the relationship between electrode size, amps and work thickness. This is only a guide as several factors can influence the selection of the amperes. A housewife cooking Sunday lunch can have an effect on a welder operating off the domestic ring main.

Electrode–amperes chart. (S.I.P Products Ltd)

DIAMETER OF ROD		RECOMMENDED CURRENT RANGE	APPROXIMATE MATERIAL THICKNESS TO BE WELDED
(MM)	(S.W.G.)	(AMPS)	
1.6	16	25– 50	20–16 S.W.G.
2.0	16	50– 75	16–12 S.W.G.
2.5	12	75–105	12– 8 S.W.G.
3.25	10	105–135	$\frac{1}{8}''-\frac{3}{16}''$
4	8	135–190	$\frac{3}{16}''-\frac{1}{4}''$
5	6	190–240	$\frac{1}{4}''-\frac{3}{8}''$
6	4	240–290	$\frac{3}{8}''-\frac{1}{2}''$

There are no hard and fast rules by which a particular gauge of electrode is selected. This is usually determined by the type of weld required in relation to the thickness of the workpiece. The above table is meant for guidance purposes only and should not be taken as an authority on the selection of any combination of the variables in question.

The correct way is to test the setting on a scrap piece of metal of the same size as your work and adjust the welder until the right setting is found. I would recommend that this is done every time you begin welding, even if the welder has been left at a setting that proved suitable for the same gauge metal as you are intending to weld. This applies particularly when welding thin metal as a slight variation in output can burn through the metal.

The metal core of the electrode should be coated with flux, which melts as the weld progresses. The molten flux forms a fluid coating over the weld, which protects the molten weld pool from the oxidising effect of the atmosphere. Some of the ingredients of the flux form a gas shield around the arc, which helps to stabilise it. The fumes given off by the flux should not be inhaled for long periods and it is advisable to ensure adequate ventilation to remove these.

The metal core of the electrode should also be matched to the metal being welded; low carbon rods for low carbon steels, alloy steel rods for alloy steels, nickel rich or monel for cast iron. Non-ferrous metals are welded with electrodes having a similar composition to the metal being welded.

Successful arc welding is very much a question of 'practise makes perfect' and plenty of time should be devoted to practising the techniques required to produce a satisfactory weld before attempting to weld something important. The first technique to be learned is striking the arc between the electrode and the work. One method is to scratch the tip of the rod on the surface of the metal and then lift the rod sharply to create a gap of between 1/16 in and ⅛ in (1.6–3 mm). Another method is to tap the end of the rod onto the work and lift it quickly to produce the arc. If the rod is not 'bounced' quickly off the metal it may stick to the work, resulting in a direct short circuit. The transformer should then be switched off and the rod loosened by bending from side to side. Should there be difficulty in striking the arc, the earth clamp should be checked for a proper connection with the work and the welding current also checked, as this may be too low for the rod selected.

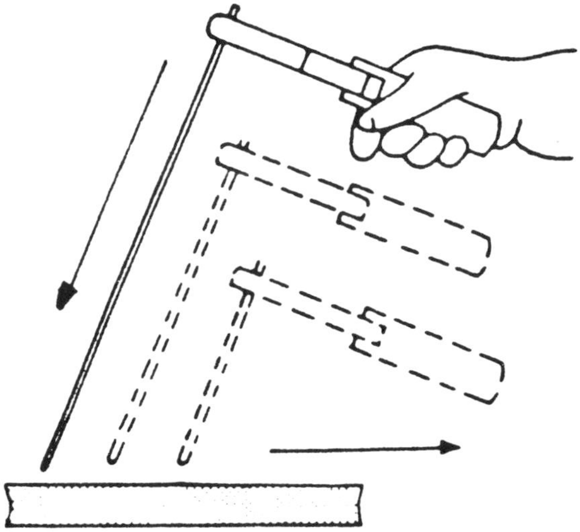

Fig. 36 Electrode angle for M.M.A. welding. S.I.P. Products Ltd)

Fig. 37 Cross-sections of different welds. (S.I.P. Products Ltd)

To produce a satisfactory weld bead only two movements are required, a steady movement in the direction of the weld and a slow downward movement to maintain the correct arc length as the electrode melts, see Fig. 36. It is important to maintain the arc length and correct rate of travel at all times. If the rate of travel is too slow, the slag formed will flow in front of the weld pool and become trapped within the weld, weakening it with impurities and gas pockets. A correctly-made weld is the same width throughout its length, has good penetration, and is uniformly rippled. If the current setting is too low, a thin bead will be deposited, having little or no penetration into the metal. The sound the arc makes will be an intermittent crackling with irregular spluttering. Too high a current will provide plenty of penetration but the bead will be undercut and the electrode will burn away very fiercely, and there is the possibility of burning through the work, especially

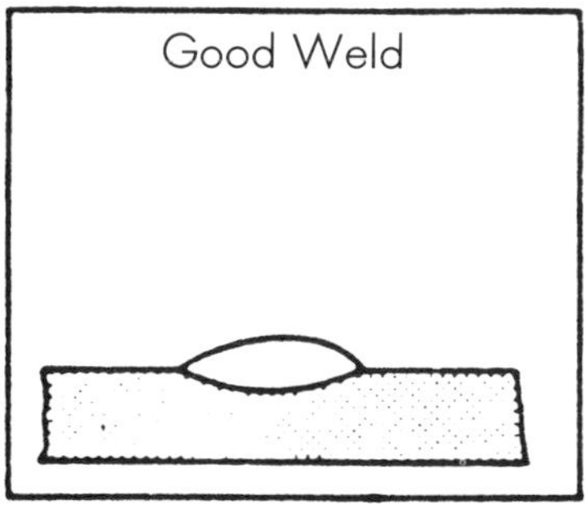

NORMAL CONDITIONS
Uniform ripples on surface of weld. Arc makes steady crackling sound.

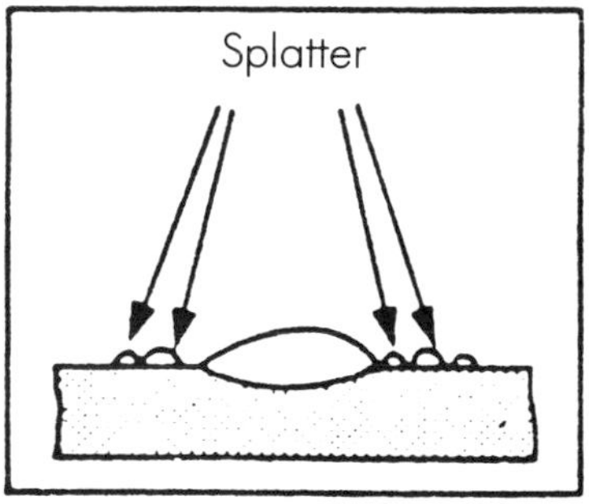

ARC TOO LONG
Surface of weld rough. Rod melts off in globules. Arc makes hissing sound.

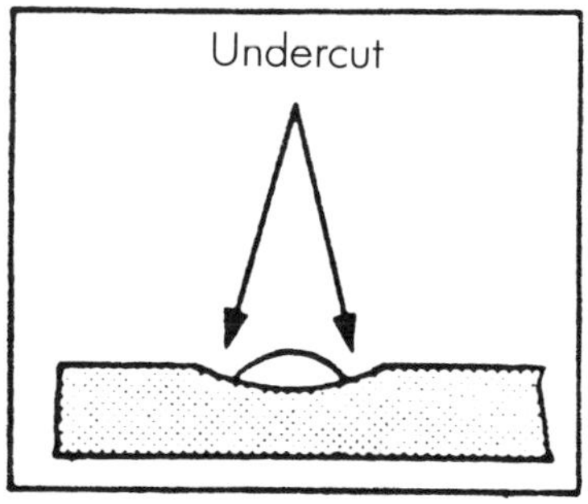

TRAVEL TOO FAST
Small bead undercut in some places. Rough surface and little penetration.

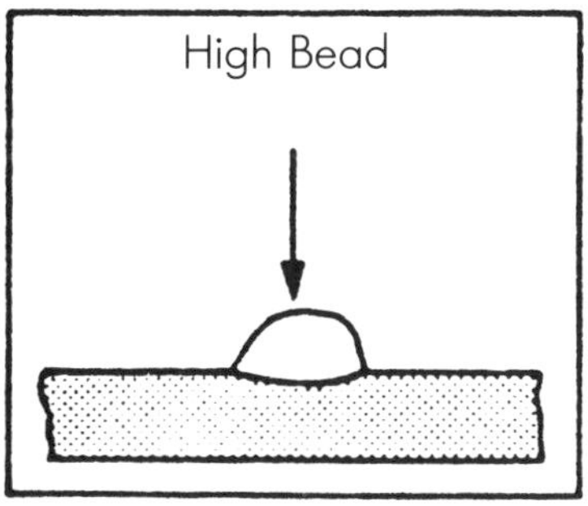

CURRENT TOO LOW
Arc is difficult to maintain. Very little penetration.

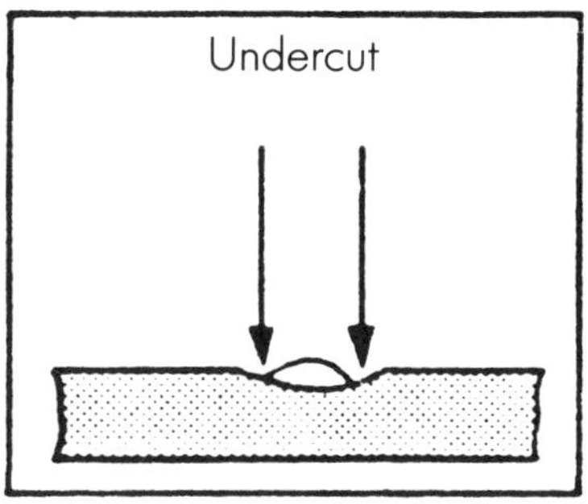

CURRENT TOO HIGH
Wide thick bead, undercut. Crater pointed and long. Rod burns away very quickly.

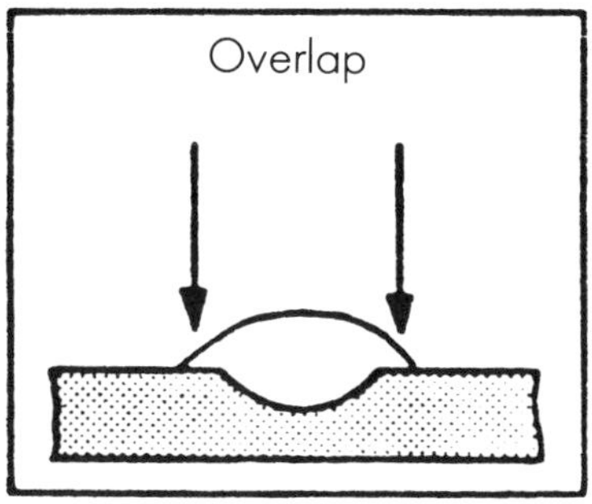

TRAVEL TOO SLOW
Metal builds up producing a wide heavy bead which noticeably overlaps at sides.

if it is fairly thin. When the travel is too fast, a very small bead will be formed; too slow will produce a wide bead and the overheating caused could lead to distortion of the work. When the electrode is held too far away from the work, producing a long arc, the rod will shoot off in globules, with scarcely any penetration and give an irregular surface. The arc itself will make a hissing sound and may peter out from time to time. Fig. 37 shows a cross-section through the different types of welds.

Metal Inert Gas (M.I.G.) This type of arc welding has gained in popularity in recent years with the introduction of smaller units and the appreciation of its qualities. The consumable electrode is in the form of a thin wire which is fed automatically into the weld pool from the welding torch assembly. At the same time, an inert gas is passed through the torch assembly to form a shield around the electrode and weld pool. It is this gas shield which gives M.I.G. welding its great advantage over M.M.A. welding. Because the gas protects the weld from the oxidising effects of the atmosphere, the electrode does not have to be coated with flux. This in turn means that the welding wire can be supplied from a reel on the equipment, obviating the need to stop welding every time an

IDEAL 120N USED WITH ARGON/CO_2 MIXTURE

WIRE THICKNESS	**30.6MM**						**0.8MM**			
PLATE THICKNESS	22SWG 0.7MM	20SWG 1.0MM	18SWG 1.2MM	16SWG 1.5MM	14SWG 2.0MM	1/8" 3.0MM	18SWG 1.2MM	16SWG 1.5MM	14SWG 2.0MM	1/8" + 3.0MM
VOLTAGE SETTING	1	2	3	4	5	6*	3*	4	5	6
WIRE FEED SETTING	2	2½	3	4	5	8*	2½	3½	4	5

IDEAL 120N USED WITH CO_2 GAS

WIRE THICKNESS	**0.6MM**				**0.8MM**		
PLATE THICKNESS	22SWG 0.7MM	18SWG 1.2MM	14SWG 2MM	12SWG+ 3MM+	16SWG 1.5MM	14SWG 1.0MM	12SWG+ 2.5MM+
VOLTAGE SETTING	3	4	5	6*	4*	5	6
WIRE FEED SETTING	1½	3	4	5	2½	3½	4–5

IDEAL 150

											SPOT WELD	**STITCH WELD**
WIRE THICKNESS	0.6					0.8					0.8	0.6
PLATE THICKNESS	22SWG	18SWG	1/16"	1/8"	3/16"	22SWG	18SWG	1/16"	1/8"	3/16"	18SWG	18SWG
VOLTAGE SETTING	1	2	3	4	5	1	2	3	4	5	5	2
WIRE FEED SETTING	1½–2	2½–3	3–4	4–5*	7–8*	1–½*	1½–2*	2–3	2½–3	4–5	4–5	2–2½
WELD TIME	–	–	–	–	–	–	–	–	–	–	6	3
PAUSE TIME	–		–	–	–	–	–	–	–	–	–	1
BURNBACK SETTING	0–1					0–1					0–1	0–1

Preferred settings shown without asterisk*

electrode is used up.

The second advantage is that the gas shield also helps to cool the welded metal down, which reduces distortion and the spread of heat, so making it possible to weld much closer to inflammable materials such as interior trim without recourse to stripping most of it out. This does not, of course, apply to petrol tanks, which should always be emptied and removed from the vehicle before any welding is done in their vicinity, unless you wish to meet an untimely end in a very impressive explosion.

There are two gases that can be used, either argon or carbon dioxide. These can be used in the pure state though argon is usually mixed with 5% Co_2 and 2% oxygen. This is sold as 'Argoshield 5' by the British Oxygen Company or 'Cougar 95/5' by Air Products Ltd. For welding steel, carbon dioxide is the cheaper of the two, but because it is a cooler gas, the welder will need higher settings to cope with the cooling effects.

Aluminium has to be welded with pure argon while stainless steel requires argon mixed with 1% or 2% oxygen. Naturally the correct welding wire must also be used.

The rate at which the wire is fed through the torch assembly, the current setting, and the gas flow, will depend on the thickness and type of material being welded; full instructions for this should be in the booklet that accompanies the welder.

The table shows the settings used for the S.I.P. Ideal 120 & 150 M.I.G. Welders. These should be used as a basic guide and fine adjustment either side of these settings will find the best results. A steady purr from the torch with little spatter is the indication that all is correct.

It is possible to produce a type of spot welding with an M.I.G. torch. Most sets have a spot welding nozzle which has two legs protruding from its end. When these legs are placed onto the metal, the nozzle is held static and when the welding wire strikes the metal

Left *Settings for M.I.G. welders.* (S.I.P. Products Ltd)

S.I.P. Mig-mate welder. (S.I.P. Products Ltd)

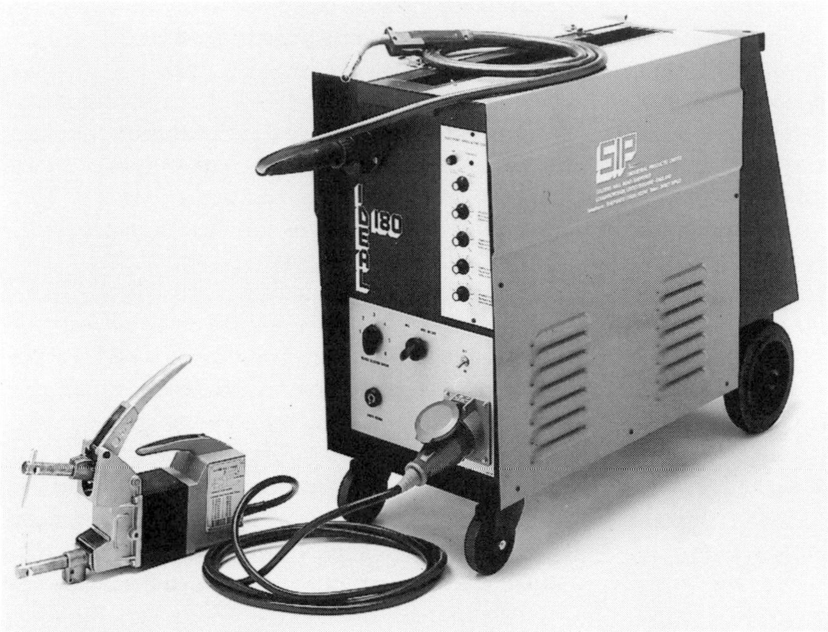

S.I.P. 180 Mig-welder. (S.I.P. Products Ltd)

it passes through the top layer into the one below. To aid the process, it is a good idea to drill a small hole in the top piece of metal and to ensure that the two plates are clamped close together. The power required to successfully weld in this situation is greater than that for seam welding and the settings required should be in the user's handbook for your machine.

Larger machines usually have a timer incorporated in them for this type of welding (and once set will produce a weld of consistent quality each time. This timer can also be used to 'stitch' a joint by giving a 'weld on' time followed by a pause or 'weld off' time.

On smaller machines, your own judgement has to be used for the length of time for the spot weld. Too little time will produce a weak weld with little penetration; too long a time will produce a large build-up of weld or a complete burn through of the plates.

Welding problems with an M.I.G.

Fault 1
Arc unstable, excessive spatter and weld porosity.
Cause
1) Insufficient shielding gas
2) Torch held too far from metal being welded
3) Grease, rust or paint on the metal
Solutions
1) Check contents gauge of gas bottle, check setting of regulator and pipes for kinks
Don't weld in a strong draught either indoors or outside
2) Don't hold the torch more than 10 mm (3/8 in) away from the work
3) Clean work off thoroughly

Fault 2
Weld deposit too thick
Cause
1) Welding voltage too low
2) Moving torch too slowly over metal being welded
Solutions
1) Turn up power until weld 'purrs' correctly
2) Move torch more quickly

Fault 3
Weld deposit stringy
Cause
1) Gas flow incorrect
2) Moving torch too quickly

Solutions
1) See fault 1.1
2) Slow movement of torch — always move in one direction, don't back track

Fault 3
Lack of penetration
Cause
1) Moving torch too quickly
2) Wire feed speed too low
3) Welding volts too low
Solutions
1) Slow down
2) Turn up power one setting at a time
3) See 2

Fault 4
Burning through the metal
Cause
1) Wire feed speed too high
2) Welding volts too high
3) Torch moved too slowly
Solutions
1) Step power setting down one step at a time
2) See 1
3) Keep torch moving continuously, smoothly

Fault 5
Wire repeatedly burns back
Cause
1) Torch too close to work
2) Wire speed too slow
3) Gas coverage poor
4) Intermittent break in welding circuit — possible causes:
   a) welding wire corroded
   b) contact tip damaged or loose
5) Wire feed slipping, possible causes:
   a) pressure wire roll adjustment incorrect
   b) worn feed rolls
   c) corrosion or blockage in liner
   d) faulty contact tip
Solutions
1) Hold torch 10 mm (⅜ in) away from work
2) Adjust wire feed
3) Check nozzle not filled with spatter, see fault 1.1
4) a) Replace wire
   b) Check and replace if necessary
5) a) Adjust pressure
   b) Replace feed rolls
   c) Check and replace if necessary
   d) Check and replace if necessary

Gas welding

The heat source used in the most common form of gas welding is a mixture of oxygen and acetylene known universally as oxy-acetylene welding. Mapp gas and oxygen can also be used and the techniques of welding are the same with either gas.

The gas is stored under pressure in cylinders colour-coded black for oxygen and maroon for acetylene, 'Mapp' gas bottles being labelled with their name. The rubber hoses connecting the cylinders to the torch are also coloured in the same way and the regulators that screw into the cylinders are also threaded differently: a right-hand thread for oxygen, left-hand thread for acetylene. The left-hand threads can be identified by small cuts on the corners of all the relevant nuts.

The regulators have two dials, the right-hand one indicates the cylinder contents, the left reads the outlet pressure. The regulators also have a pressure regulating screw which is operated once the main cylinder valve has been opened.

Before the regulators are fitted, the cylinders must be vented; that is the term used to describe the method of making sure that the threads and valve at the top of the cylinder are clean. The cylinder valve should be opened very briefly, allowing a short, sharp, release of gas which will blow out any particles of dirt.

It is important when fixing the regulators to the cylinders that no cross-threading occurs and that the correct spanner is used; do not over-tighten as this could strain the brass of the fittings. The hoses and the torch should be fitted next and the main cylinder valves can be opened.

The torch is basically a mixing chamber for the two gases; the amount of each gas that is allowed into the torch is controlled by a knob, blue for oxygen, red for acetylene. The combined gases leave the torch via the nozzle, to be burnt at the nozzle tip.

The nozzle of the torch is removable and nozzles

are available with different hole diameters at the tip. It is the size of the hole that determines the thickness of metal that can be welded.

The most common sizes are: 1, 2, 3, 4, 5, 7, 10, 13, 16, 25 and 35. The larger the number, the larger the hole in the tip. For thin sheet metal work such as car panels, the number 1 nozzle is the most suitable. Over 1.0 mm (20 s.w.g.) a number 2 or 3 will be required. Commercially available sets of nozzles usually incorporate a chart, matching nozzle size to metal size, but this should only be regarded as a guide rather than a hard and fast rule, because the flame adjustment and the material can also affect the tip size.

For most welds, a filler rod will be needed and should be the same composition as the metal being welded. Mild steel rods are copper-coated to help reduce oxidation; the most common size is 1.6 mm diameter and they are generally sold by weight.

When everything is ready, the main cylinder valves should be turned on and the pressure regulated to the required setting. Once set, the torch valves can be opened and the pressure levels re-adjusted if necessary. After closing the valves, the torch is ready for lighting.

The acetylene control should be opened slightly and the torch lit. The flame should then be increased in size until it begins to smoke. Then the acetylene control should be gradually closed until the flame just ceases to smoke. The oxygen control can now be opened gradually. As the amount of oxygen is increased, a white cone will become visible in the centre of the flame. The oxygen control on the torch should be adjusted until the cone is only a few millimetres long, with a rounded tip. This type of flame is called a neutral flame. There are two other types of flame that can be produced by adjusting the proportions of oxygen to acetylene. An oxidising flame is produced by reducing the flow of acetylene, which will reduce the overall size of the cone and flame; and a reducing or carburising flame which is achieved by increasing the acetylene flow until a feather-like haze appears around the central cone.

These different types of flame are required for welding different types of metal. An oxidising flame is used for welding brass and bronze the excess oxygen helps to prevent the zinc in the brass from vapourising out. The reducing flame is used for welding cast iron and the neutral flame is ideal for mild steel, stainless steel, copper and aluminium.

There are two main methods of welding with a gas

Fig. 38 Leftward and rightward welding.

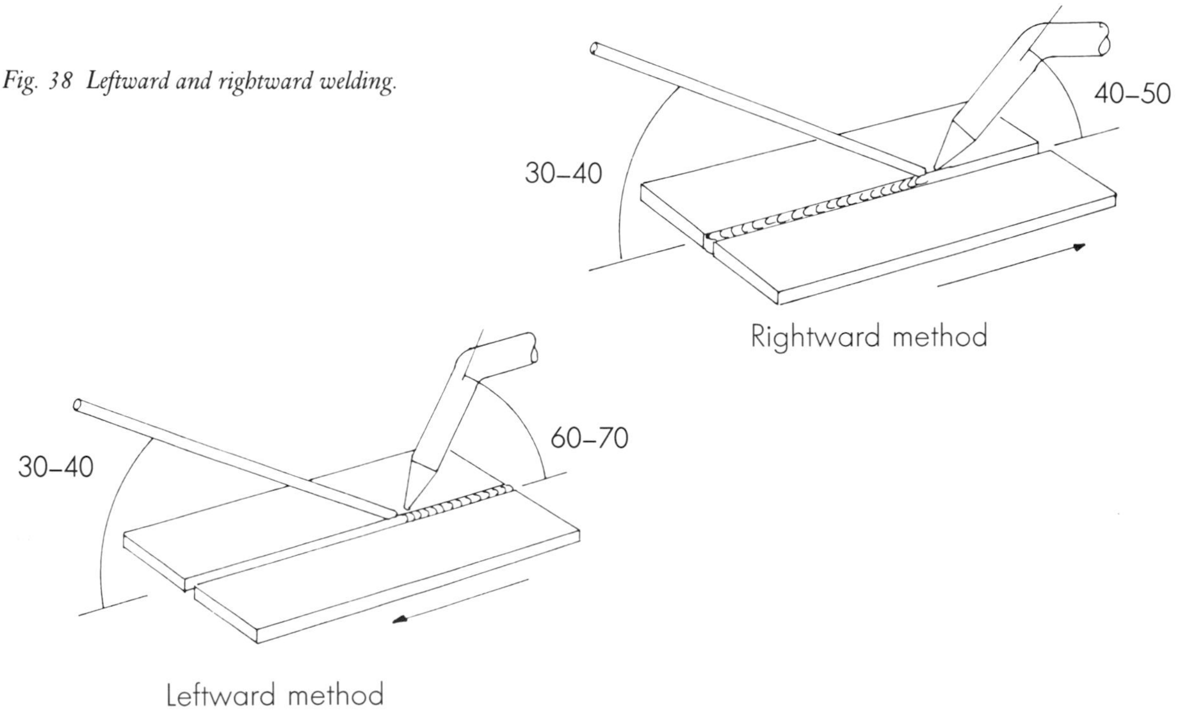

torch, known as leftward and rightward welding, see Fig. 38. For thinner metal below 5 mm 3/16 in thick, leftward welding is used with the filler rod introduced in front of the flame. The flame should be kept moving forward at all times coupled with a slight zig-zag movement to ensure that both sides of the joint are kept molten. The filler rod is fed into the centre of the weld pool to produce a satisfactory joint.

Rightward welding is used on work that is over 5 mm thick; in this instance the torch is moved to the right in a circular movement and the filler rod is fed into the weld pool behind the torch. This method enables the torch to pre-heat the metal and ensure a fluid weld pool that joins the two parts together.

One of the main problems with gas welding is heat distortion and the thinner the metal being welded, the greater the distortion. The main precaution used to overcome this distortion is to tack weld the joint prior to the final weld; the thinner the metal, the closer the tacks should be. They should be kept as small as practicable to prevent obstructions when completing the joint.

The metal for gas welding does not have to be completely clean as the torch will weld through a small amount of debris, but it can cause spitting and spluttering which may be disconcerting when you are concentrating on producing a sound joint.

Flat welding includes all joints in which the weld is laid horizontally and the electrode or filler rod is fed downward into the joint. Flat welding is the easiest form of welding since there is no tendency for the molten weld pool to run under the force of gravity which can make other forms of welding difficult. Therefore it is preferable wherever possible to arrange the work so that the joint is flat.

However, it is not always easy to achieve a flat position and welding vertically and overhead should be practised. Vertical welding can be done vertical-up or vertical-down. The basic problem is the sag of the weld pool; for this reason vertical down is preferable as the cold metal beneath the weld prevents the weld pool sagging too easily. Fine control is necessary whichever type of welding you are using and practice is essential on similar thickness material until you are satisfied that the weld can be accomplished correctly.

Overhead welding is probably the most difficult to achieve successfully. Avoid trying to lay too much weld at one time as this leads to a larger weld pool which is more likely to drop. You may find it easier to weld the join with a series of tacks, gradually filling in the gaps.

A head screen, leather apron and gauntlet gloves should be worn as a protection against spatter and molten metal dropping from the joint.

T.I.G. welding (Tungsten inert gas)

T.I.G. welding is not a method of welding available to the amateur but a brief description of the process will at least remove the confusion that often exists in people's minds over the different forms of welding. In the T.I.G. welding process, the heat is supplied by an electric arc from a tungsten electrode which will withstand the high temperatures without melting. The electrode is surrounded by a nozzle which conducts the shielding gas to the weld area; the gases used are either argon or helium. A filler rod is fed into the weld area by hand or, in an automated set up, by machine.

T.I.G. welding is used extensively in the aircraft and atomic energy industries because it will produce high quality welds in light alloys and other difficult metals.

It is also very versatile, using current from as little as 0.5 amps to as high as 750 amps. Very small currents used with specialised air-cooled torches can weld metals as little as 0.05 mm thick.

Spot welding

Most motor cars built with all steel unit-construction bodies have the seams between the panels spot welded together. A spot weld is achieved by clamping the parts to be joined firmly between a pair of heavy electrodes which are connected to the secondary circuit of a step-down transformer. The maximum resistance in the circuit is at the point of contact between the two parts being joined and localised heating occurs. The rise in temperature is sufficient for the metal to fuse together forming a rigid joint. Fig. 39 shows, in diagrammatic form, a section through a spot weld being formed.

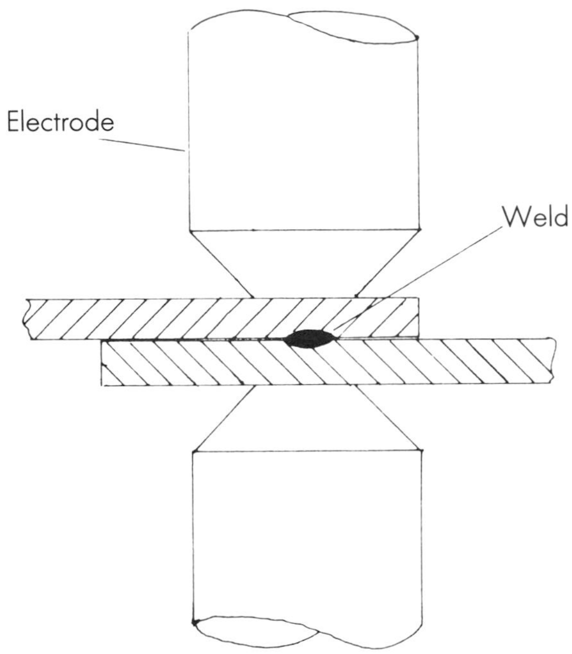

Fig. 39 Cross-section through a spot weld.

Spot welding faults

Fault 1
Holes burnt through work
Cause
1) Weld time too long
2) Weld settings too high
3) Distance between the metals being joined too wide
4) Weld too close to the edge
Solutions
1) Reduce weld time
2) Reduce settings
3) Clamp close together, ensure plates are flat, use self-tapping screws if necessary
4) Use a seam weld if the spot weld position cannot be moved away from the edge

Fault 2
Insufficient penetration
Cause
1) Weld time too short
2) Weld settings too low
3) Distance between the metals too wide
Solutions
1) Increase time
2) Increase setting. If CO_2 is being used, the low temperature of the gas could make welding difficult with thicker metals
3) See solution 1.3

Spot welders are usually rated at 25 amps and if run from a domestic 13 amp ring main could blow the fuses. An uprated circuit is needed to cope with the extra load. They can only work when access is possible to both sides of the metal. This in turn gives rise to the need for interchangeable arms for the welder to reach into awkward places and over longer distances. To produce satisfactory spot welds, the metal must be clean and the joints close fitting. The parts should be clamped together in several places to ensure that the panel cannot move out of alignment during welding. The position of the welds should be marked out along the join to give an even spacing. If you are not sure of the spacing, measure the ones on a similar area of the bodywork as a guide.

The faces of the electrodes should be clean and smooth to achieve a good contact between them and the metal panel. The electrodes are brought into contact with the work and pressure applied before the current is allowed to flow. Once the joint is formed, the current is switched off and the joint allowed to cool sufficiently to prevent movement before the pressure is removed. The more expensive spot welders incorporate a timer which can be set to switch the current off when the weld is complete, depending on the thickness of the metal being welded. This makes the process easier and the welds more uniform in quality.

Carbon arc torch

A useful addition to an ordinary arc welder is a carbon arc torch. This consists of an insulated handle which has two metal rods passing through it. At the end of one rod is a clamp for holding a copper-coated carbon electrode. The other rod, which can slide in and out of the handle, has a clamp for holding the second electrode. The two rods are connected by electrical cable to the positive and negative clamps of the arc welder.

The welder is set to a low amperage and when the sliding carbon electrode is brought into close contact with the fixed electrode, an arc flame is formed between the two. It must be emphasised that a full head shield is needed plus gloves and long sleeves for this operation. The arc gives off strong ultra violet radiation which can burn the skin in the same way as a long session of sun bathing.

The actual process of brazing with the carbon arc torch is the same as that when using an ordinary blow torch; the metal being joined must be clean and the joint close fitting; flux must be used to prevent the metal oxidising in the flame.

The main disadvantage of using the carbon arc torch is the difficulty of seeing when the metal being joined is at bright cherry red because of the dark glass of the eyeshield. It is possible to burn through thin metal without realizing how hot the metal is becoming. This can be avoided by cutting off small pieces of brazing rod and placing them on the joint. When the metal reaches the correct temperature, the pieces of spelter will melt and run along the joint. A second disadvantage is the large amount of distortion caused by the flame. This can be minimised by careful clamping of the work or by the use of self-tapping screws where possible to hold the parts together. For this reason, I would not recommend using a carbon arc torch for body repairs in situ.

Fig. 41 Edge preparation.

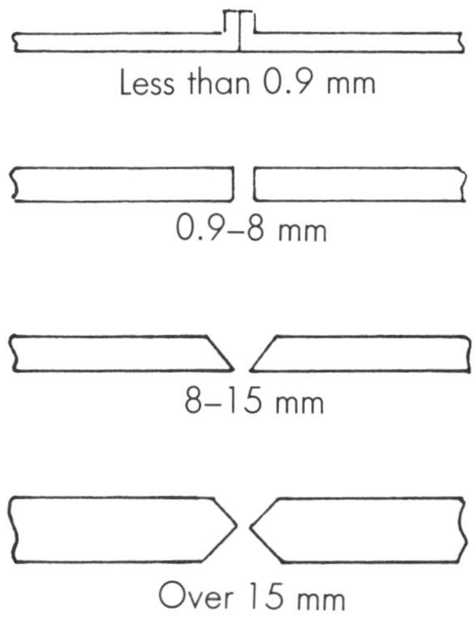

Welding joints

No matter what type of welder you use, apart from a pure spot weld, the different types of joints are given the same name. Before trying any new type of joint it is best to practise on some scrap metal first. See Fig. 40.

Before welding butt joints together the edges of the metal must be prepared to achieve adequate penetration of the weld into the joint. See Fig. 41.

Fig. 40 Different welds. (S.I.P. Products Ltd)

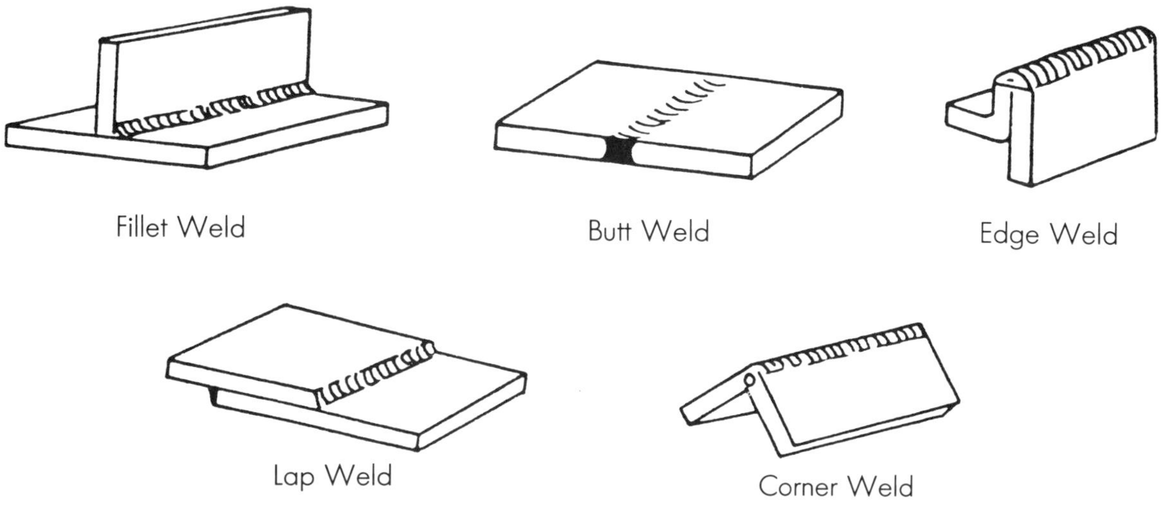

Welding safety

It is important to remember that whichever type of welding is used, there are some important safety precautions that must be taken.

Suitable clothing must be worn; a cotton boiler suit that secures at the neck and wrists is ideal. Do not use nylon because any hot sparks or molten slag will melt through it, increasing the danger from burns. A strong leather apron and gloves will also give added protection; metal that has been welded retains the heat for some time and gloves can save many painful burns.

Eye protection is essential and it is important that the correct grade of dark glass is used for the type of welding undertaken. Ensure that onlookers are protected from the flash of electric welding and the glare from carbon arc brazing. If you are using an extension lead connected to an arc-welder, make sure all the lead is unwound from the drum. The high current passing through the cable can cause over-heating if it is left coiled.

Gas bottles should always be used upright and checked carefully for leaks before lighting the torch.

When welding direct onto a car body, check carefully that there is nothing inflammable near the weld such as underseal, carpets, electrical wiring, petrol or brake pipes. Always have a suitable fire extinguisher handy in case the worst happens.

Never weld in a confined space where you could be trapped in the event of a fire. If you have to weld in such a position have someone standing by to help in an emergency.

Always provide adequate ventilation when welding. It is not healthy to breathe the fumes produced by welding fluxes, and some metals, particularly galvanised steel, can produce fumes that cause temporary breathing problems and uncontrolled tremors of the hands. If you have to weld galvanised steel and you do not have adequate ventilation or extraction equipment, restrict your welding to very short periods, allowing plenty of time between them to let the fumes disperse.

CHAPTER 10

Sheet metal and tube work

Sheet metal and beaten metalwork is an area of vehicle restoration that many people feel very unsure of. The mysterious art of the skilled panel beater who is able, with the help of a few odd shaped hammers and the assistance of lumps of smooth metal called 'dollies' to produce beautiful flowing bodywork with voluptuous compound curves, seems beyond the meagre ability of us ordinary folk. Though none of us will turn into panel beaters overnight there is a lot that can be achieved with a few simple tools, careful thought and some practice on scrap metal. Hopefully, this will leave only the difficult pieces to be taken to the professionals.

Sheetmetal work can be broken down into three stages: marking and cutting out, shaping and joining. The joining of sheet metal has already been dealt with in other sections of this book so I shall concentrate on the other two.

Normal marking out tools are required for sheet metal and the only point to remember is that when marking out soft metals or coated steel — i.e. tinplate, etc — a soft pencil should be used unless the metal is going to be cut along the marked line. Soft metals scratch very easily and the blemish is difficult to remove, while cutting through the protective coating on sheet steel will encourage rust to spread under the coating and lift it off. Most body panels on modern cars are 20 or 22 S.W.G. with 18 or 16 S.W.G. for the chassis pressings. Older cars used thicker gauge material, which is one of the reasons they have lasted so well. When making replacement parts, do not use a thicker gauge material than the original. It is not necessary from the strength point of view and the thicker the gauge, the harder it is to work.

Hand-held tinsnips for cutting sheet metal are usually adequate up to 18 S.W.G. in steel or 16 S.W.G in copper and aluminium. Beyond this it is very hard work and accuracy is very difficult.

A pair of bench shears will cope with thicker sections, but along with the tinsnips they distort the metal that is being cut off. In many instances, this does not matter but where both pieces are needed, the distortion can cause problems. A hand tool such as the 'Monodex' cutter will cut without distortion as will bench shears that are designed to remove a strip of metal as they cut. A 'nibbler' fitted to an electric drill will cut through metal easily, reducing the effort required enormously.

Tin snips.

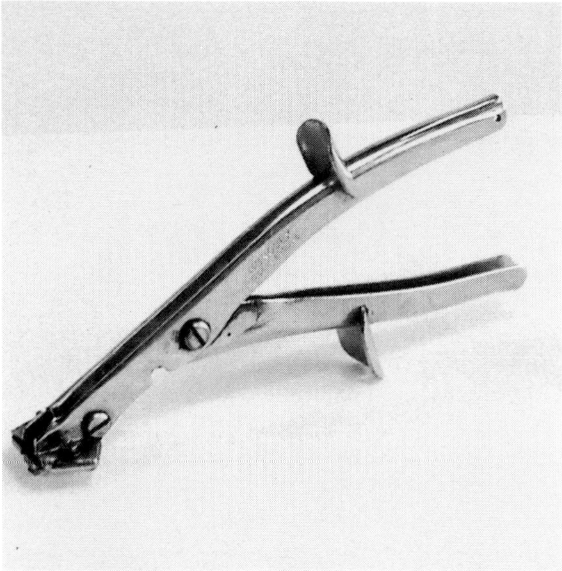

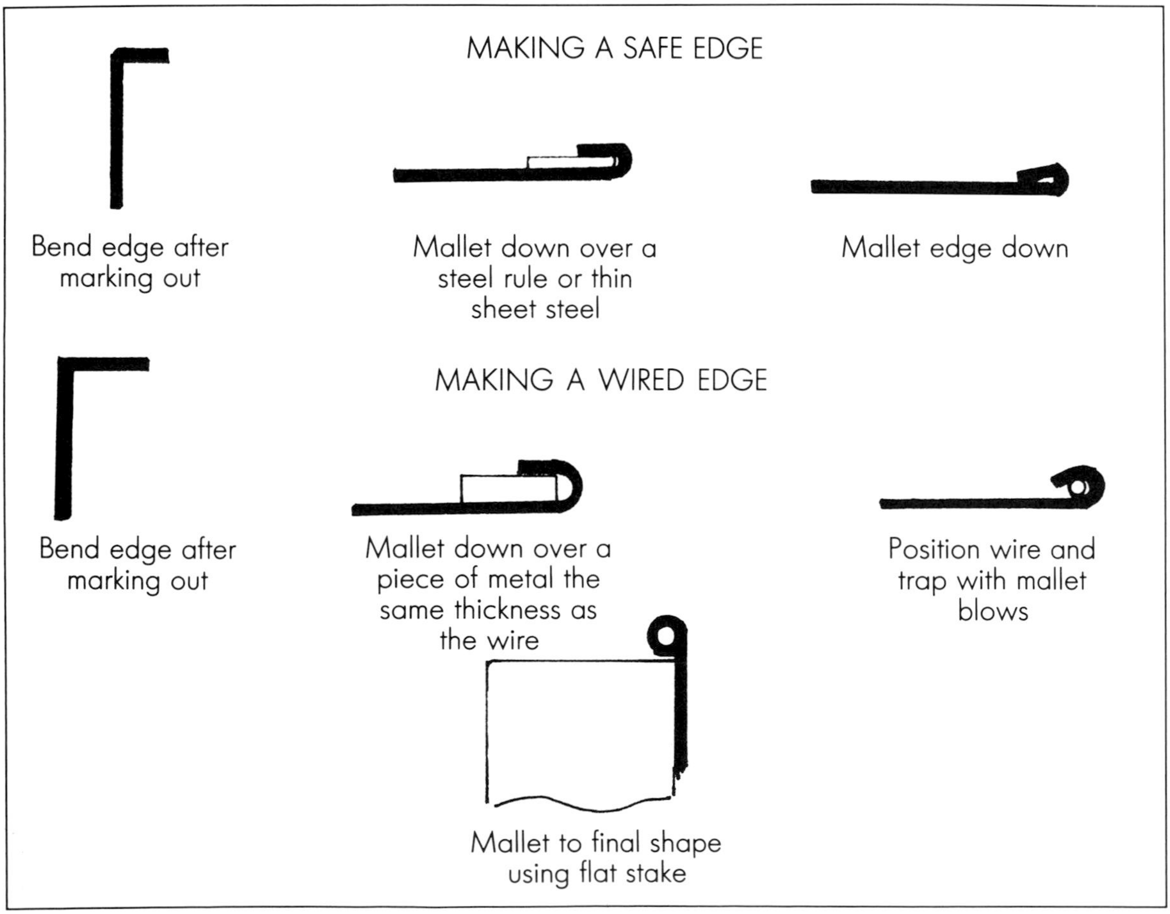
MAKING A SAFE EDGE
Bend edge after marking out
Mallet down over a steel rule or thin sheet steel
Mallet edge down
MAKING A WIRED EDGE
Bend edge after marking out
Mallet down over a piece of metal the same thickness as the wire
Position wire and trap with mallet blows
Mallet to final shape using flat stake

Far left *A Monodex cutter.*

Left *A bench guillotine.*

Fig 42 **Below left** *Edge treatment of sheet metal.*

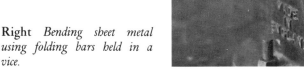

Right *Bending sheet metal using folding bars held in a vice.*

There are various hammers and mallets available for working on sheet metal but you do not need to buy more than one or two. Hammers for sheet metal work should not be used for normal nailing or other hammer work; if the faces become damaged, they will transfer the marks to the metal every time they are used. For general shaping of a panel, a mallet made from hide, wood or rubber is the best tool to use. It will not bruise the metal in the same way as a hammer yet has sufficient weight to form the panel.

Dollies are shaped lumps of steel with polished faces; they are available in different shapes and sizes and are used to support the metal on the opposite side to the hammer blows.

After sheet metal has been cut, the raw edge is often sharp and jagged. A pair of leather gloves are invaluable when handling sheet metal and save many an annoying and painful cut or snag on the hands. It is not often that the edge of a piece of sheet is left raw on a finished piece of work. Usually the edge is treated in such a way as to increase the strength of the panel or to provide a decorative edge. The simplest method of treating the edge of a panel is to produce a 'safe edge' by bending the edge of the metal back over itself and malleting it down flat. Mark a line ¼ in (6 mm) from the edge and first bend the metal at right angles for the length of the panel. Then working from one end, mallet down the edge. Do not bend the edge right over in one place before you move on but gradually bring the whole edge over, working from one end to the other. This will avoid producing a pucker in the sheet which is hard to remove.

A wired edge is produced by forming the edge of the panel over a length of wire; this not only provides a smooth edge but increases its strength substantially. A line is drawn 2½ times the diameter of the wire in from the edge of the panel. This edge is then bent at right angles, the wire inserted and the metal formed round it. The diagram opposite gives a step by step guide to forming both these edges.

Forming a right angle bend can be achieved with a pair of folding bars or by clamping the work to the edge of the bench using a strip of angle iron or wood secured by 'G' clamps. As has already been mentioned, the metal must be malleted over gradually, working backwards and forwards from one end to the other. If the bend is in the middle of a piece of metal and there is sufficient to get hold of, force the metal down with one hand while using the mallet in the other. Obviously a folding machine would make light work of such a job and if you have access to one your work will be that much easier.

Where the edge has to be formed on a curve, it can be tackled in two ways. The first way is to cut the shape out of a piece of wood and clamp the metal to

Left and below left *Bending sheet metal using the bench edge, G-cramps and a bar.*

it. This will provide a positive guide for the metal. The second way is to use a narrow piece of wood or metal that has a slight curve at the end; this can be moved round the panel while the edge is gradually formed up. Before we leave the treatment of panel edges, one other forming operation is used where two panels overlap. To ensure that the two panels are flush with each other, the edge of one panel is swaged down so that the edge of the other panel sits on it. This operation is best done in a swaging machine which will give an accurate swage the length of the panel. A hand tool that does the same job is a pair of joddlers; these have to be moved along the panel edge forming the swage each time the handles are gripped together.

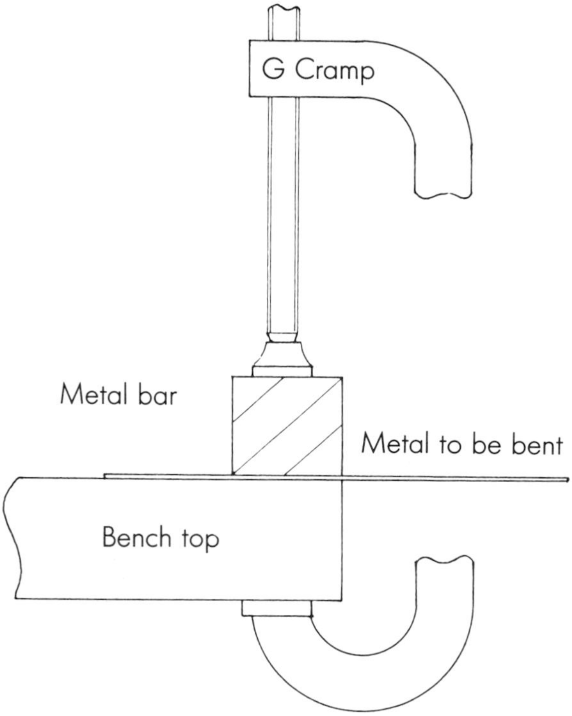

When forming curves in a single plane, a set of bending rolls is the ideal method. However, a lot can be done using tube of the correct or smaller diameter — the metal can be formed by pressing the sheet over the tube and malleting where necessary. Obviously soft metals such as aluminium and copper can be formed more easily than steel. If you find this process does not work well, most sheet metal firms have bending rolls and if you take your sheet ready cut with the precise instructions as to the dimensions of the curve, it should be a relatively cheap operation. When making replacement panels or sections of chassis for a moncoque body, it is always best to make a paper pattern of the part before you commit yourself to cutting metal. Offer up the pattern, make sure it is a good fit and that there is an allowance for treating the edge of the metal. You may find it easier to make patterns for pieces that require folding out of cardboard as this holds its shape much better when you are checking the fit on a car.

Right *A swaging machine.*

Below right *A close-up view of the rollers.*

Bottom right *A piece of metal in the process of being swaged.*

In many instances where a body frame of wood or metal tube is to be covered, it is possible to clamp the metal sheet after it has been cut out, directly to the body frame and dress the edges of the panel over the frame. This will work for curves in a single plane and also compound curves, providing the curve is a shallow one over a large area. For this operation, you will need a number of 'G' clamps and pieces of wood packing to prevent the clamps marking the metal. The body panel should be clamped into position, making sure the correct overlap is present all round the frame and that the metal is held in contact with the edge of the frame where it is to be malleted over.

The metal is then malleted over using a rawhide or rubber mallet, remembering to work the metal over gradually along the frame. If you haven't enough 'G' clamps to hold the metal all along the edge, the part of the metal that has been dressed over can be fixed to the frame before moving the clamps along the frame. The method of fixing will depend on the material of the body frame. Panelling on wooden frames can be held in place with wood screws or pins. If the frame is of metal tube or angle, then 'pop' rivets, self-tapping screws or small nuts and bolts can be used. Avoid using, if possible, steel fixings in an aluminium body — this will prevent any problems in the future with electrolytic corrosion.

To produce a compound curve using hand tools you will need: a sand bag, a bossing mallet or ball pein

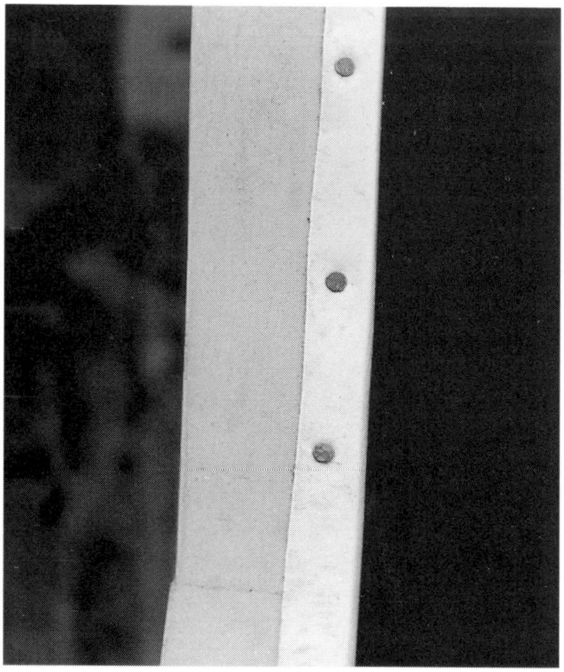

Body panel malleted over the frame and pinned into place.

hammer and a planishing hammer for finishing the surface. If a sand bag is not available, a stout piece of wood with a hollow of the shape required carved into it will be a useful substitute.

The first stage is to work out the size of blank necessary to form the required shape. Fig. 43 shows two methods of achieving this. Do not cut the metal too large as this will make the forming difficult, particularly at the edges, where the excess metal will tend to pucker into unwanted folds.

After the blank has been cut to size, file the edges to remove any burrs that may have been produced during the cutting out. The next step is to anneal the metal as described in the section on heat treatment so that it can be easily shaped. Before the metal can be beaten, it must be cleaned of the oxides that have formed on its surface. Aluminium is the easiest to clean; it will only require the blackened soap washed off the surface of the metal.

If you are working in brass, copper or gilding metal, a pickle bath made up from a 10% solution of sulphuric acid should be used. Remember when making up dilute acid solutions to ADD THE ACID TO THE WATER not vice versa or it will explode. The solution is best kept in an earthenware or plastic container with a well fitting lid. For the best results, the metal should be dipped when it is warm, not hot, or it may spit and injure you. Brass tongs are the best for use in acid baths as they do not discolour the acid in the same way as steel or copper.

Fig. 43 Estimating the size of a blank required for a curved shape.

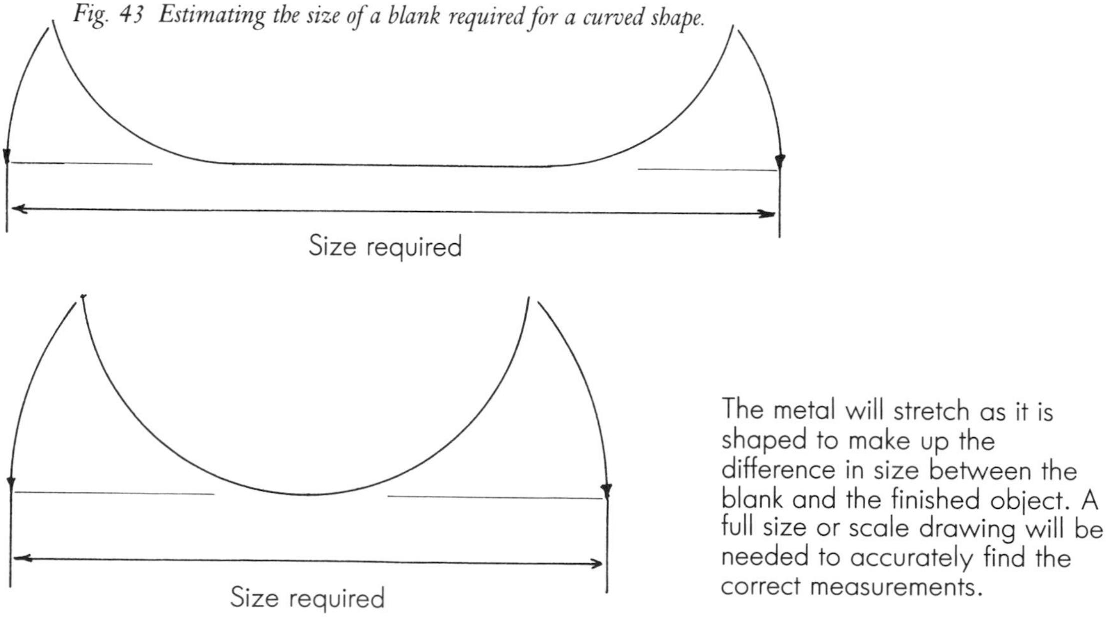

Size required
Size required
The metal will stretch as it is shaped to make up the difference in size between the blank and the finished object. A full size or scale drawing will be needed to accurately find the correct measurements.

Mild steel can be pickled but use a separate bath because the acid solution will become discoloured extremely quickly. The other method of cleaning steel is to use emery cloth to remove the oxides. It is important to remove as much of the oxides as possible, otherwise they may be hammered into the surface of the metal, which could affect the later finishing.

After the metal has been dried, a series of lines ½ in (13 mm) apart should be drawn around the blank starting from the outside and working towards the middle. These lines are used as a guide for the mallet blows to aid even shaping of the blank.

The blank is held at an angle on the sand bag or block and the blows from the mallet or hammer made a short distance in from the edge. The blank is rotated slowly so that the hammer blows are made in the same place on the bag or block. The second course of blows is made just inside the first and the shaping is continued until the required shape is obtained. The work will probably have to be annealed and cleaned during the shaping, as the metal becomes work-hardened by the blows of the hammer. The number of times the metal needs to be annealed will depend on the metal being worked and the depth of the hollowing.

When the shaping operation is complete, the work should be planished to even up the shape and remove any irregularities. It will also harden the metal and produce a more rigid shape. The work should be annealed and then hammered on a suitably shaped stake (a polished block of steel) with a planishing hammer. It is possible to use a normal hammer but the faces of both the hammer and stake must be polished, with no flaws in the surface; any flaws will be transferred to the surface of the work, marking it badly.

If you don't have any shaped stakes, a curved piece of metal can be planished from the inside on a flat block of polished steel, using the ball pien of a hammer. Planishing is started from the centre of the work with relatively light blows, working in concentric circles towards the outside. The hammer must hit the metal where it is supported on the stake, otherwise the work will be distorted. As in the first process, the work should be rotated so that the hammer is brought down in the same position each time. The facets formed by the hammer should overlap slightly to make sure that no part of the surface is missed.

When the planishing is finished you will be left with a surface that is evenly covered with facets left by the hammer. The next process depends on the final finish for the work. If it is going to be polished and then plated all the marks on the surface will have to be removed.

Normally a Water-of-Ayr stone, which is a very smooth abrasive stone available in sticks about ⅜ in (10 mm) square, is used with water to grind away the facets and produce a perfectly smooth surface prior to polishing. Should the surface of the work be fairly rough, fine emery cloth can be used followed by wet and dry paper before the final finishing with the Water-of-Ayr stone.

If the work is going to be painted, the process need not be so painstaking as the paint will need a slightly roughened surface to act as a key. Any slight irregularities in the surface can also be filled with body filler or lead loaded if the work is made from steel.

When faced with the problem of removing a dent from a part of your car, you must decide whether the job is going to be easier with the part left on the car or removed. Obviously if your car has a monocoque bodyshell, the decision is made for you where many panels are concerned. Removal of the part can be advantageous in that the damaged part of the panel may be supported more firmly than if it is left on the car. Also it is a lot easier to work upright than grovelling under a wing or in a similar awkward position.

Before starting to reshape the panel, clean off all the dirt; this is particularly important if you are working under part of the car, otherwise you will work in a continuous shower of debris. The next step is to assess how the dent was formed; the direction of the dent, whether straight in or at an angle, will tell you where to start the reshaping process. Using a dolly, sand bag or a shaped piece of hardwood on the outside of the panel, start hammering on the highest part of the dent. Do not use brute force to return the panel to shape; the blows from the hammer should be controlled so as not to stretch the metal, which would cause more problems. Only experience will tell you how best to tackle each type of dent, but do not expect too much too soon. If you expect to return a panel to perfect shape with a hammer you are going to be disappointed. It is just as important to know when to stop and finish the job with filler or lead, as it is to know where to start.

Where the metal has been stretched, usually indicated by a deep dent or crease, do not attempt to hammer out all the damage. Shrinking metal that has been stretched is a very skilled operation and requires the use of heat properly applied. In situations such as this, knock out the dent as much as possible and then use filler. Over-hammering will stretch the metal even more and lead to an ugly bulge on the outside of the panel.

Many pre-war cars with headlights mounted next to the radiator have suffered damage to the lamps through the bonnet sides being knocked into them. Before repairing these, the lamps must be removed from the car and stripped down to the bare shell. If the dents are small it will probably be possible to remove them without annealing the metal. Where the lamps are chrome-plated the annealing process will discolour the chrome, making re-plating necessary. The dents can be carefully knocked out from the inside, using a ball pien planishing hammer, with the lamp shell supported on a polished steel block.

Where the lamps have painted shells or where they are going to be re-plated, it is best to anneal the metal first. Obviously painted shells will have to have all the paint stripped off before this process.

After the dents have been removed, the surface should be smoothed off with a Water-of-Ayr stone. Where the metal has been scored or depressions left where the metal has been stretched, these can be filled in one of two ways. A shell that is going to be painted can be filled with body filler or for a better job, body solder. Both these fillers can be rubbed down to give a perfect finish to the surface.

A shell that is going to be replated should have any scores or small depressions filled with silver solder and then smoothed off. It is possible to plate over body solder but the heat and pressure from the polishing mop when the chrome is buffed can cause the solder to move, spoiling the finish.

Working with tube

When making a body frame or any other structure out of tube, the first decision that has to be made is the cross-sectional shape of the tube to be used. Square or rectangular section tube is far easier to prepare for joining as the ends of the tube can be cut at the required angle and assembled for joining. On the other hand, round tube will have to be shaped at the end to fit around the other tube to which it is to be joined.

Square tube is more difficult to bend without distorting its shape unless you have access to the specialised equipment that can deal with cross-sections of this type. There are two other ways that square tube can be bent. The first involves making a curved jig to suit the bend you require. If the jig is made of wood it should be covered with sheet metal to protect it from the red-hot tube as it is bent round the jig. This operation should be done in stages, so that the tube can

A heat-scorched wooden jig for bending square tube, together with a section of bent tube.

Fig. 44 **Right** *Bending square tube by cutting.*

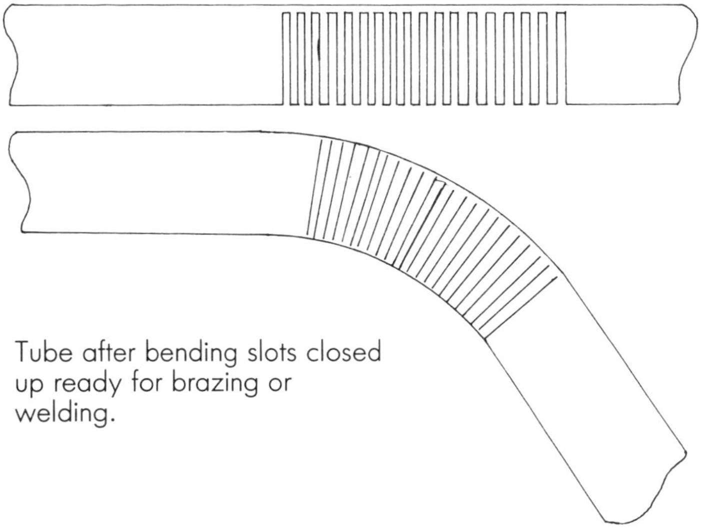

Tube cut through three sides before bending.
Tube after bending slots closed up ready for brazing or welding.

Fig. 45 **Below right** *Joining round tube.*

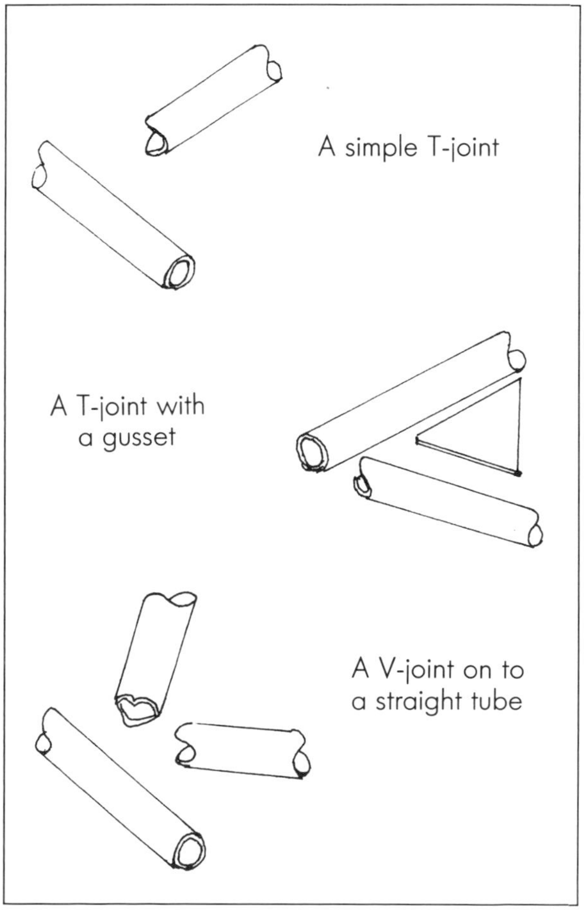

be kept in shape with a hammer should it start to distort.

The second method involves making a number of saw cuts through three sides of the tube where the bend is to be. The number and spacing of the saw cuts depends on the radius and length of the bend and is best found by experimenting with a piece of scrap tube. After cutting, the tube is bent round and the closed saw cuts can be welded or brazed together.

Round tube is easily bent using a tube bender which can be hired from most tool hire shops. Make sure that the formers and guides are correct for the tube you are using. Many firms still supply imperial size tube only, and if you order, for example, 25 mm diameter you will be supplied with one inch diameter. Though the difference in size is only about .035 in, a 25 mm tube bending former will put an ugly neck in the tube which will spoil an otherwise good piece of work. Small diameter cold drawn seamless tube can be bent without a tube bender if treated carefully, either by making up a former to bend the tube round or by drilling a hole through a piece of strong timber about 4 in x 2 in (100 mm x 50 mm). The hole should be countersunk both sides. The wood should be held securely in the vice and the tube placed into the hole and bent over. Quite complex bends can be achieved with this simple tool, but don't try using

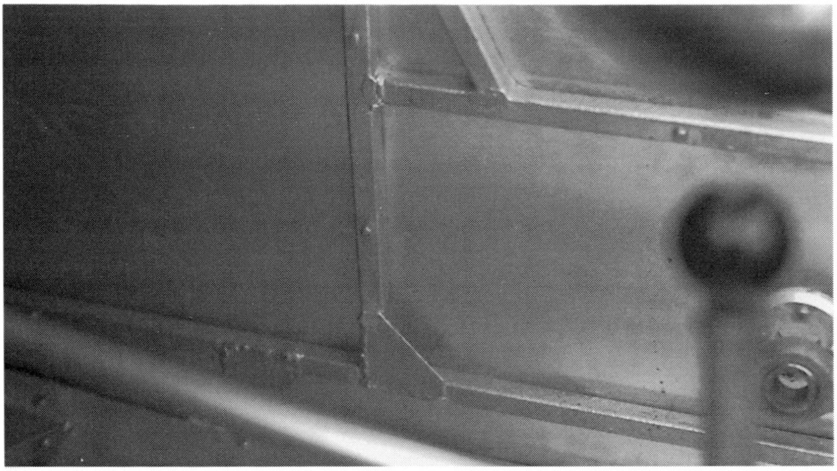

Left *Strengthening gusset on a steel tube frame.*

Below left *Louvre cutter made by the author. The main tubes are 1½" square 14 S.W.G. tube.*

Below *Close-up of the cutter wheels. They are made of case hardened mild steel. They have cut over 150 louvres before re-sharpening.*

seamed tube as the wall of the tube will collapse very easily.

Fig. 45 shows some methods of mitring tubes together. It can be seen from this that round tube requires considerably more work than square or rectangular section.

The strengthening gusset shown in the diagram can also be used on the outside of the joint where tubes of the same dimensions are used. For anyone who is at all doubtful of their ability to produce perfect welded joints every time, a simple gusset such as this is easy to weld onto a joint and increases its strength considerably.

Louvre cutting

Though louvres are best cut using a tool and a press or the louvre cutter shown, it is possible to cut and form them by hand. First, a female former the length and shape of the louvre required should be made from a suitable hardwood. Next, the lines where the metal is to be cut through are marked out and the metal cut through with a wide, sharp, cold chisel. The metal is then formed with a mallet into the former to produce the finished louvre. Obviously great care must be taken to produce a neat finish.

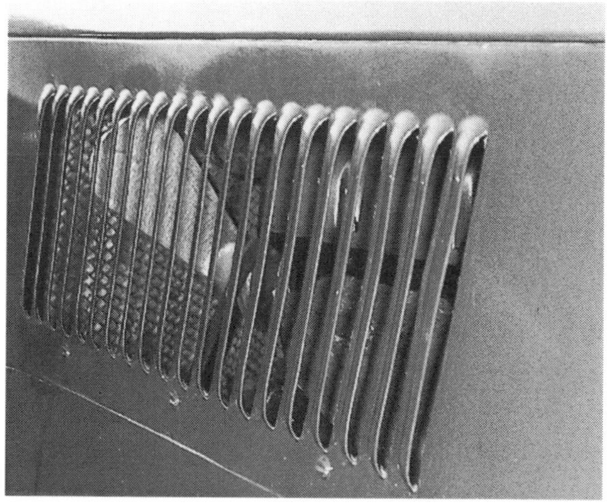

Above *Louvres cut by the louvre cutter.*

Right *The body of a 12/4 Riley Special skinned by the author.*

Right *The top part of the tail from the same special was made from sections of Morris 1000 bonnet cut and welded together.*

CHAPTER 11

Casting and pattern making

Although casting is generally thought of as a specialised skill beyond the range of the amateur restorer, the production of simple castings is not beyond the abilities of most reasonably competent people. The lack of facilities need not be a handicap; there are many foundries around the country who would possibly be willing to undertake a 'one-off' job at a reasonable price. If you have been able to join a night school class as mentioned in the introduction, you may find you have all the facilities you need.

The most expensive part of the operation is the making of a pattern to use in the production of the mould. If it is possible to make this yourself, casting costs will be greatly reduced. It is not possible to use an original part for a pattern because the copy will be smaller as the molten metal shrinks as it cools. Also, many patterns have to be made in several pieces so that they will lift out of the mouldings and without breaking the mould. The table given here shows the shrinkage rate of various metals, which in the case of steel is quite considerable.

APPROXIMATE SHRINKAGE OF SOME CASTING ALLOYS	Shrinkage (mm/m)
Cast Iron	10
Steel	20
Brass	15
Aluminium	13
Magnesium Base	13

Unless the casting is very simple and dimensional, accuracy is not important; a pattern larger than the final object must be made not only to allow for shrinkage but also to allow for machining where necessary. Pattern makers allow for this shrinkage by using a contraction rule which is calibrated to produce the correct increase in length of the pattern. The simplest patterns to make and cast are those known as flat-backed patterns; these as their name implies have a flat back. This makes them easier to make and cast.

More complex shapes such as circular sections or those having holes through the casting require a split pattern. This may be split into two pieces, or in the case of an intricate casting, several pieces, which are slotted together to produce the final pattern.

Pattern makers are amongst the most highly skilled people in the industry as they have to interpret a two-dimensional drawing into a three-dimensional object, making sure that the pattern will lift cleanly from the sand and that the mould is positioned in such a way that the mould cavity will fill correctly and produce a sound casting.

It will probably clarify the process more easily to describe the procedure involved in producing patterns and the completed moulding box for the two types of casting.

Patterns should be made from a good close-grained wood which can be sanded to a smooth finish. The wood must then be varnished or painted, otherwise the damp moulding sand will raise the grain of the wood and it will not lift from the sand cleanly. If the pattern is being made for casting by a foundry, it is best to paint the pattern in the correct colour code. This will help the foundry decide the best way to cast the component.

Colour Code for Casting Patterns	
Red	— unmachined surfaces
Yellow	— machined surfaces
Black	— core prints

Colour code for casting patterns

Any surface imperfection on the pattern, even visible wood grain, will be reproduced on the surface of the final casting.

The pattern must also be given a very slight taper of 3° to 5°, called the draw, to enable it to lift from the sand cleanly. If you have an original part to work from, study it carefully. It is often possible to see the moulding line where the pattern was split.

Simple patterns can be made from one piece of wood, whereas complex shapes are more easily made by building up the pattern from smaller pieces of wood fixed together. Any internal corners should be radiused using car body filler, or similar. This will produce a stronger casting and also reduce the risk of sand breaking from the edge of the mould.

Shown top right are the two patterns needed to produce a door hinge for a post-war special. They are flat back and have a taper from the base to the top. Because of their size, they can easily be cast together.

To produce a mould ready for pouring you will need: moulding boxes or flasks, mansfield sand, parting powder, sprue pins and some simple moulding tools.

Moulding boxes, or flasks as they are called in the trade (see illustrations) are normally made from metal when used in industry, but quite adequate ones can be made simply from wood. The important point to remember is that they should be approximately 50 mm wider and longer than the pattern and at least 50 mm or more deeper than the pattern, otherwise the sand will not have sufficient strength to stay in the box when the pattern is removed. The flasks are used in pairs; the top box is known as the cope, the bottom one as the drag.

The mansfield sand used in the moulding is sand

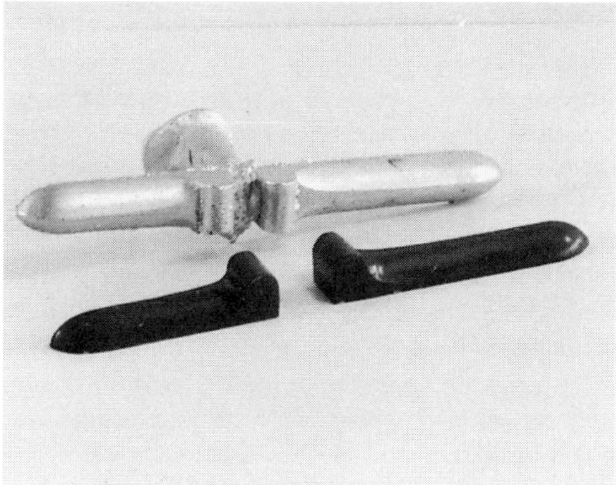

Top right *Flat-backed casting patterns for a door hinge, with the finished casting behind.*

Middle right *Commercial metal moulding flasks.*

Right *Home-made wooden moulding flasks.*

with a thin layer of clay around each grain. When this is moistened, it has the ability to bind together firmly and hold its shape, even when the molten metal comes in contact with it. The sand is prepared by passing it first through a sieve to remove and break up any lumps until it is smooth in texture. Water is then added a small amount at a time, and mixed thoroughly with the sand. In industry, this is done by special mills but an equally good result can be achieved by hand. The most simple test for the correct amount of moisture (about 5%) is by squeezing a handful of sand. The sand should hold together but when broken in two the break should be clean not crumbly. Also the hand should not feel wet. It is important that the moisture content is correct. If it is too dry, the mould will crumble as the pattern is removed or as the molten metal flows into it. If it is too wet, the molten metal will turn the excess water to steam which will either stay trapped in the mould and produce a casting similar in appearance to gruyere cheese or blow the molten metal back out of the mould often with dire consequences for the person pouring the metal. Obviously, therefore, proper safety clothing should be worn for this process. Parting powder is used to prevent the moulding sand from sticking to the pattern and the sand in the cope and drag from sticking together. Dry sand can also be used though it is not so effective. The sprue pins are tapered wooden pegs used to make the holes to allow the molten metal into the mould and the air out. These holes are usually referred to as the runner and riser.

Moulding tools come in a bewildering array of shapes and sizes, some of which are shown in Fig. 46. It is also possible to make usable tools from small spoons or cut pieces of metal.

Producing a mould

Using the door hinge described earlier as an example, a mould can be prepared in the following manner.

The bottom flask or drag should be placed upside down on the moulding bench and the patterns placed centrally in it. Because of the small size of the parts, they can easily be cast together. A thin layer of parting powder should then be sprinkled over the patterns and the area of the bench inside the drag. Next, a layer of moulding sand about 50 mm deep should be sieved into the drag; this should be pressed firmly down with the knuckles of one hand while holding the patterns in place with the other. The sand should then be rammed firmly with the pein or pointed end of the rammer, taking particular care at the edges of the drag. Another layer of sand should then be sieved

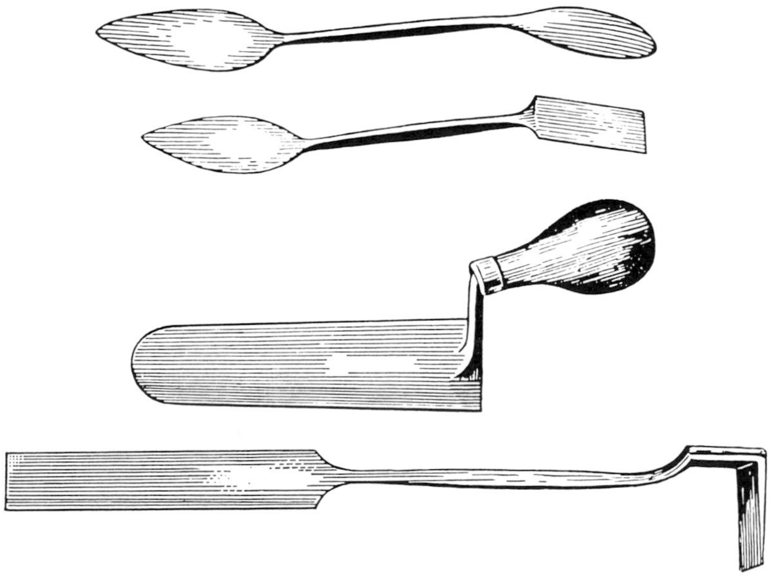

Fig. 46 Various moulding tools. (F.L. Hunt Ltd)

in and the process repeated except that the rammer can be used straight away. Once the pattern is covered, there is no need to sieve the sand into the drag, as the purpose of this is to ensure as smooth a finish as possible to the surface of the mould. It is important that too much sand is not put into the flask at any one time as there is the possibility that the bottom layers of sand will not be rammed firmly enough, causing the mould to be weak. Ramming too hard can also cause problems since the gases from the molten metal and the sand will not be able to escape by permeating out through the sand.

When the drag is over-full it should be rammed with the flat or butt end of the rammer to produce a smooth surface. The reason why the butt end of the rammer is not used until the final stages is that it produces a smooth surface which would prevent the next layer of sand sticking to it. The consequence of this is a pile of sand either on the bench or more likely in your boots when the flask is picked up.

The surface of the sand should now be scraped flat with a piece of wood or metal that is long enough to span the flask in one go. Any concave depressions must be filled in and scraped flat otherwise they could cause problems later. The foundryman's term for this is 'strickling'.

Next, turn the drag over (if your technique is correct all the sand will stay in the box) and place the cope in position.

The sprue pins should now be put in place; it is important that the sprue pins are placed near the thickest part of the pattern and preferably one either side of it. They should also be larger in cross-section than the thickest part of the pattern so that the runner and riser can remain molten to provide a reservoir of molten metal as the casting cools and shrinks. If the runner and riser cool before the casting, shrinkage cavities will occur, spoiling the casting.

For a small job such as these hinges it is possible to use only one sprue pin placed between the thickest ends of the patterns.

Parting powder should be sprinkled inside the cope to prevent the sand from the two flasks sticking together and the cope filled and rammed in the same way as the drag. After strickling of the surface, the mould should be vented with a thin rod to help the gases from the mould escape. The rod should not be pushed through the sand to touch the pattern, otherwise the casting could come out resembling a porcupine; ½ in (12 mm) away is near enough. The easiest way to achieve this is to hold the rod between finger and thumb the correct distance from its end and push it down till the hand meets the sand. Only a small number of holes is needed, about one every 2 sq in (50 mm square) is adequate.

The sprue pin should then be loosened and removed, and the pouring basin cut, which will prevent the metal passing into the mould too quickly and perhaps causing some damage to any frail parts. Then the edges of the runner can be smoothed off.

The cope and the drag should now be parted and the bottom of the runner rounded off. Next the channel from the runner to the mould cavity should be cut and smoothed off. Now the patterns are removed, the draw spike can be screwed into the pattern and gently rapped to loosen the pattern in the sand. It can then be lifted carefully out of the sand. Any damage to the mould can be carefully repaired and all sharp edges in the path of the molten metal smoothed off. Finally a small vee-shaped groove should be scraped from the ends of the pattern to the edge of the moulding flask. With small patterns such as these, this will be sufficient to allow the air to escape from the mould cavity. After gently blowing away any loose grains of sand, the two flasks should be placed together and the cope weighted to prevent it being lifted by the pressure of the molten metal. The mould is now ready for pouring. See Fig. 47.

Castings that have holes cast in them require a slightly different technique, in that a solid object the same shape as the holes must be placed into the mould cavity for the molten metal to flow round. This shape, or core to give it its correct name, is made from sand mixed with a binding agent which is then cured so that it is strong enough to withstand handling and the pressure of the molten metal when it is in the mould.

The making of the simple tubular shape shown in Fig. 48 should be undertaken as follows. First a split pattern should be made, the two halves located correctly by two small dowels. Note that the pattern has a circular extension at each end — these are called core prints and they produce the cavity in the mould for the core to rest in. Next, a core box should be made

Fig. 47 Making a mould with a flat-backed pattern.

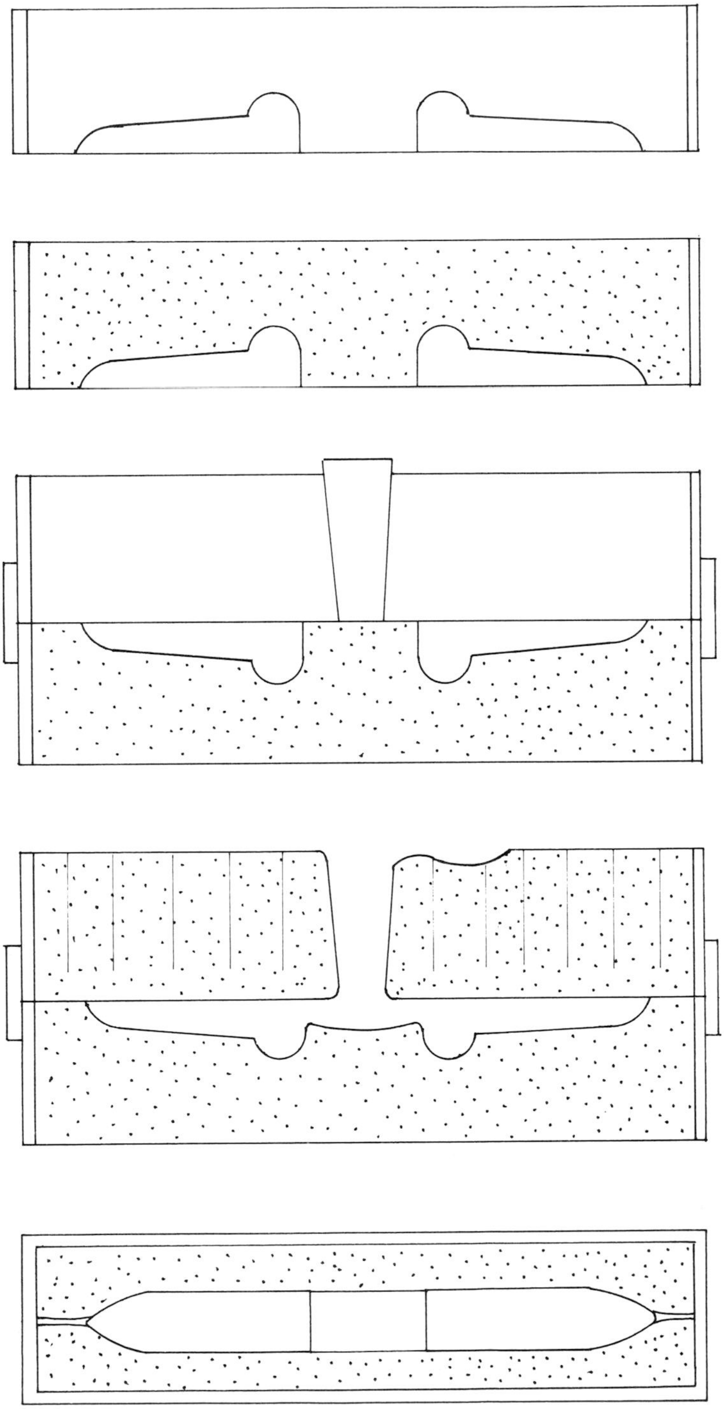

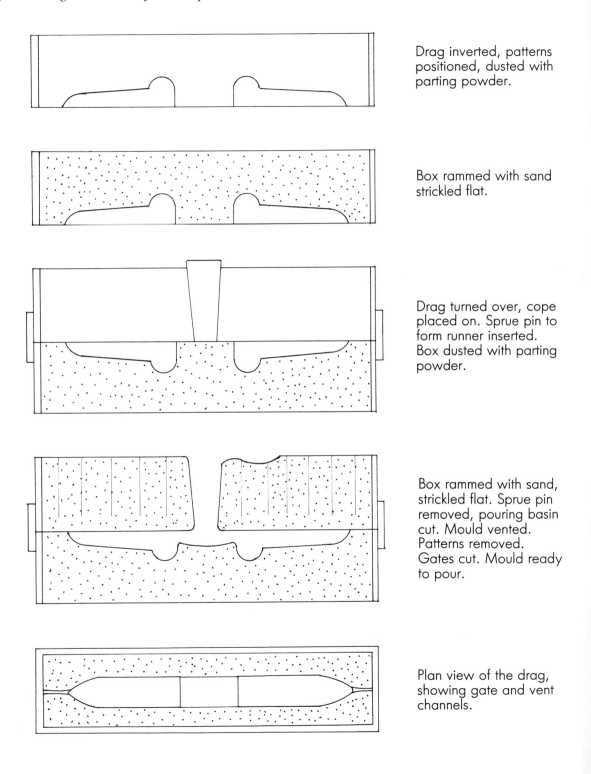

Drag inverted, patterns positioned, dusted with parting powder.

Box rammed with sand strickled flat.

Drag turned over, cope placed on. Sprue pin to form runner inserted. Box dusted with parting powder.

Box rammed with sand, strickled flat. Sprue pin removed, pouring basin cut. Mould vented. Patterns removed. Gates cut. Mould ready to pour.

Plan view of the drag, showing gate and vent channels.

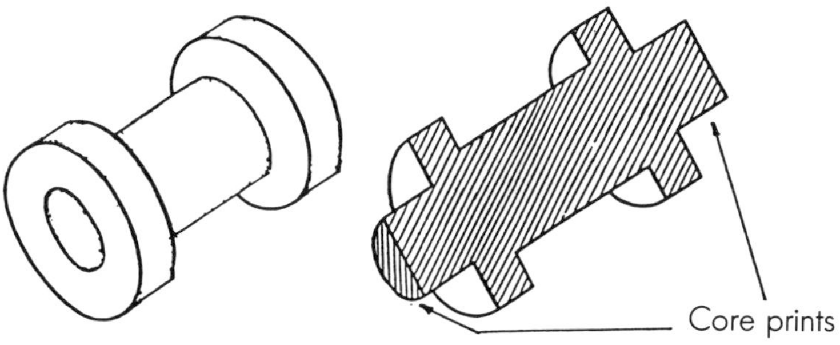

Fig. 48 Tubular component with half a split pattern.

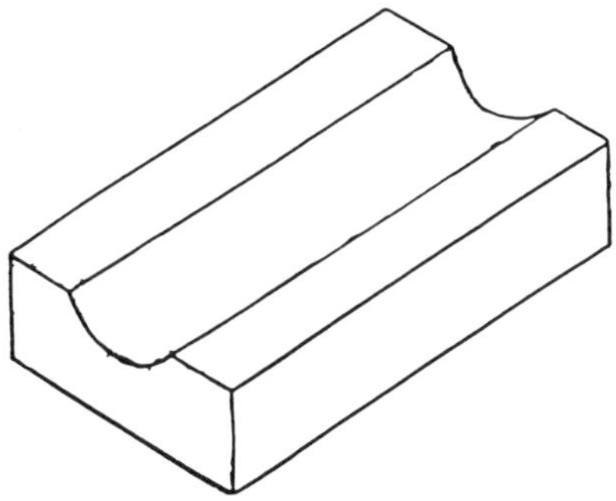

Fig. 49 Half a core box.

(see Fig. 49). Again dowels are used to locate the two halves of the core box so that an accurate core can be produced. If the hole through the casting is going to be machined, the core box and core prints should be made smaller to allow for the machining. The length of the core box should be slightly less than the length of pattern and core prints; this will give some necessary clearance when positioning the core into the mould cavity.

There are two methods of producing cores. The first uses linseed oil as the binder and sharp silica sand. They are mixed in the ratio 40 parts sand to 1 part linseed oil by volume. When the mixture is thoroughly mixed it can be rammed into the core box after the cavity has been dusted with parting powder. Next a thin rod should be pushed through the centre of the core to provide a vent before the two halves of the core box are separated and the core gently removed. The core must be handled with care as it is very fragile in its green state. It must now be baked at about 200°C until it has the appearence of milk chocolate. Do not overheat as this will destroy the bond and weaken the core considerably. When the core has cured it can be placed into the mould cavity and the casting poured.

Core-making using linseed oil is time consuming, and if a domestic oven is used to cure the mixture it is likely, because of the smell, to be very unpopular with the rest of the family. The second method, the cold process, using carbon dioxide gas and sodium silicate as a binder, has two great advantages: the core can be cured in the core box and therefore is hard when handled and it is very quick, taking only a few seconds to cure.

Carbon dioxide is readily available either in small cylinders or even the small bulbs used for fizzy drink makers. Sodium silicate is available from most chemists, usually under its more common name,

Fig. 50 Fitting for applying CO_2 to core sand.

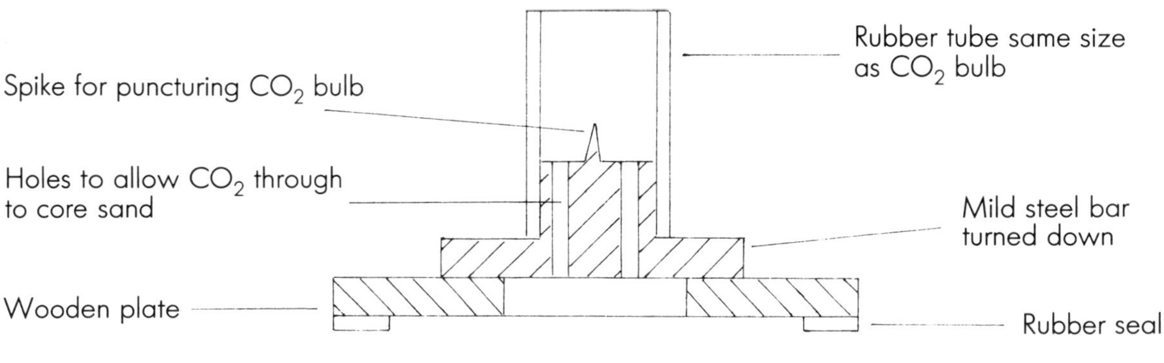

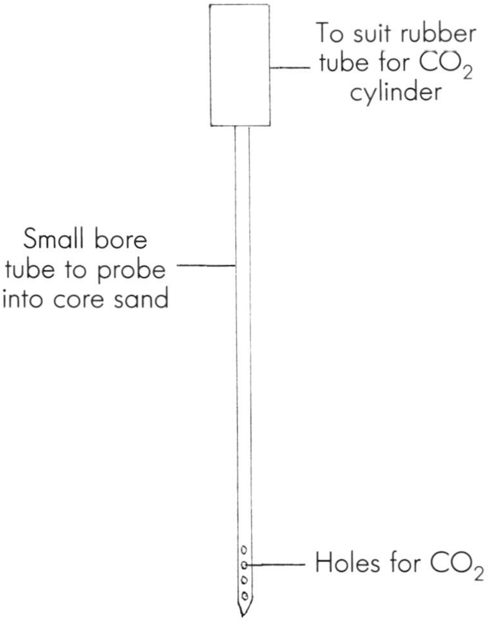

Waterglass, used in days past to help preserve new laid eggs.

Silica sand is mixed with about 5% of sodium silicate: for small scale use a tablespoon provides a satisfactory measure, 20 spoonfuls of sand to one spoonful of sodium silicate. The mixing should be thorough so that each grain of sand is coated with the sodium silicate. Rubber gloves should be worn as the skin can react to the chemicals, and the gloves enable you to rub the mixture through the fingers to ensure a good mix.

The core box should be dusted with parting powder and the sand carefully rammed into the box, making sure there are no parts of the box left soft. Vent holes should be made right through the core to enable the gas to penetrate the sand. The carbon dioxide is then passed through the sand at a low pressure for a few seconds — the larger the core, the more the gas that will be needed; the box should be gassed from both ends if possible. This will turn the sodium silicate to silica gel and bond the sand grains together. Figs. 50 and 51 show two simple fittings that can be used

Fig. 51 **Above left** *Lance fitting for gassing deep cores.*

The split pattern, core box, core, and finished casting for a post-war Singer rear light made by the author.

Assorted casting patterns made by the author.

to transfer the gas to the core box. The photograph shows the core box, core, pattern and finished casting of a rear light holder for a postwar Singer made by the author.

Low melting point alloys

While sand casting is ideal for a vast range of work, it is not suitable for castings that require thin sections or fine detail such as mascots, badges and name scripts. Normally, items such as these would either be made by the lost wax process or by using metal moulds to obtain the fine definition. Both these methods are perhaps beyond the scope of the amateur restorer, though a brief description of the lost wax process will be included later. Metal moulds are very expensive to produce and the expense would be difficult to justify for a one-off job.

There is one method of casting that can be accomplished successfully on the kitchen table if necessary, and that is with low melting point alloy using silicone rubber for the mould. These alloys have melting points that range from 185°C to 245°C and are capable of being melted in a ladle over a gas stove.

There are two different methods of casting with L.M.P. alloys, either using a small centrifugal casting machine or by hand. Naturally the machine will produce castings that have very thin sections that require pressure to fill correctly and will also produce several different castings at the same time if necessary. The one drawback is that the best machine costs several hundred pounds. However, it is possible to obtain equally good results by hand casting, providing care is taken in the type of work undertaken and in the production of the moulds.

The material used for mould making is called room temperature vulcanising (R.T.V.) silicone rubber. There are several types of silicone rubber and the two most suitable for hand casting are known as RTV11 and RTV31. Mixed with a catalyst they will produce a cure within one to 24 hours, though they should not be used for casting before 72 hours have elapsed to allow the rubber time to achieve its full working properties.

The pattern for the mould can be made from almost anything as no heat is involved in the mould-making operation. If you are using an original mascot or badge

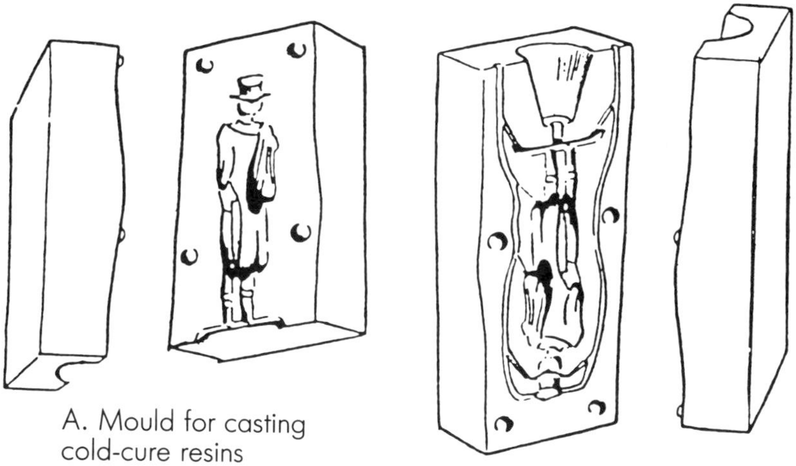

A. Mould for casting cold-cure resins
B. Mould set up for casting hot low-melt metals
The long funnel on top of B allows a good head of pressure to force the metal into the mould; the air goes up the risers and helps the metal to flow freely.
All the sprues and air vents are cut with the sprue cutter after the mould has cured. Do not make them too big to start with; they can always be enlarged later.

Fig. 52 The two different methods of producing a mould using R.T.V. rubber. (Alec Tiranti Ltd)

it must be cleaned up and all imperfections removed. Any pitting or corrosion must be filled with a suitable material such as car body filler and smoothed down to a perfect finish. The level of finish required can be judged by the fact that the rubber will reproduce even a smudgy finger mark. As with patterns for sand casting, time spent getting one pattern correct is less time-consuming than having to correct every casting produced.

If the pattern has a flat back such as a badge or name script, a simple mould box ½ in (13 mm) bigger all round than the pattern can be produced out of wood, cardboard, metal or even Lego bricks pressed firmly together.

The box should be sealed to a smooth base with double-sided Sellotape. If the pattern is a badge or something similar, with legs or lugs on the back for fixing purposes, wood is the best material for the base board. Holes can be drilled in the board to locate the legs, allowing the pattern to fit flush with the board. Location key formers are also needed. These provide depressions in the face of the mould. Any domed or conical object can be used if it is large enough to form a suitable depression.

A release agent should be brushed onto the inside of the box and on the pattern to ensure ease of stripping. If plasticine is used anywhere it must be varnished first and then treated with a release agent as the rubber will stick readily to it.

The silicone rubber should then be mixed with the correct amount of catalyst. When it is ready it should be poured slowly into a corner of the box and allowed to flow round the model, then over it. Allow the rubber to settle for a few minutes then continue pouring until there is at least ½ in (13 mm) of rubber covering the highest part of the pattern. Leave the rubber to cure, making sure the box is standing level. When the rubber has cured, lift the mould and the mould box off the base board and invert both onto the board. If the pattern stays on the base board, it should then be replaced in the mould. A second mould box of the required depth should then be fixed to the first with double-sided tape. The inside of this box and the surface of the first half of the mould should be given a coating of release agent before the box is filled with catalysed rubber. The rubber will flow into the depressions made by the location formers on the first half of the mould. These will ensure that the two halves of the mould will locate together perfectly each time it is assembled.

When the rubber has cured completely, the two halves of the mould can be removed from the mould boxes and the necessary gates and risers cut into the mould with the sprue cutter. For hand poured castings, the ingate where the molten metal is poured in must not be too small. A reasonable head of metal is required to provide enough pressure to force the metal into the mould.

When the object to be cast is a more complicated shape such as a mascot, two different methods of mould making can be used. In the first method, the pattern is half embedded in modelling wax or plasticine. This should be done carefully so that the surface of the wax follows the centre line of the pattern. Location key formers are placed on the surface of the wax and the procedure is then the same as for the simple mould.

When the rubber has cured, the mould box should be inverted, the modelling wax or plasticine removed and the pattern cleaned up. After the release agent has been applied to the pattern, rubber and mould box, the second half of the mould can be poured. After the recommended cure time, the mould box can be removed, the two halves of the mould parted and the pattern lifted out. Where required, sprue and vent holes can be cut.

The second method involves making a box with a clear perspex front tapered to the top on all sides. The box should be at least ½ in (13 mm) taller than the pattern plus an allowance for the ingate. The pattern should be stood inside the box and the parting line drawn on the perspex with a felt pen. This line should then be re-drawn on the inside of the perspex so that it will mark the rubber of the mould.

After the box has been re-assembled and secured with the pattern to the base board, the catalysed rubber can be poured carefully into a corner of the box until it is full. Slow pouring will ensure that no air is trapped in the mould. When the rubber has completely cured, the perspex front can be removed and the mould taken out of the box. A sharp scalpel or craft knife should then be used to cut down the parting line to the pattern. The mould can then be opened out and the pattern removed. Before casting, the

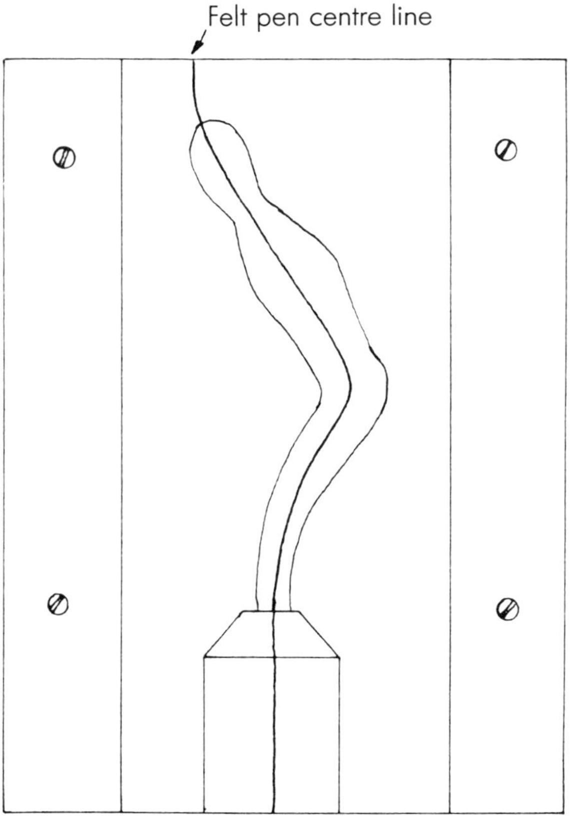

Fig. 53 Mould box with a perspex front.

mould should be replaced in its box to hold the two halves of the mould together. See Fig. 53.

Casting in low-melt metals

The two halves of the mould should be dusted with talc or graphite. Brush the powder in to all sections of the mould. Bang the two halves of the mould together to get rid of any excess powder. The use of graphite helps eliminate porosity in the finished casting. Assemble the mould and securely clamp it together ready for casting. The mould should be stood on a metal tray when pouring to contain any spillage that may occur.

Heat sufficient metal in a flat bottomed ladle on a stove or other suitable source of heat. Do not overheat the metal — a good test of temperature is to use a spent matchstick or cocktail stick, which, when dipped into the molten metal, should smoke slightly. When the metal is ready, it should be poured in one go without a break. Do not flood the metal into the mould as this could cause air to become trapped; a steady pour will give good results. When the mould is full, it should be carefully tapped to shake down the metal and more added if required. If you are undertaking a run of castings using the same mould, always allow sufficient time for the casting to cool completely before removing it from the mould. Do not attempt to water-cool the mould; it can be extremely dangerous, and may cause an explosion. Allow the mould time to cool down by itself after every few casts, otherwise it may overheat and become damaged.

There are several different low melting point alloys available, each suitable for different applications. As a general rule, high tin content alloys have better flow and definition, but are more expensive. Generally it will be found that the more delicate castings will require the higher range of temperature. Bulky castings require lower temperatures; experiment to find the most suitable. The following grades of low melting point alloys are available:

Lead-free pewter metal alloy

Made to BS 5140 (Spec A), pewter is a very high grade alloy, lead-free and tin-rich, suitable for highly detailed castings where good flow properties and polished finish are required. Castings are reasonably malleable. Pewter is a metal in its own right and because of the high degree of finish it takes, it does not need plating or painting. Melting point 245 °C. Suggested operating temperature 280 °C - 295 °C (can go to 310 °C).

KA low-melt metal alloy

A tin-rich alloy, ideal for thin sections and fine delicate castings where good flow properties and detail are needed (e.g. filigree). Widely used in the jewellery trade. Castings have a good shiny surface and are malleable. Very prone to porosity if overheated. Particularly suitable for hand gravity casting. Melting point 185 °C. Suggested operating temperature 240 °C - 280 °C.

No. 1 Low-melt metal alloy

A good all-purpose lead-rich tin alloy. Suitable for casting larger bulk where detail is more important than flow properties. Useful,like KA, for jewellery manufacturing. Castings are malleable. Melting point 228 °C. Suggested operating temperature 280 °C - 300 °C.

No. 2 Low-melt metal alloy
A general lead-rich tin alloy, pouring at higher temperatures than No. 1. Suitable for figures, jewellery components and model making, giving good reproduction of detail and very malleable castings. Melting point 243 °C. Suggested operating temperature 290 °C - 310 °C.

No. 3 Low-melt metal alloy
An alloy developed especially for flat surfaces, where porosity is giving problems. Good flow properties give very good reproduction of detail and good surface finish on flat areas. Ideal for making model kits of locos, cars, trams, other vehicles, etc. Low malleability. Melting point 225 °C. Suggested operating temperature 275 °C - 295 °C.

Lost wax casting

Although the silicone rubber mould will produce high quality castings of intricate shapes in low melting point alloy, it is unable to cope with metals having a melting point much above 300 °C. If castings are required in zinc, aluminium or brass, some other method of producing a mould is needed.

Lost wax casting utilises a pattern made from wax which is placed in an open-ended box, then investment material made from a refactory plaster is poured over the wax pattern. When the plaster has set, the wax pattern is melted out of the plaster, leaving a cavity into which the molten metal is poured.

The wax pattern can be carved from a block of modelling wax, or if you want to copy an original casting, a silicone rubber mould will have to be produced as already described. The wax should be melted and poured into the mould and left to cool before removal from the mould.

Runners and risers made from wax should be attached to the pattern; this can be done with a small piece of hot metal. The pattern should then be stuck on a metal plate by melting some of the wax, this prevents the pattern moving when the plaster is poured. A suitable size of metal tube is then placed over the pattern and sealed to the base plate with wax. Next the refactory plaster should be carefully mixed and poured slowly into the tube; do not pour it directly onto the pattern as this could damage it. The outside of the tube should be tapped as the plaster is poured to help any trapped air to escape. In industry the mould is placed on a vibratory table while pouring.

Vauxhall Griffon cast by the author using the lost wax process.

Allow the mould to dry for about four hours. Then remove the base plate and place the mould in an oven set at 100 °C - 150 °C. This melts the wax, leaving a mould cavity in the investment material. When most of the wax has been removed, the mould should be pre-heated before receiving the molten metal. The object of the heating is to remove the last traces of wax and ensure that all the remaining moisture is driven out of the investment plaster. A temperature between 200°C – 220°C is needed; higher than this will cause shrinkage or distortion of the mould, whilst a lower temperature will not remove all the moisture, making the pouring of the molten metal very dangerous.

Once the casting has cooled, the investment material can be broken away to remove the finished casting.

Small flat-backed castings can also be produced in a two-piece plaster mould by using a wooden pattern, well-painted to prevent the moisture from the plaster affecting it, or with an original of the part you wish to reproduce.

A wooden frame should be made, large enough to take the pattern and the runner and riser plus about one inch (25 mm) all round. This should be placed on a sheet of glass or metal, after the inside has been greased to act as a release agent. The frame should then be sealed to the glass with double-sided tape or plasticine. The pattern should be smeared with thin lubricating oil and put in the frame; it can be held in place by a nail through a piece of wood which is itself nailed to the top side of the frame.

Mix the plaster carefully according to the instructions and pour it into the box. The box should be gently tapped to help any air bubbles rise to the surface. When the plaster has set it can be carefully pressed out of the frame. Using a penny, cut out four locating dowels by screwing the penny into the plaster. Smear the surface of the plaster with grease and lightly coat the surface of the pattern with thin oil.

The wooden frame must also be coated with grease on the inside and then pressed down over the top of the first plaster cast. The bottom edge should be sealed with plasticine and the second mix of plaster poured into the frame. When this has set, the wooden frame can be removed and the two halves of the plaster mould separated. The runner and riser can be cut into the plaster and the pattern removed. The plaster should then be heated as already described in the lost wax process before clamping the two halves together and pouring in the molten metal.

CHAPTER 12
The lathe and lathework

Buying a lathe

The lathe is a very versatile and useful tool to have in one's workshop and the amount of time and money that can be saved by being able to repair or make your own spare parts is considerable.

Not everyone is able to go out and buy a brand new lathe, complete with all the necessary accessories. The vast majority will have to rely on the second-hand market or use the machines at local night school classes.

Buying a second-hand lathe is very like buying a second-hand car. There are certain questions and tests you must apply to a machine before you make your decisions.

The first concern is the size of lathe that is best suited both to your needs and the space available to house it. Lathes are sized according to their capacity for machining metal; a 6-inch lathe is capable of turning a piece of metal 12 inches in diameter. In America, and increasingly in Europe, machines are being designated by the largest diameter they can swing, which avoids confusion. The largest diameter capable of being turned can be increased if the lathe has a 'gap bed'. This is where a short portion of the bed near the headstock can be unbolted and removed, allowing a relatively short, larger diameter item to be machined, a very useful addition if flywheels or brake drums need attention.

The physical size of the complete machine must also be taken into consideration. A 4½ in Boxford lathe is 3 ft 6 in long and 1 ft 8 in wide and weighs approx 3 cwt. In contrast to this a 7½ in Colchester is 7 ft 6 in long, 3 ft 6 in wide and weighs over 1 ton.

The next question concerns the electric motor — is it single or three-phase? Household electricity supply is single-phase and considerable expense is required to run a three-phase cable out to the workshop. It would also be expensive to swap the three-phase motor for a new single-phase one, particularly as the output of the motor must be quite high.

The condition of the lathe should be checked. The

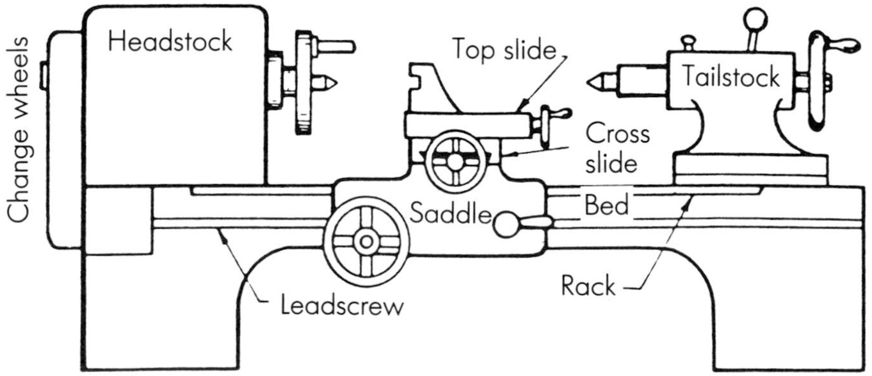

Fig. 54 The centre lathe.

Right *A 7½-inch Colchester lathe.*

Right *A 4½-inch Boxford lathe. Note its size in comparison to the Colchester behind it.*

Below *A unimat modelmakers lathe. While these are excellent machines they cannot be expected to produce the same work as a larger lathe.* (Elliott Machines Ltd)

Lathe bed with the 'Gap' piece in place.

The same lathe with the 'Gap' removed. Note the increased space to swing larger pieces of work.

bearings in the headstock should have no play in them; check these by attempting to shake the chuck. On some machines which use taper roller bearings, these are adjustable to take up any wear.

The saddle, cross slide and top slide must also be checked for play. Try lifting the saddle and pulling and pushing the top and cross slides in their direction of travel. There should be little or no free play. If there is and there is no method of adjustment, the replacement of parts could be costly or, if the machine is old, impossible, without having the parts made. The bed-ways and other castings should be checked for any damage that could affect the accuracy of the machine.

The accessories that come with the machine should also be checked. The minimum you will require is a three-jaw and four-jaw chuck, a tailstock drill chuck and a tailstock centre. Face plates etc are useful but are not usually used as much as a chuck. If either of the chucks is missing, it is as well to remember that a good quality 4 in (100 mm) diameter three-jaw chuck can cost upwards of £100.

It is important that you see the lathe working so that you can check the accuracy of the machine. A piece of round bar should be held in the chuck and machined along its length. The lathe tool should be moved by operating the carriage rather than the top slide. After the bar has been turned down, its diameter should be checked at either end of the machined portion with a micrometer. The readings should be the same; if they are not and the lathe is producing a taper, do not buy it unless it is the type of lathe where the headstock is a separate casting to the bed. If it is, then it may be possible to realign the headstock to produce an accurate machine.

Do not worry too much if the piece of test bar you have turned down is not concentric to the original size. A three-jaw chuck after some use is not expected to hold work perfectly true and an allowance has to be made for this when machining. Obviously if the difference is great, new chuck jaws or a new chuck may be needed. It should be remembered that any accurate work is usually set up in a four-jaw chuck where the independent adjustment of each jaw can ensure that the work is set up accurately before machining begins.

Try taking a fairly heavy cut on the test bar; this will give you some indication of the state of the motor. There should not be an appreciable change in speed and the lathe should not go slower and slower. If there is a drop in speed and the lathe is belt driven, check that the belt tension is correct and the belts are in good condition before blaming the motor.

Finally, don't be in a rush to buy the first lathe that comes along. With the rapid change in manufacturing industry over the last few years, there are plenty of good second-hand lathes available.

Lathe tools

The correct type of lathe tool must be used if the lathe is to machine efficiently and accurately. The cutting edge must be correctly ground and set at the correct height.

Lathe tools can be made from either high carbon steel (H.C.S.), high speed steel (H.S.S.) or tungsten carbide, the last of which is usually used as a cutting tip brazed onto a steel bar or as an insert that is held in a special holder.

High carbon steel lathe tools are cheaper than the others but they are only suitable for the softer materials; tackle anything harder than mild steel and the edge will dull very quickly.

High speed steel tools will cut more effectively than H.C.S. at higher speeds and greater depth of cut, but on hard materials such as alloy steels they need to be sharpened frequently.

Tungsten carbide tipped tools will cut all materials more efficiently than H.S.S. and will last longer between re-sharpening. These tools need a special green grit grinding wheel for sharpening because the ordinary type of wheel will not grind them satisfactorily.

The angles ground on a lathe tool to produce the cutting edge will differ, depending on the hardness of the material being cut, the amount of metal to be removed and the quality of the finish required. The harder and tougher the material, the greater the tool angle must be to support the cutting edge of the tool. A large tool angle gives maximum strength to the cutting edge and helps to dissipate the heat produced by the cutting action. It also requires greater power to force the tool into the work. A smaller tool angle gives a better finish to the work with less tearing, but does weaken the cutting edge.

The top or front rake is the angle formed between a horizontal line and the top face of the tool. Tools used for turning some brasses and cast iron need little or no top rake, while those used for aluminium need a large top rake for efficient cutting.

The side rake is the angle ground on the top face of the tool away from the cutting edge. The size of the angle depends on the material being cut; in general hard metals require a small angle while soft materials have a larger angle. The side rake will also determine the direction that the swarf will follow off the cutting edge. Because of this, some tools such as parting off tools have no side rake.

The front clearance angle is ground on to prevent the front of the tool rubbing on the work. As with other angles, it is kept to a minimum with hard materials to give extra support to the cutting edge.

The side clearance angle also depends on the material and the rate of feed used. A coarse feed needs a larger clearance than a fine one.

Fig. 55 shows a selection of lathe tool-shapes and

applications and Fig. 56 gives a chart showing cutting speeds and tool angles for various materials.

Having selected the correct tool for the work in hand, it must be set up in the tool post correctly. If the tool is set too high, the front clearance angle will be reduced, perhaps to a point where the tool is rubbing rather than cutting. Setting the tool too low will reduce the top rake angle and also leave a small portion unmachined in the centre of the work.

Fig. 55 Selection of lathe tool shapes.

Types of turning

Facing off

This is the term given to machining the face of the work parallel to the chuck. All work should be faced off before it is drilled or centre drilled and any other machining undertaken.

Parallel or plain turning

This is the term used to describe turning at right angles

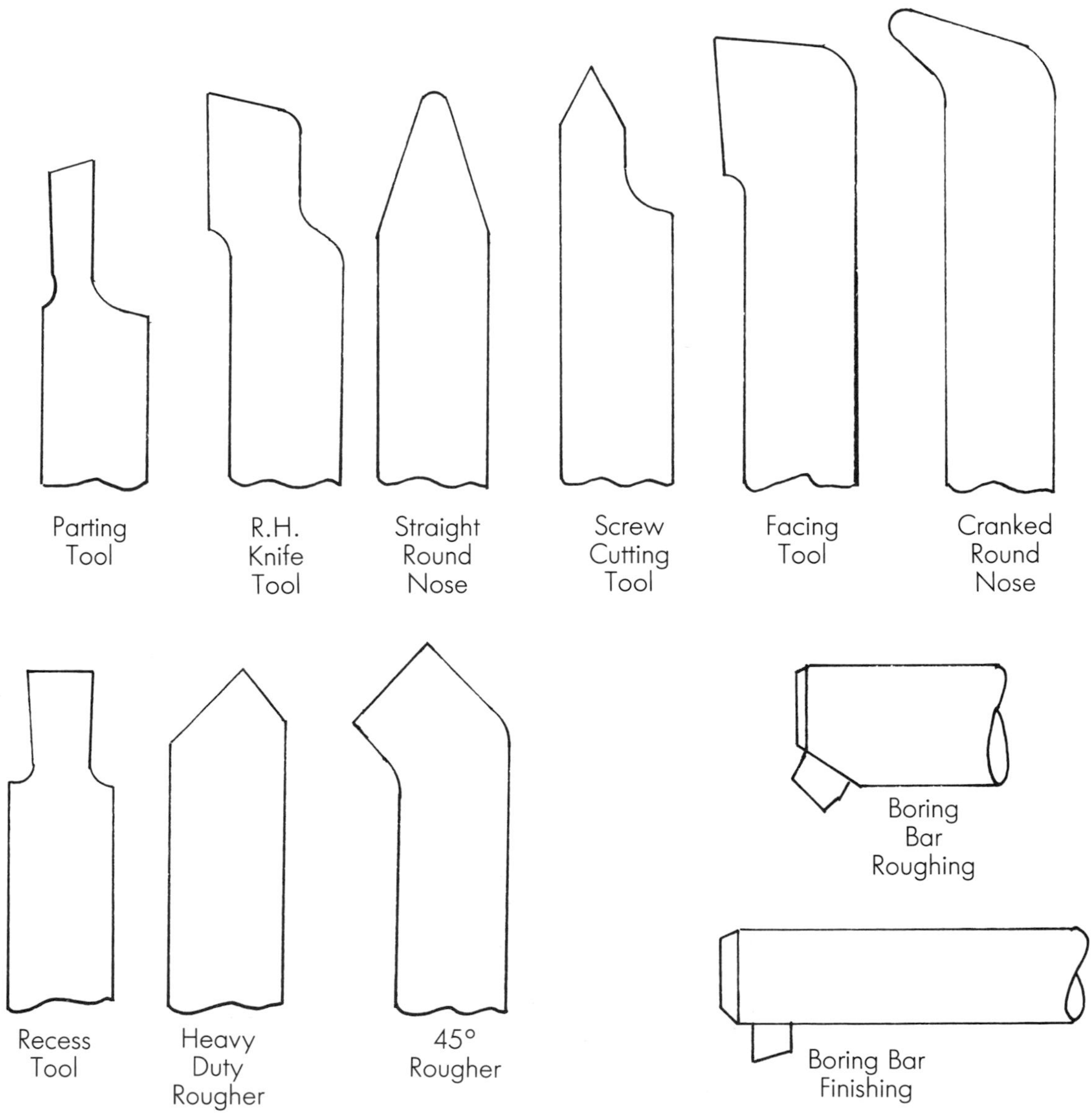

MATERIAL	CUTTING SPEED		TOOL ANGLES IN DEGREES			
	METRES PER MINUTE	FEET PER MINUTE	FRONT CLEARANCE	SIDE CLEARANCE	BACK OR TOP RAKE	SIDE RAKE
ALUMINIUM – SOFT ALLOY	120–240	400–800	9	9	30	15
ALUMINIUM – HARD ALLOY	90–180	300–600	9	9	30	15
BRASS	90–180	300–600	7	6	0	5
BRONZE – FREE CUTTING	90–180	300–600	5	5	0	2
BRONZE – TOUGH	30– 60	100–200	10	12	8	10
CAST IRON	20– 30	60–100	5	4	10	9
COPPER	20– 45	60–150	5	5	20	25
DIE-CASTINGS (ZINC)	60– 90	200–300	8	8	8	10
MAGNESIUM ALLOY	180–300	600–1,000	10	10	8	6
PLASTICS – CAST RESIN	60–180	200–600	10	12	30	25
PLASTICS – LAMINATED	60–180	200–600	7	7	25	25
STEEL – MILD	30– 60	100–200	8	6	20	15
STEEL – HIGH CARBON	10– 25	35–80	6	5	10	5
STEEL – STAINLESS	20– 45	60–150	8	6	8	5
WOOD	150–300	500–1,000	15	15	25	25

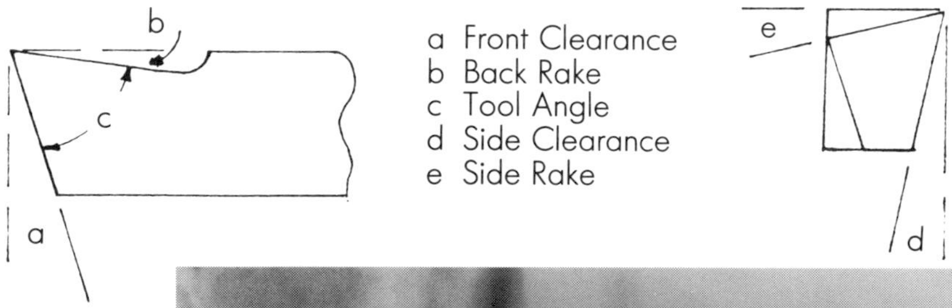

Fig. 56 **Above** *Tool angles and cutting speeds.*

Right *Facing off.*

Taper turning using the compound slide.

to the chuck i.e. parallel to the bed of the lathe. On a short piece of work the job can be supported by the chuck alone. For longer work the end of the metal is often supported by a centre held in the tailstock of the lathe.

Work can also be held between two centres, one end held in the headstock and the other in the tailstock. The work is driven by a dog which is clamped around the metal and a catch or driving plate screwed onto the headstock spindle.

Taper turning

There are three methods of producing a taper. For short tapers the compound slide should be loosened, set to the correct angle and then re-tightened. The taper can then be cut using the compound slide feedscrew by hand. Long tapers can be cut by one of two methods. That it first involves setting over the tailstock so that it is out of line with the centre line of the lathe. The amount of set over has to be calculated carefully. One method of finding the set over is to take the total length of the work piece and divide by the length of the part to be tapered. Multiply the answer by one half the difference in diameters to obtain the amount of set over. This form of cutting tapers can only be used if the work is set up between centres.

The second method uses a taper turning attachment which bolts on the rear of the lathe saddle and is also clamped to the lathe bed at its other end. The cross slide can then be disengaged from the saddle and clamped to the taper attachment.

If the taper attachment is then adjusted to the correct angle, and the saddle moved along the bed, the cross slide will slowly move across the bed of the lathe as it travels along it. The method of attachment and adjustment varies between different makes of lathe but the basic format remains the same. One of the big advantages of the attachment is that it enables internal tapers to be bored.

Screw cutting

One of the great advantages of owning or having the use of a lathe is the ability to cut screwthreads of any size or pitch very accurately.

If the lathe has a gearbox, it is only a matter of selecting the appropriate gears to achieve the correct relationship between the speed of the lathe chuck and the lathe leadscrew.

If there is no gearbox, the change gear wheels mounted on the back of the headstock will have to be changed to suit the type of screw thread you wish to cut. The correct wheels to use are usually marked on a plate fixed to the headstock. Where there is no indication of gear wheels to use, you will have to work out the relationship yourself. For this you will need to measure the pitch of the leadscrew and then decide which gearwheels are necessary to cut the correct thread, i.e. if the leadscrew is 8 T.P.I. and you wish to cut 24 T.P.I. thread, the gearing must be set up so that the chuck revolves three times quicker than the leadscrew. The thread is produced with a single point lathe tool that has been ground to suit the profile of the thread to be cut. A threading tool gauge should be used to check the profile of the ground lathe tool. This gauge has vee slots cut into it, corresponding with the angle of different types of thread. It should also be used to set the threading tool square before machining is started.

Once the tool is set up correctly the point can be brought in until it just touches the work. The micrometer collar should then be set to zero so that the depth of cut can be measured accurately.

Before the thread is machined it is usual to cut a groove where the thread is going to end. This is to give a small run out area at the end of the thread where the leadscrew of the lathe can be disengaged and the screwing tool wound out away from the work.

The lathe should be set on the slowest speed and a very light cut taken to check that the thread is correct. If it is, the rest of the thread should be cut until it is the correct depth.

The leadscrew must be engaged at the correct place each time and this can be achieved using the thread dial indicator. The handbook for your lathe will tell you which lines on the indicator to use for different threads.

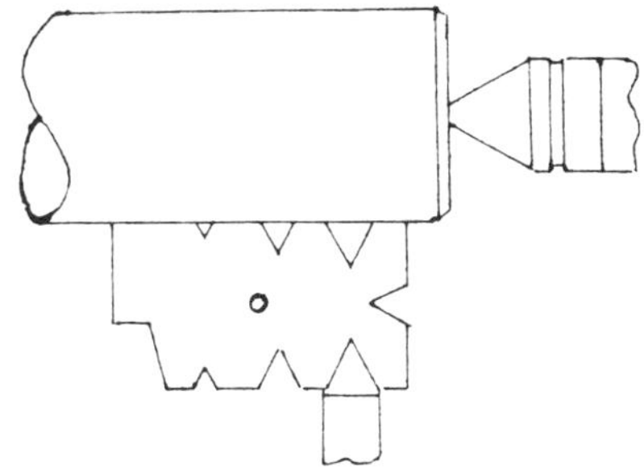

External tool bit set square using threading gauge

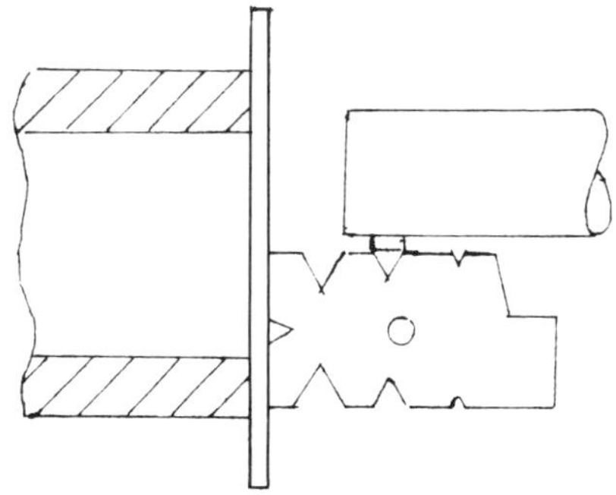

Internal tool bit set square using threading gauge

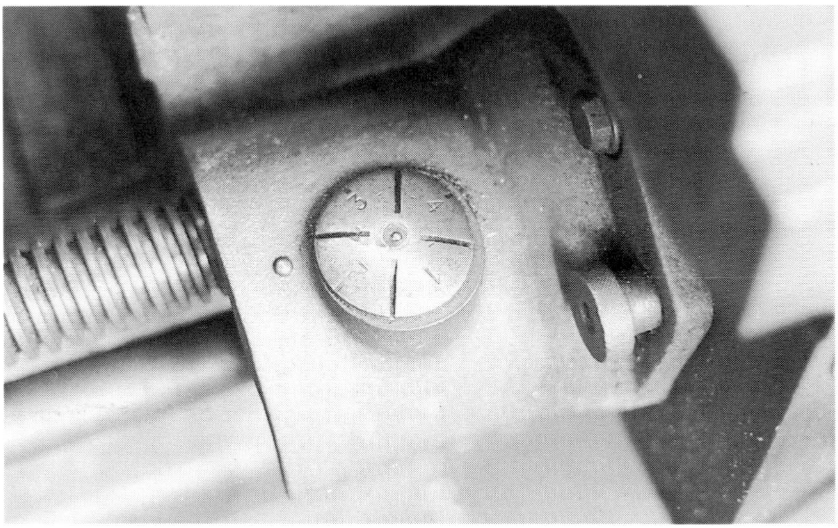

Fig. 57 **Above right** *Threading gauge.*

Right *Thread dial indicator.*

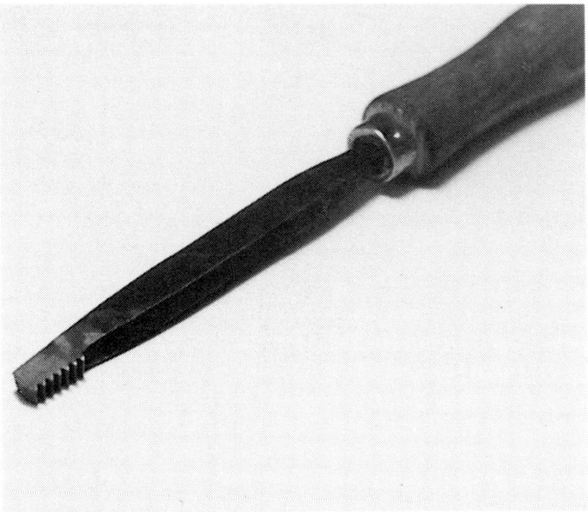

A hand thread chaser for internal threads.

If you have no handbook then it will be a question of testing on a piece of metal and making a note of the results, or using the same line each time you take a cut.

Once the thread has been cut to the correct depth, a thread chaser should be used to round off the crest and root of the thread to produce the correct thread form. The easiest to use are hand chasers; Held in contact with the thread as it revolves they will remove a very small amount of metal. It is essential to check the thread after each pass of the chaser as it is easy to remove too much metal and produce an undersize thread.

Drilling and boring

The most common method of drilling in the lathe is for the work to be held in the chuck and the drill to be held stationary in the tailstock chuck. The second method used involves mounting the work on the carriage of the lathe and holding the drill either in the chuck or the tapered headstock sleeve. This second method is rarely used because in many cases it is easier to use a drilling machine rather than take the time required to mount the work piece accurately in line with the centre line of the lathe.

Before drilling a hole in the end of a round bar, the metal must be faced off. When the work is ready, a combination drill should be put in the tailstock chuck and the workpiece drilled with this first. This will locate the twist drill accurately in the centre of the metal and enable it to start cutting correctly. A drill will not be able to start cutting accurately on its own. The point will wander and most likely start to drill off-centre.

Drill sizes beyond the capacity of the tailstock chuck, usually ½ in (13 mm) can be held in the morse taper of the tailstock spindle.

Reamers can also be held in the tailstock to ream holes to the correct size. Small straight shank reamers are held in the drill chuck while taper shank reamers are held directly in the tailstock spindle.

A boring tool can be held in the toolpost for boring large diameter or non-standard size holes. Before boring a hole in a solid piece of metal, the work will have to be centre drilled and then drilled to a large enough size to allow the boring tool to enter the work. It is usually quicker to drill the hole as large as possible, leaving only a small amount of metal to be removed with the boring tool.

When a deep through hole has to be bored that is beyond the capabilities of a normal boring tool, it is possible to set up a special boring bar held on centres between the headstock and tailstock. The work is mounted on the lathe carriage and moved along the bed of the lathe to produce the cut.

Knurling

Knurling is the method of raising the surface to provide a grip for holding or turning. Two types of knurling are available; diamond knurling or straight knurling, and they are produced by a knurling tool that has one or two wheels with straight or angled teeth cut into them.

The knurling tool should be mounted in the toolpost with the centre line of the wheels in line with the centre of the work. The lathe should then be set on a low speed and when it has been started the knurling wheels will be forced into the work and then moved along, preferably using the automatic feed for uniformity of speed. Plenty of oil should be used during knurling to help produce good definition. More than one pass may be needed to give a knurl of satisfactory depth.

Parting off

Parting off is the name given to the process of cutting off a piece of work while it is being held in the lathe. A special narrow lathe tool is required usually consisting of a blade of H.S.S. clamped into a holder.

The parting tool must be set up correctly; if it is below centre, the workpiece will try to climb over the tool, usually snapping the end of it off.

The lathe should be adjusted to a low speed and the parting off tool fed straight in. Coolant should be used on all metals except cast iron and great care taken not to force the tool into the work.

Should your lathe have play in the cross-slide, it may not be possible to part off work without difficulty. In this case it is much better to saw through the metal and face off the cut surface.

Mandrel work

When machining the outside of a hollow piece of work, it is often necessary to mount the work on a mandrel.

Standard lathe mandrels, hardened and tempered, can be bought in various sizes. The mandrel should be ground to a taper of 1 in 2000 (.0005in per inch). The surface of the mandrel should then be lubricated and driven into the workpiece and the work set up between centres.

Manufactured mandrels are expensive to buy and

Top right *A knurling tool, showing the two sets of wheels. One gives a straight knurl, the other a diamond knurl.*

Middle right *A parting tool.*

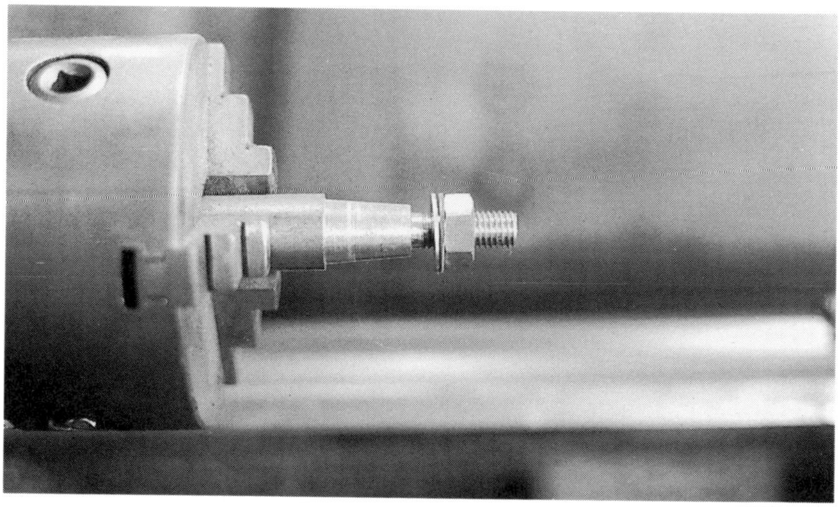

Right *A stub mandrel.*

it is possible to make a satisfactory mandrel for one-off jobs.

A short stub mandrel can be made from mild steel, by turning down a larger diameter bar to the size wanted. One method of clamping the workpiece to the mandrel is by turning down the end piece of the mandrel, threading it, and using a nut and washer to clamp the work against the shoulder of the mandrel. The second method involves drilling a hole into the end of the mandrel and threading it with a taper tap only. The end of the mandrel should be cut down the centre line to beyond the depth of the hole. When a bolt is screwed into the hole, it will thus expand the mandrel and grip the inside of the work.

It should be understood that only a brief outline of the lathe's uses can be given in this book. Anyone wishing to know more about lathe work will find there are several specialist books dealing with this subject.

CHAPTER 13
Cleaning and protecting metal

Whenever motor vehicles are dismantled there is always the problem of cleaning the parts before work on them can begin. There are several ways of cleaning metal ranging from a brush and paraffin bath to more sophisticated equipment.

High pressure water washers can be obtained using cold or hot water with possibly the addition of a detergent to aid grease removal. These types of cleaner will only remove dirt, oil or grease from the vehicle; they do not have the cutting power to remove corrosion or paint from metal. They are an ideal way of cleaning down the engine compartment and underside of a vehicle before dismantling or for removing the salt and debris of winter motoring.

Where corrosion, paint or similar hard substances have to be removed from metal, abrasive cleaning equipment must be used. This equipment falls into two categories: dry blast or wet blast.

Dry blast equipment uses air under pressure to shoot an abrasive at the component being cleaned. Wet blast equipment uses air and water under pressure to shoot the abrasive. The abrasives used can be silicon carbide, aluminium oxide, emery, shot, glass beads or any other abrasive material, depending on the material being cleaned and the substance being removed.

There are two main differences between the systems. Wet blasting surrounds the abrasive with a layer of water; this means the cutting action is reduced, producing a smoother finish, but also increasing the time taken to clean the component and adding to the cost. Dry blasting is quicker but much more aggressive, which can cause problems with thin or rust-weakened components. Dry blasting with coarse grit can cut through thin aluminium or rust-weakened body panels, so care must be taken to choose the right system.

Vaqua blasting is a water/air grit system which is ideal for aluminium castings. Apart from the advantage over the dry system of removing less stock from the casting, any grit from the cleaning process is washed away by a clean water/air spray at the end of the process, leaving a bright lustre on the surface.

Apart from cleaning anything from a spark plug to a large chassis frame, components can be strengthened by wet or dry blasting with lead shot or glass beads. These processes are known as shot peening, or vapour bead blasting when using a wet blast system. The process compacts and smooths the surface of the metal, removing scratches and other imperfections that could be the cause of stress failures. Whatever cleaning process you decide to use, make sure it is suitable for the article involved.

Remember if it is steel that has been cleaned, paint it as soon as possible, because rust will start to form extremely quickly on the surface.

Electroplating

Electroplating is used to provide a bright decorative finish that will resist tarnishing or to build up worn components by providing a hard, wear-resistant surface.

Chromium plating is the most widely used form of electroplating for motor vehicles, though more manufacturers are using stainless steel in its place. On older cars, such as those built up to the late 1920s, only nickel was applied as the final finish. Hidden parts of the vehicle that need protection against corrosion can be zinc or cadmium plated. Of these zinc is the cheaper and its ability to protect steel is the equal, if not superior, to cadmium.

Other plated finishes that can be used are: copper, brass, silver or even gold if your taste is that extravagant. Whatever finish you require, the component must be prepared first. Do not expect to be welcomed with open arms by the plater if you thrust a dirty, rusty piece of metal into his hands, and ask him to plate it. The component should be clean, grease-free, and in rust-free condition. If the object is made of several parts, it should be dismantled as far as possible. If you are in any doubt, ask the plater for advice.

One of the most difficult metals to replate is diecast zinc, used for many items such as door handles, rear light holders, etc. The problem arises from the swelling and cracking of the casting as described in Chapter 2. If the corrosion is too bad, don't bother wasting time on it; try to find another in better condition.

While it is possible to electroplate most metals, including aluminium and some plastics, not all plating shops have the equipment to undertake this work. Should you find a good plating firm, treat them well as by all accounts they seem to be few and far between.

Anodising

Aluminium components can be protected from corrosion by anodising. This produces an oxide of aluminium on the surface of the metal which prevents further corrosion. The anodic layer can be self-coloured or dyed to any number of different colours.

Many plating firms will undertake anodising, but one word of warning. Make sure that the alloy is of anodising quality, otherwise the component could be ruined. The plater should be able to tell you, but if in doubt don't try it.

Stove enamel

This is an extremely tough finish that is suitable for wheels and engine parts as it is proof against hot oil. The components are cleaned, painted with enamel and then baked, or stoved, in an oven. Most shot blasting firms offer stove enamelling as part of their service.

Vitreous enamel

Many high quality cars use this heat-resisting finish on cast iron exhaust manifolds. Though the finish is quite tough, it is possible to chip it, particularly on exposed edges.

Plastic coating

Any metal can be coated with plastic using the hot dip method. The metal is cleaned and heated to a temperature between 190°C–230°C depending on the type of plastic used. The metal is then dipped into a tank of plastic powder that is being fluidised by having air blown through it. The plastic powder sticks to the hot metal and melts to a uniform thickness.

The equipment needed is quite simple and many night schools possess it.

Metal spraying

While metal spraying is often used to build up worn components, it can be used as a decorative or protective finish. Most metals can be sprayed on to another metal base; the finish is matt and will require careful polishing.

Exhaust systems can be sprayed with aluminium to give a rust-proof coating.

Painting

One of the most obvious ways of protecting metal is by painting. The painting of motor vehicles is a very large subject and it is not possible in a book of this nature to go into it in any great detail. I can only recommend that anyone who requires chapter and verse on the subject should read one of the many books on the market that deal solely with this aspect of car restoration.

Before starting the preparation work on a motor vehicle, it is necessary to decide whether you are going to brush paint or spray the finish onto the vehicle. Don't be put off brush painting by the horrific vehicles you may see that look as if they have been painted by the roadside with a scrubbing brush. They probably have. With a decent brush and the correct method of use, a very good result can be obtained.

The author's 1934 Austin 7 special, brush-painted with Tekaloid enamel.

My own Austin Seven special was brush painted with 'Tekaloid' synthetic enamel and as can be seen from the photographs the results are pleasing.

The main problem to overcome when using synthetic enamel, irrespective of whether it is applied by spray gun or brush, is the longer drying time before it becomes dust proof; it will take approximately 1½ to 2 hours compared to the very short space of time for sprayed cellulose.

If you intend to use a spray gun, it is possible to hire one from most hire shops, to avoid the expense of buying a spray gun and compressor outright. Where only part of the body needs repainting, the decision is made for you. You must match the existing finish of the vehicle.

When you are undertaking a total repaint of a vehicle from scratch, it is best to buy the materials you require from a paint specialist. All paint manufacturers supply technical information sheets with their products and these will enable you to ensure that you buy the correct primers, undercoats, etc. The information will also include thinning ratios and drying times — everything in fact you need to know to produce a good result.

Problems can arise when only part of the car needs re-painting. All paints fade due to the effects of sunlight and pollutants in the atmosphere. Buying the original colour, either in bulk or in the small aerosol tins available from accessory shops, will not match the faded paint on your car. The best way round the problem is to go to an accident repair shop and ask them to match the colour of your car. Obviously you will need to take the car with you, or part of it if it is not mobile. Specialist sprayers such as these have paint matching cards that have a range of shades from the original paint. The cards can be placed on the bodywork and the nearest match selected. On the back of the card the ingredients for making up that particular shade of paint should be listed.

Whatever method of painting you use, the preparation of the car is the same. If you are stripping the entire car down to the bare bodyshell be prepared for a lot of mess. Choose the paint stripper carefully, particularly if the bodywork is made of fibreglass. Some strippers will attack the gel coat. Do give the paint stripper time to work and wear protective gloves and clothing. To make a thorough job of it, all the exterior trim, windows and interior trim should be removed. They are best removed anyway if you want to make a good job of the re-paint, particularly if it is in a different colour to the original.

When all the paint has been removed, the body shell must be cleaned thoroughly to remove any traces of paint stripper. This is particularly important if there are any areas of the body shell which could trap the stripper. If it is not removed, it will cause continual problems with the re-painting.

Once all the stripper has been removed, inspect the body panels carefully. Be prepared to find all manner of nasty things that have been covered by layers of paint. Don't skimp on the repair work; make sure the bodywork is as sound as you can make it before contemplating applying any paint. Remember paint will not hide defects, only make them more visible, so ensure that the bodywork is as smooth as possible, using body solder or filler paste to fill any small blemishes. Now you can start applying the paint following the maker's instructions carefully.

If you do not have the facilities for re-painting the vehicle yourself, and that includes a garage big enough to walk round the vehicle with room to spare, then it is advisable to have the job done professionally. Painting in the open air will not achieve good results. You will at least have the satisfaction of knowing that your own preparation work has been properly done and that you will have saved a considerable amount of money as a result.

CHAPTER 14
Glues

Although I have mentioned glues in several chapters of this book, a separate section dealing with all the different types would, I feel, be advantageous.

The following list, though not exhaustive, gives suitable adhesives for most jobs. When faced with an unusual combination of materials, it may be necessary to experiment with various glues. Perhaps the quickest and surest way is to get in touch with one of the major glue manufacturers, most of whom have an information service to answer such queries.

Metal to metal	– epoxy resin
Metal to others	– epoxy resin or contact adhesive
Wood to wood	– a wide range of wood glues suitable for all purposes
Wood to others	– epoxy resin or contact adhesive
Leather to leather	– epoxy resin, contact adhesive or P.V.A.
Leather to others	– contact adhesives or epoxy resin
Textiles to textiles	– natural latex (e.g.'Copydex')
Textiles to others	– natural latex, P.V.A. or contact adhesive
Acrylic to acrylic	– 'Tensol' cements
Acrylic to others	– acrylic is not usually glued to others. Use screws, etc, or experiment with various types of 'Bostik'.
Rubber to rubber	– rubber solution, natural latex or contact adhesive
Rubber to others	– natural latex or contact adhesive
Glass to glass	– epoxy resin
China to china	– epoxy resin
Glass or china to others	– contact adhesive or epoxy resin. Glass should not be glued to wood. If the wood warps or shrinks, the glass may crack.
P.V.C. to P.V.C.	– P.V.C. cement
P.V.C. to others	– P.V.C. cement or contact adhesive
Polystyrene to polystyrene	– polystyrene cement
Polystyrenc to others	– contact adhesive

Surfaces that are to be joined must be clean, dry and grease-free. Old paint, varnish, glue, etc, must be removed to enable the glue to form a good bond with the material.

Plastics should be washed in warm water with a small amount of detergent added to it. They should be rinsed in clean warm water and left to dry.

Smooth surfaces must be roughened slightly to improve the glue bond; this does not apply when joining plastic to plastic because the cements used work by dissolving the surface layer of the plastic. Always put the work together dry to ensure that the various parts fit together closely before glueing. Use cramps, weights, etc, to hold the parts together until the glue sets. Joints that move during the drying process will fail easily. Follow the manufacturer's instructions closely, particularly in respect of mixing and the working time available before the glue starts to cure. The setting time is also important. Some glues may appear or feel hard but do not reach full strength for some time; to put stress on the joint before a full cure is achieved may well weaken the bond and cause premature failure.

Excess glue should be wiped from the joint before it sets. Most wood glues can be removed with a damp cloth; some other glues have solvents which can be used sparingly to remove the excess. Glues that contain a high proportion of solvent, e.g. contact adhesive and plastic cements, should not be used in a confined space or near a naked flame. The solvents are not only detrimental to your health but are highly inflammable.

Recently hot glue guns have become available on the market. These comprise a heating element within a holder shaped like a gun, hence the name. Sticks of hot melt glue are placed into the gun and when melted can be forced from the nozzle of the gun onto the surfaces to be joined. These are excellent for quick small jobs, but it is inadvisable to try them on long runs as the glue begins to set before the parts can be assembled.

Glues for wood

When considering glues suitable for wood in a motor car body, it is essential that only glue that is waterproof be used where there is any possibility of the timber becoming damp or wet.

A hot glue gun. A useful piece of equipment for quick gluing jobs.

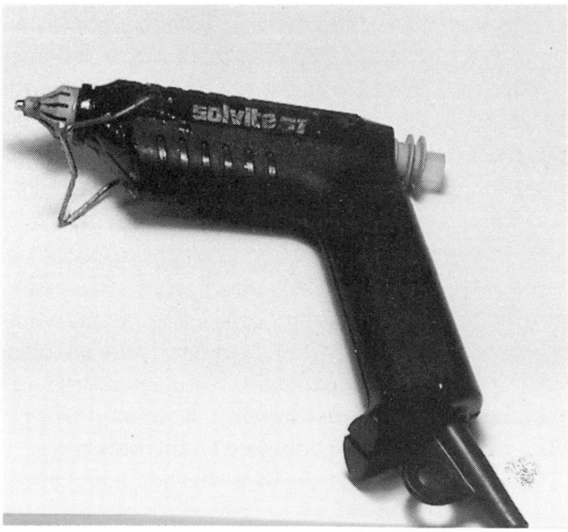

Polyvinyl Acetate glue (P.V.A.) is a white liquid usually sold in plastic containers (e.g. Resin W). It is probably one of the most widely used wood glues and is also suitable for some other materials. It has an unlimited shelf life and is reasonably quick setting; approximately two hours will give a strong joint. Though the glue is water-resistant, it is not waterproof and for this reason I would not recommend its use anywhere on a car where it may come in contact with water.

Synthetic resin glues are made from plastic resins and come in two main types. The one-shot type (e.g.'Cascamite') are in powder form and have to be mixed with water to activate the resin and hardener. The two-shot type (e.g.'Aerolite 306') consist of a liquid hardener and a resin powder. The resin has to be mixed with water and spread on one half of the joint and the liquid hardener spread on the other half before the joint is cramped together.

These glues produce a waterproof joint that is stronger than the wood itself and are ideally suited for motor vehicle work. The one disadvantage they have is that they stain some woods, of little importance if the wood is not seen when in use.

Resorcinol and phenol glues are considered the strongest glues for wood and are especially suited for laminating work and highly stressed joints. They are completely waterproof but are very expensive and leave dark brown glue lines on the work.

Impact or contact adhesives (e.g. 'Bostik', 'Evostik', 'Thixafix') are made from synthetic rubbers and solvents. They are best used for glueing dissimilar materials together such as leathercloth to wood. They are ideal for large areas or awkwardly-shaped items which are difficult to clamp. The main disadvantage with these adhesives is their relatively low strength, making them unsuitable for joints under stress. They also have a short shelf-life after their containers have been opened.

Glues for plastics

Most thermoplastics can be joined by a suitable cement that contains a powerful solvent for the material being joined. There are, however, several thermoplastics that cannot be joined in this way because suitable solvents are not available.

Polypropylene, polythene and P.T.F.E. are examples of these.

Though other adhesives are capable of joining plastics to each other and other materials, the joints are usually not as strong as those produced by plastic cements. Acrylic (e.g. Perspex, 'Oroglass') can be joined to itself using cement. The most widely used are the 'Tensol' range from I.C.I. 'Tensol No. 12' is a ready-mixed cement which is suitable for most purposes but it does not produce a clear joint. 'Tensol No. 10' is a two-part cement which gives a clear and waterproof joint that is suitable for outdoor use.

Rigid polystyrene can be joined with polystyrene cement, readily available in small tubes from any model shop that sells polystyrene model kits. It is quick-drying and gives a clear joint. Excess glue can be removed with acetone (available in many a home under the guise of nail polish remover). Do not attempt to join expanded polystyrene with this cement; it will dissolve before your eyes as the solvent gets to work.

Polyvinyl Chloride (P.V.C.) can be joined using 'Tensol 53' cement or a number of other proprietary P.V.C. adhesives. Some of these, such as 'Gloy' P.V.C. repair and 'Vinyl' weld, will stick P.V.C. to other materials. Acetone can be used to clean off excess glue.

Adhesives for metal

For many people the thought of sticking metal to metal has had no place in a properly ordered workshop, but in recent years, great strides have been made in adhesive technology. Not many people realise that the wing sections of their package holiday aeroplane are literally stuck together with adhesive or that the rotor blades of helicopters are also very successfully bonded together. There are now several adhesives that are very useful to engineers and in many instances, like those mentioned already, they can out-perform more traditional ways of joining metals.

Epoxy resins are possibly the most well-known of the adhesives suitable for joining metals, the most common type being the two-part epoxy which is comprised of a resin and a hardener. A good example of this is 'Araldite'. These should be carefully mixed, applied direct to the work surface and allowed to cure. In single-part epoxies, these two components are already mixed and simply require heating to cure.

In many applications, the new single-part epoxies, such as 'Permabond ESP', offer a real challenge to brazing and soldering. They are easier to use, free from lead and flux, and eliminate the need for refinishing.

Anaerobic adhesives are often known as sealants or 'locking compounds'. Acrylic based, they normally set in the presence of metal and absence of air (to be exact, atmospheric oxygen). They are used to lock, seal and retain all manner of turned, threaded and fitted parts, and often to seal flanges.

The 'Permabond A' range of adhesives only require the joint to be clean and dry and are applied straight from the container to the workpiece. 'Permabond A136' can be used instead of a thin gasket, saving the time and difficulty of making gaskets.

Cyanoacrylate adhesives are very versatile. With one drop it is possible to bond a wide variety of materials together – plastics, metals, rubber and ceramics. They are solvent-free and cure as a result of contact with the very small quantities of moisture found on all surfaces exposed to the atmosphere.

As single-part adhesives, cyanoacrylates do not require mixing. They can be applied straight from the bottle to the workpiece and they cure rapidly. One drop will cover up to one square inch with a 0.001 in glueline thickness. The surfaces to be bonded must be clean and free from oil or grease. Use alkaline solvents (acetone or methy ethyl ketone) or if there is persistent surface contamination, remove it by abrasion. Apply the adhesive sparingly to one surface (usually one drop is sufficient) and bring the components together quickly and correctly aligned until curing is achieved, normally in a few seconds. Any surplus adhesive can be removed by the use of acetone or methyl ethyl ketone, observing the usual precautions with these solvents.

Where difficult surfaces are to be bonded, such as acidic, porous or unreactive ones, a surface activator can be used to extend the capabilities of cyanoacrylates. It is usually only necessary to treat one surface, applying adhesive to the other.

Cyanoacrylate adhesive bonds skin and eyes in seconds, so wear polythene gloves. If contact with the skin does occur, warm soapy water will gradually remove the adhesive. In the case of contact with eyes, bathe with copious amounts of water and seek medical advice at once. Keep cyanoacrylate adhesive out of the reach of children.

The very latest types of adhesives are known as toughened adhesives and their development in this country has been pioneered by Permabond Ltd. Toughened adhesives combine the best features of anaerobics, cyanoacrylates and epoxies with exceptional toughness. They will withstand shock, peel and impact forces that destroy other adhesives. The toughness is obtained by the incorporation of a low-modulus rubber phase which prevents cracks from spreading by absorbing their energy before they effectively start. Toughened adhesives can be used to join the majority of materials such as metals, plastics, wood, glass and ceramics to themselves and each other. They can be obtained in various grades of single-part epoxies, two-part epoxies and acrylics.

The strength of these new adhesives can be gauged by the fact that Permabond 'Flexon 241' holds the rare M.O.D. full type approval for bonding metallic and reinforced plastic components in primary and secondary airframe structures.

As with any other method of joining materials, the strength of the joint is dependent on good joint design. Fig. 58 points the way.

Fig. 58 Joint design. (Permabond Ltd)

Right

These are good examples of adhesive joint design.

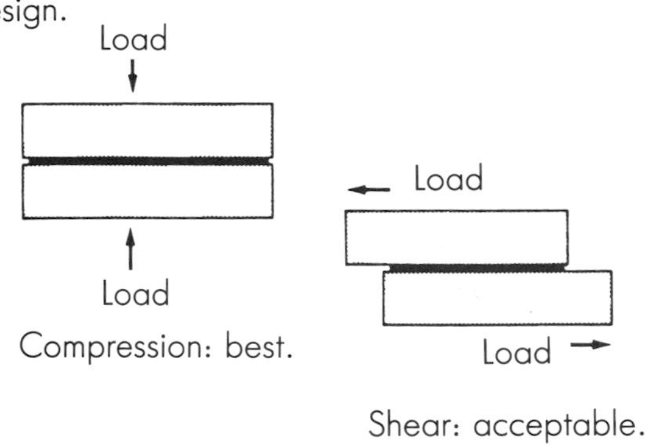
Load
Load
Compression: best.
Load
Load
Shear: acceptable.

Design to use the benefits of adhesives

There are many ways to reduce or avoid destructive cleavage forces. The 'wrong' examples can be avoided in any of the ways shown, with dramatic improvements in performance.

It is important to remember that adhesives are a separate technology. Joints that are perfectly suited to welding may be unsuitable for adhesives, and vice versa. Here is a brief guide to better joint design.

Wrong

Joints which are subject to peel and cleavage forces should be avoided.

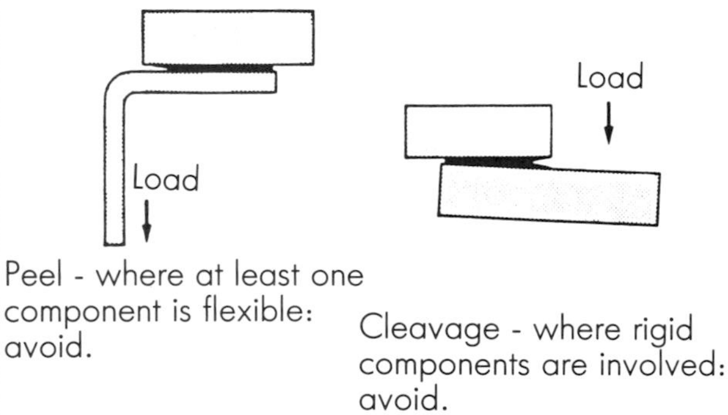
Load
Load
Peel - where at least one component is flexible: avoid.
Cleavage - where rigid components are involved: avoid.

Is the joint heavily or lightly loaded?

Conventional adhesives may be used wherever loads are light, and components are not expected to suffer heavy impacts. Where there is a risk of impact and/or heavy loading, you should use an appropriate toughened variant.

Wherever possible, adhesives should be loaded in compression and shear, so as to minimise or avoid peel or cleavage forces.

Good practice

1. Do use an adequate overlap, as this gives a stronger joint.
2. Do choose a rigid adherend where loads are carried. Joints formed from thick, rigid sections perform better than thinner ones, as they lower peak stress to the joint.
3. Do avoid butt joints
4. Do talk to the manufacturer. The old maxim 'the thinner the glue line, the better the joint' is not always true. Your supplier will be able to advise you on the optimum amount to use.

Wrong

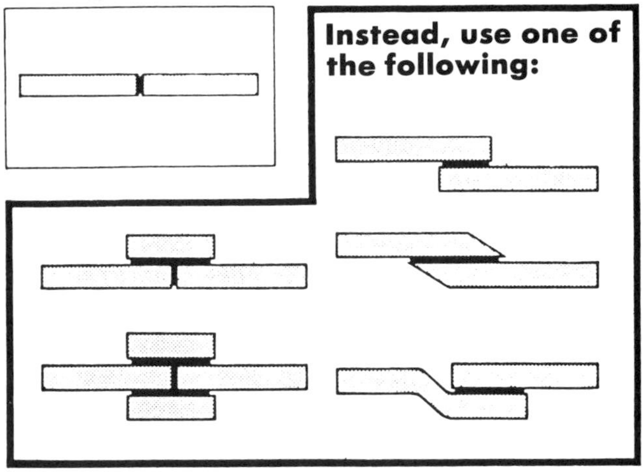

Wrong

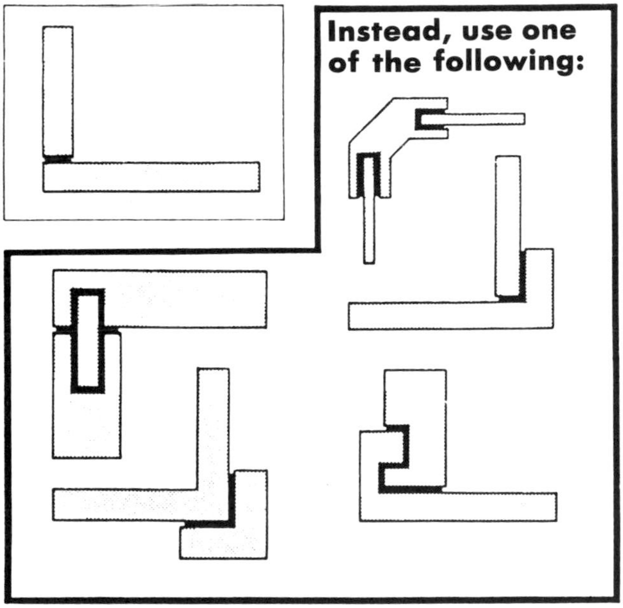

CHAPTER 15

Woods for motor vehicles

Woods fall into two basic groups: softwoods, which belong to the conifer family (gymnosperms), have needle-shaped leaves and are usually evergreen, and hardwoods, which belong to the broad-leaved family (angiosperms) and have their seeds contained in a seed case, e.g. an acorn or chestnut. They can be deciduous or evergreen.

In certain examples the name hardwood or softwood is rather a misnomer since balsa is a hardwood that is very soft and yew is a softwood that is harder than several hardwoods.

For motor vehicle work, all the softwoods can be ignored, except for certain methods of roof panelling in some pre-war cars, because their open grained structure and lack of strength make them unsuitable.

Only a few hardwoods are normally used in vehicle work: ash, elm, oak and beech for body framing, walnut and mahogany for dashboards and door cappings, and plywood for floor and running boards.

Ash This is a tough durable timber, cream to pale brown in colour. It has good bending qualities and an excellent strength-to-weight ratio. It is without doubt the best timber to use for body framing. The main defect to look for in ash is Black Heart; this occurs in the heartwood of the tree and looks like a black patchy stain. Avoid buying boards that have this appearance.

Oak There are three basic types of oak available in this country: European, including English oak, American and Japanese. Of the three, European and American are the stronger and are more suitable for coach-building work, although well-seasoned Japanese oak is also suitable. The main disadvantage with all oak is its tannic acid content, which will corrode iron and steel quickly. This can be overcome by using stainless steel screws and fittings.

Elm This timber has similar properties to ash in that it will bend easily and works well. It contains more knots than ash and you should check that you can cut what you need out of a board without running into the knots.

Beech This is a dense, heavy wood, that needs sharp tools to work well. It has good steam bending properties and withstands wear and shocks. Beech will split if nailed too near to the edge and it is not very durable if exposed to changes in moisture. For this reason, it must always be well protected when used in a car body frame.

Mahogany (Brazilian) The colour of this species of mahogany varies with its density from yellowish-brown to a deep reddish-brown. Its texture is finer than African mahogany and it is usually straight grained. This wood has excellent working and finishing properties and it can be nailed, screwed and glued satisfactorily.

Walnut This timber is yellowish-brown to golden-brown in colour and is sometimes marked with dark streaks. It can be worked well and takes a good finish, being excellent for fine joinery and veneers.

Hardwoods are priced by the cubic foot and whatever size boards you buy will be converted to this for costing. A convenient way to visualise a cubic foot is to remember that four boards six feet long, six inches wide and one inch thick add up to a cubic foot.

When buying timber, make sure you check the boards carefully; if they are warped or wet reject them. Wet wood can, if dried very carefully, be used, but it will warp if the drying is carried out too quickly. Boards that are split can be used if nothing else is available, but check that you can cut out the parts you need and ask for a discount on the price. It is normal to find splits, or shakes as they are called, in the end inch or two of a well-seasoned board. While on the subject of cutting boards, remember to allow for the width of the saw cut and some more for planing up afterwards in your calculations. Most hardwoods in timber yards are sold rough sawn, so if your timber needs to be 1 in. (25 mm) finished size you will need to buy a thicker board.

Reject boards that have a bleached appearance, which often means that the timber has been left out in the weather unprotected. This usually causes a multitude of fine shakes along the entire length of the board.

Plywood This is made by glueing thin layers of timber, called veneers, together. The layers or plies are glued with their grain directions at 90° to each other. Because of this cross-bonding, shrinkage and warping are minimal. Plywood is made up from an odd number of veneers to give even stresses in the sheets. Plywood with five or more layers is called multi-ply.

For use in motor vehicles it is essential that only exterior grade or marine ply is used, because moisture will attack the adhesive of interior plywood and soften it, causing the sheet to de-laminate and fall apart.

Exterior grade plywoods are marked as follows according to the type of adhesive used in their manufacture.

M. R. Moisture resistant and to some extent weather resistant. Will stand exposure to water for a short period, but boiling water will cause the adhesive to fail.

B.R. Boil resistant. These plywoods will accept exposure to weather conditions.

W.B.P. Weather and boilproof. The adhesive used in these plywoods will resist all weather conditions. They are the best to use for such items as floorboards and running boards.

Plywoods are manufactured in a range of thicknesses from 4–25 mm and in sheets normally 8 ft x 4 ft (2,440 mm x 1,220 mm) or 6 ft x 3 ft (1,830 mm x 915 mm). Some plywoods are also available with a hardwood veneer on one side for more decorative work.

Veneers

Veneers are thin slices of wood cut from the main trunk or large branches of the tree. They are used to enhance the surface of plainer timbers or, more usually, for plywood and other man-made boards.

There are several different types of veneer, each giving a different effect to the grain of the wood:

Burl These come from growths on a branch caused by injury, and provide a very decorative pattern.

Quarter These are taken from a quarter section of log, giving an attractive striped effect.

Curl A veneer taken from the junction of a branch and the main trunk, producing an attractive cut.

Oyster Produced by cutting a branch at an angle of 45°.

Butt These are taken from the swollen base of the tree. Slices are cut from half the log.

Half round The log is mounted off-centre on a rotary lathe to produce a broad grained pattern.

Flat The log is sliced along its length, exposing the marbled heartwood.

Rotary The whole log is brought against the cutting knife and a veneer cut in a continuous sheet. This produces the 'birds-eye' effect in maple.

CHAPTER 16

Woodworking tools

If your car has wood in its construction, and the majority of pre-war cars have, you will need some basic woodworking tools as an essential part of your tool kit. Planes come in a wide variety of shapes and sizes and it would be very expensive and unnecessary to collect a full set. Jack planes are the maid-of-all-work and all the general planing can be accomplished with them. A smaller version of the jack plane is the smoothing plane; this is used for cleaning-up work to remove tool marks and for planing end grain. Because of its short sole (250 mm) it will not produce a flat surface over a long length of timber.

The foreplane, jointer plane or tryplane is the long version of the jack plane. The length of the sole is usually 18–24 in (450–600 mm) and this plane is used for trueing up large surfaces and long edges. The long sole will produce an accurate flat surface whereas the shorter planes will follow the contour of the wood as it cuts (see Fig. 59).

A plane capable of cutting rebates is very useful; this will allow plywood panels to be let in flush with the body frame. There are several planes which will cut rebates, such as the plough, combination and rebate. Any one of these, together with a small block plane for getting into awkward places, will satisfy your basic requirements for planes.

Use of the plane

Wood should always be planed with the grain to produce the smoothest possible surface. It will soon become apparent if you are planing the wrong way. The wood will tear and leave a rough surface. To achieve a good finish on wood that has awkward grain, the plane must have a sharp blade that is set very fine.

Stand in a position where you can plane without leaning over the bench, with your left foot parallel

Fig. 59 Using the correct plane.

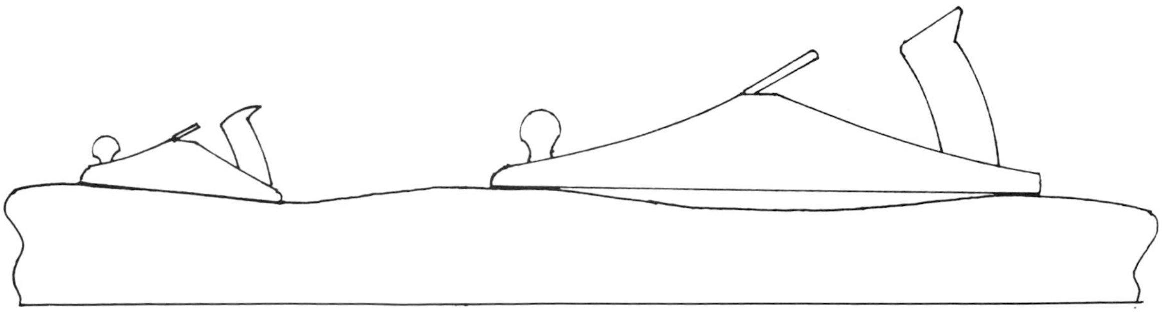

Jack, try and smoothing planes.

A compass and router plane.

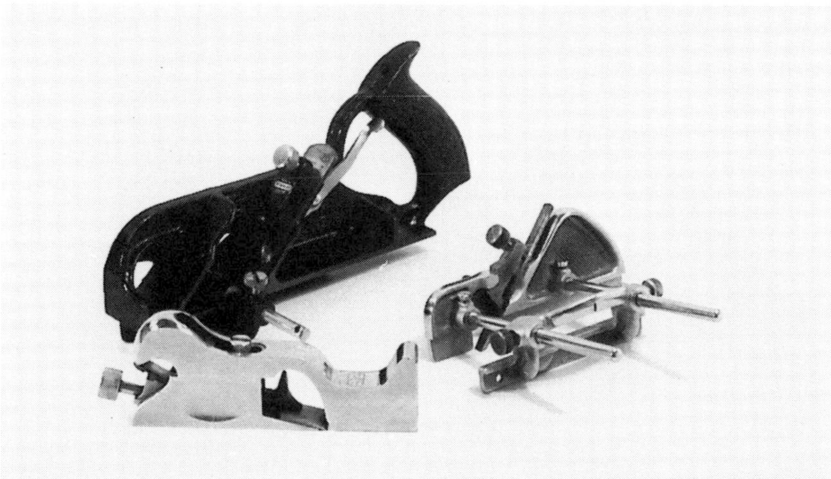

A shoulder plane and combination plane with a rebate plane in the background.

to the wood being planed (right foot if you are left-handed). Your bodyweight should move on to this foot as you push the plane forward. Make sure you feel balanced throughout the length of the cut; any tendency for your body to wobble will make planing an accurate surface very difficult.

The plane should be gripped with the thumb and first finger of the right hand guiding it, the other three fingers gripping the handle. The other hand grips the knob. If you are left-handed, the grip will be reversed.

When you are planing narrow edges, do not grip the knob at the front of the plane as this could cause the plane to wobble. Grip the toe of the plane and use the fingers as a fence. Frequently check the side of the timber you have chosen to plane first with a straight edge until it is flat. Next, look at the two edges and decide which one will need the least planed off it to produce a good edge. When you have decided which edge you will plane first, the side you have just finished planing should be marked with the face-side mark *ƒ* with the tail pointing towards the edge to be planed next.

This edge should now be planed and should be checked frequently with a straight edge for flatness and with a try-square from the face side for squareness. When the edge has been planed smooth, flat and square you can put on the face edge mark ^, with the point of the inverted vee touching the tail of the face side mark. The face side and face edge should be used for all subsequent marking out of the timber and this will ensure that the finished piece will be as accurate as possible.

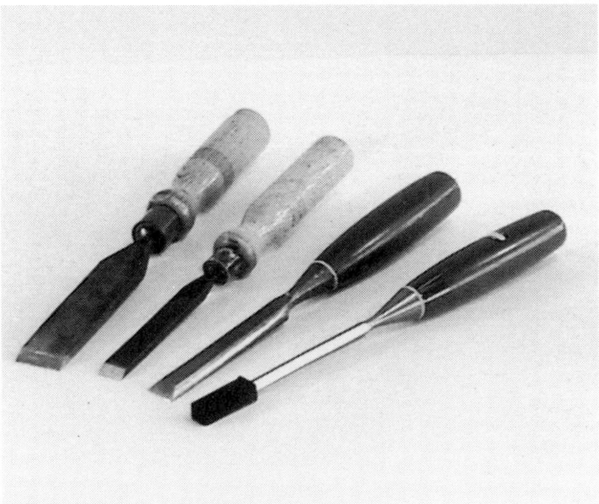

When planing across the grain at the end of a piece of wood, do not plane right the way across otherwise the grain will split at the edge as the plane passes over it. To prevent this happening, a scrap piece of wood can be either cramped to the edge of the board with a sash cramp or, if the wood is narrow enough to fit sideways in the vice, placed in the vice with the wood to be planed. This scrapwood supports the grain at the edge of the board, preventing it from splitting away. If the wood is wide it is possible to plane from the sides towards the middle, so preventing the splitting.

Chisels

A selection of chisels will be needed for cutting joints and shaping timber where planes cannot be used. Chisels are classified by type and by width.

Firmer chisels are for general purpose work and are available from ⅛ in (3 mm) to 2 in (50 mm) width. They are used for cutting with hand pressure, called paring, or with light blows from a mallet.

Bevel-edged firmer chisels are available in the same sizes as the firmer chisel, the only difference being that the sides of the blade are bevelled for cutting into acute angles such as the corners of dovetails. Because of its bevelled edge, the blade is not so strong as the firmer chisel and must be treated with care.

Mortise chisels are used for heavy duty work such as the cutting of mortise joints. They are specially designed to withstand heavy blows from a mallet. The thick blade prevents twisting in the mortise and enables the waste to be levered out of the joint without straining the blade. A leather washer is fitted between the handle and the blade to act as a shock absorber. The width of the blade varies from ¼ in (6 mm) to ½ in (13 mm).

Plastic end caps are available that fit over the end of the blade to protect the cutting edge from damage while being stored in a tool box or rack — one is shown in the illustration on the left.

Spokeshaves are extremely useful tools for shaping timber and will produce a smooth surface that does not need sanding if they are kept sharp and adjusted properly.

There are two basic types of spokeshave: a flat-faced spokeshave for flat surfaces and convex (outside) curves and a curved-faced spokeshave for concave (inside) curves.

Spokeshaves take practice to use well and many people resort to a rasp and glass paper rather than persevere. While a rasp will do the job, it takes longer and requires a great deal of cleaning up.

Before using a spokeshave, make sure the blade is sharp and set correctly. The cap iron should be no more than 2 mm from the cutting edge for use on hardwoods and it should be tight to reduce the risk of chatter. The blade should be adjusted so that it appears as a dark hair line when looking along the sole of the spokeshave. When using the spokeshave it is important to apply plenty of downward pressure as the spokeshave is moved forward. It also helps to hold the spokeshave at a slight angle to its direction of travel, giving a slicing action to its cut.

Cramps Whenever you work on building or repairing a body frame, there are very many occasions when you need three or more hands to hold everything in place. This is when the 'G' cramp becomes an invaluable tool and anyone trying to work without one or a similar cramp faces an uphill struggle.

There are times when you feel you can never have enough 'G' cramps, but half a dozen of varying sizes up to 150 mm should cope with most occasions. Cramps over 6 in (150 mm) are not needed so often but two or three of about 10 in (250 mm) capacity

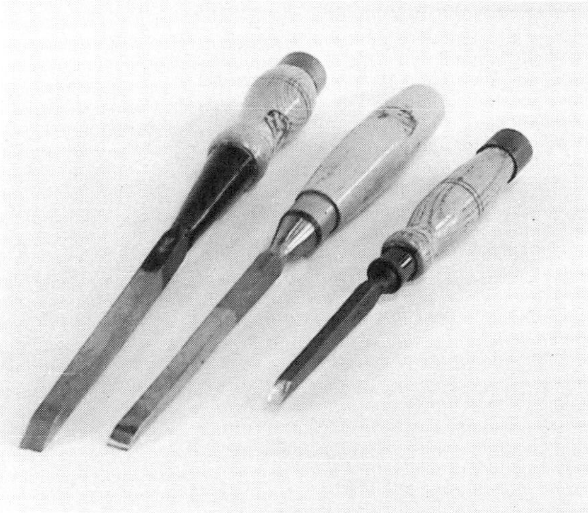

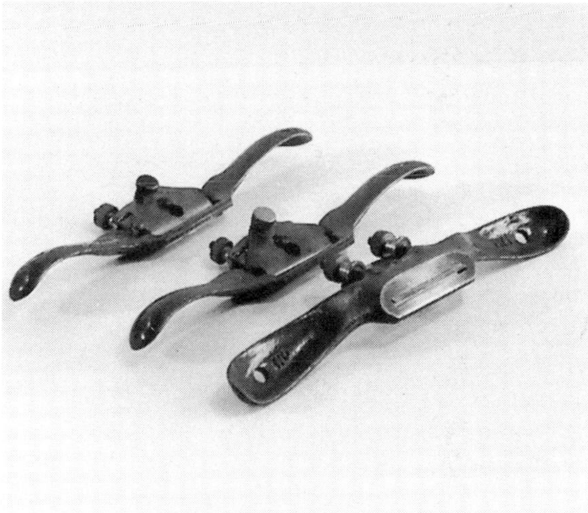

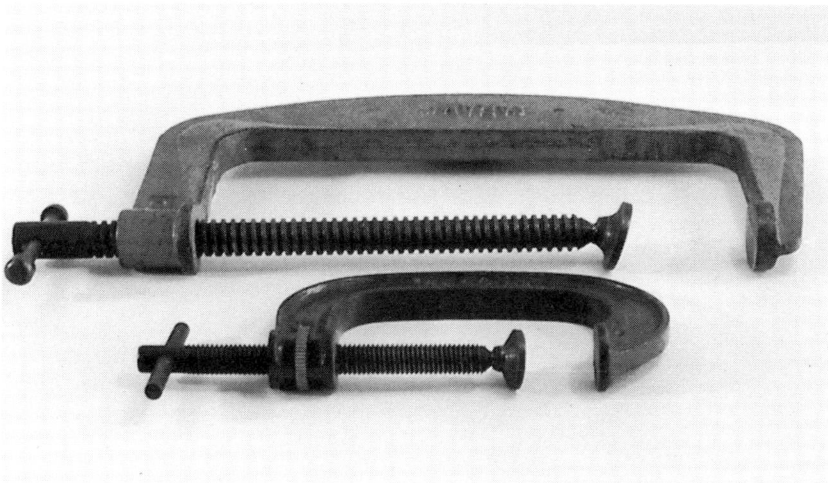

Far left *Firmer and bevelled edge chisels.*

Top right *Mortise chisels.*

Above right *Spokeshaves.*

Right *G-cramps.*

Left *Sash cramps and cramp heads for use on long pieces of wood to make cramps of any length.*

Below left *Corner cramps for cramping pieces of wood at right angles.*

Bottom *Rip and cross cut saws.*

will be useful for larger work.

Grab clamps are a very useful alternative to 'G' cramps. With these clamps the two jaws are screwed together in a pincer movement gripping the work. They can be more convenient to use, in some instances, than a G-cramp because of their shape.

For even larger work than the capacity of your 'G' cramps, sash or T-bar cramps are needed. Sash cramps are available in sizes from 18 in (450 mm) to 48 in (1,220 mm). It is possible to bolt two sash cramps together to increase their capacity. T-bar cramps are a heavier version of the sash cramp in sizes from 48 in (1,220 mm) to 72 in (1,980 mm) and extension bars are available to increase their capacity.

It is possible to buy the two heads that fit on the

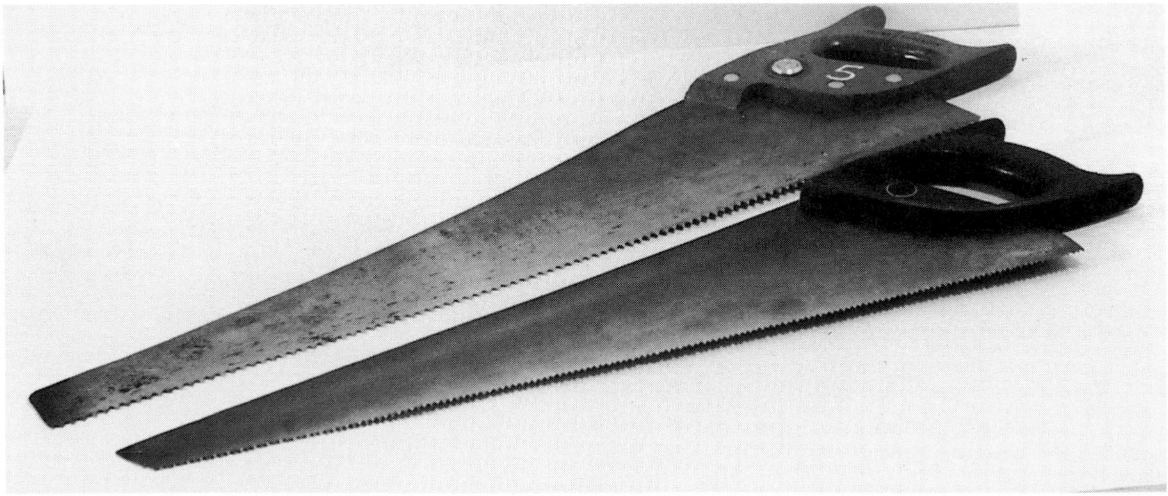

Tenon and dovetail saws.

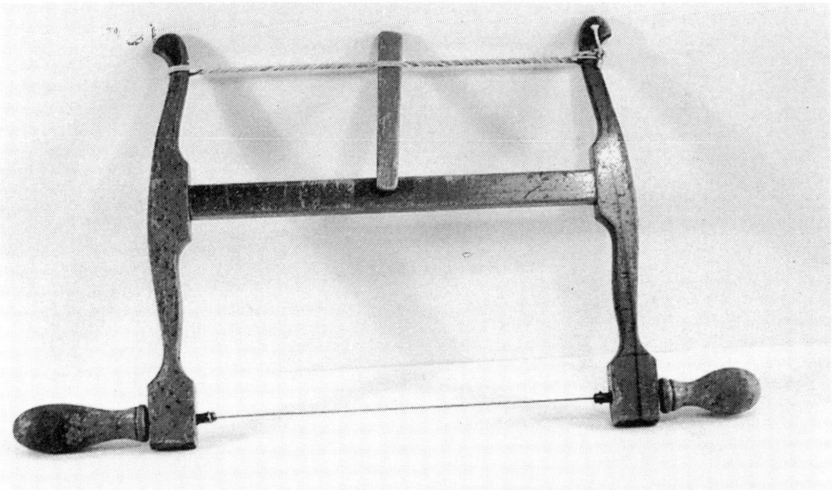

A bow saw for cutting curves.

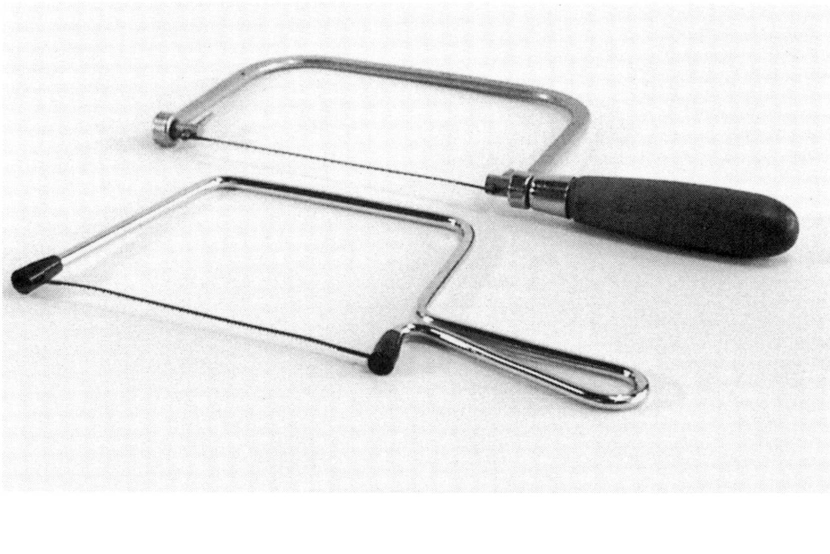

Coping saws for cutting small curves.

metal bar of the cramp; these can then be fitted to a length of suitable-sized timber to make up a cramp of any length required.

Always use some scrap timber between the 'G' or sash cramps' faces and the timber of the frame, to prevent the cramps damaging the timber.

Saws Good quality hand saws are needed if you are going to cut a large amount of timber and you do not have access to powered machinery.

For cutting down the grain of timber, a rip saw will cut the most efficiently. A panel or cross cut saw will cope with cutting across the grain and a tenon saw will be needed for joint work. For cutting curves, a bow saw will be necessary, the smaller coping saw being too small for all but the lightest work.

Making friends with the local timber merchant can pay great dividends. If you know what basic sizes of wood you want, he will usually put it through his saw for a very reasonable cost and this could save hours of hard work with a handsaw.

Tool Maintenance Planes and chisels must be kept sharp if you are going to produce neat, accurate work. Working with hardwoods means that the tools will require sharpening more frequently.

A good quality India oil stone will, if used regularly, put a keen edge on the blades. There is no mystery about sharpening blades; they must be held at the correct angle of 30°/35° and moved backwards and forwards along the stone. A few drops of oil on the surface of the stone helps the cutting action and keeps the fine particles of metal that have been ground away from clogging the grit of the stone.

Should you have difficulty in obtaining a good flat edge, one of the honing guides that are available from most ironmongers will solve the problem. Once the edge has been sharpened, there will be a fine feather of metal on the underside of the edge. This has to be removed by stropping the blade on the palm of the hand or a leather strop. Alternatively, the blade can be placed flat on the stone and the feather ground off gently.

CHAPTER 17

Repairs to wooden body frames

When faced with the task of repairing a wooden body frame or even making a completely new one, don't allow despair to engulf you. The basic skills are quite straightforward; you do not have to be a master craftsman at cutting fancy joints such as dovetails because they don't appear in body frames. The most commonly used joint is the halving joint, where, as its name suggests, half the thickness of the two pieces of timber are cut away so that when the joint is put together the pieces of wood are flush with one another.

There are two types of halving joint: one where the ends of two pieces of timber are joined; the other where the end of one piece of timber meets another piece somewhere along its length.

Halving joints are marked out using a marking gauge set to half the thickness of the timber. The length of the joint should be marked out with a square and then the centre line marked with the gauge. It is a good idea to mark with a pencil the part of the joint to be cut out, to eliminate the frustrating discovery that you have removed the wrong piece of wood! A tenon saw can then be used to cut across the timber, first down to the line and secondly down the length of the timber to remove the waste. Remember to keep to the waste side of the line otherwise your completed joint will be thinner than necessary and the faces of the two frame members

Above right *Marking and mortise gauges.*

Right *A selection of marking out tools. From left to right: a square, a sliding bevel, a marking knife and a bevel or mitre square.*

will not be flush with one another. Once the bulk of the waste has been removed with the saw, the joint should be pared down to the line, if necessary, with a sharp, wide-bladed chisel.

When removing wood from the middle of a piece of timber, saw down to the centre line at each end of the joint. Depending on the width of the waste wood to be removed, it may be possible to use the saw at an angle to saw some of the remaining waste out of the joint. After this, use a chisel with a wide blade to cut out the remaining waste. The joint should be pared out at an angle, working from the sides of the timber towards the middle. Do not chisel straight across the timber as this could cause the grain of the wood to split on the far side of the joint. Ensure that the faces of the joint are true, otherwise the timbers will be angled in relation to each other.

There are times when a joint has to be cut to achieve an angle between the timbers. Doors, for instance, are built with a certain amount of twist so that they do not rattle when shut. This twist is referred to as 'wind' or 'slam' and is carefully arranged so that the door makes contact with the dovetail rubber just a few millimetres in advance of the lock meeting the striker plate.

If you are rebuilding a door, take careful note of the joints in any remaining pieces of timber and reproduce them as accurately as possible. It is not necessary to cut each item to the finished size, indeed it is an advantage to leave them oversize which will allow for adjustments to be made without spoiling the finished piece. The final shape of the door can be achieved by planing off the excess wood. Always cramp the door together dry and offer it up to the frame. If the 'slam' of door is incorrect, small wedges of timber can be placed in the appropriate joints until the door is correct. This will then show which joints need adjusting and the amount of wood to be removed.

Halving joints should be screwed together as well as glued, to ensure that they withstand any stress that is put on them. I would advise the use of stainless steel screws in any body frame. They are more expensive than other types of woodscrew but once they are in place you can forget them with peace of mind. Normal mild steel screws will rust very quickly, especially in an acidic timber such as oak. Even plated screws will rust in the end and brass screws, while non-rusting, are not really strong enough for the job.

Do not use a screw direct into the timbers. Not only will it be very difficult to drive in, but the joint will not be pulled together properly. The outer half of the joint should be drilled to provide a clearance hole for the screw to pass through. This hole should then be countersunk, deep enough for the head of the screw to be below the level of the surrounding wood. The second half of the joint should be drilled to suit the core diameter of the screw, and its depth exclusive of the tapered point of the screw. The table shows the sizes for clearance and core diameter drills. The timber can then be glued and screwed together. (Make sure you use the correct size screwdriver on the screw otherwise the slot will become damaged and you will have difficulty driving the screw fully home.)

It is not every time that a whole frame member has to be renewed because of rot. You may find that only a portion of timber is affected and that a replacement section can be fitted in.

The first thing to do is to assess the extent of the damage or rot. Be generous with your calculations — 'if in doubt cut it out' must guide what you do. Having decided what needs to be replaced, take all the necessary measurements to enable you to reproduce the part. Do not cut out the old timber from the frame until the new part has been made and compared to the original.

There are two joints you can use to join the new wood to the old, a halving joint, which has already been described, and a spliced joint. The latter is basically a butt joint that has a rebate in the face of each piece of timber. A tongue, usually of plywood, is tapped into the rebates to provide the strength of the glued joint (see Fig. 60). You may find this joint more awkward to cut than a halving joint if the rebate that has to be cut on the wood in situ is in a difficult position.

Whatever joint you decide to use, do not glue the joint before you have had a 'dry run' at assembly. The

Screw sizes.

GAUGE NO.	2	4	6	8	10	12	14
CLEARANCE	2.2	.8	3.6	4.4	5.0	5.8	6.4
CORE	1.2	1.4	1.8	2.2	2.6	3.0	3.2

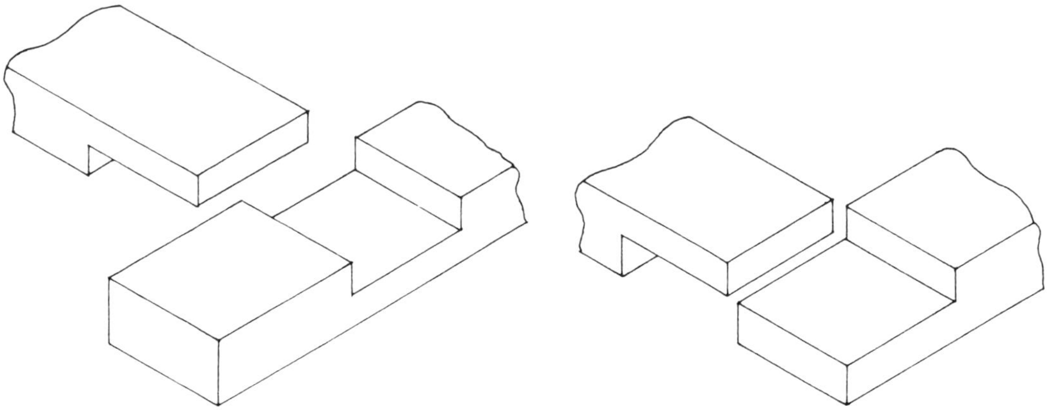

Fig. 60 Above *Halving joints.*

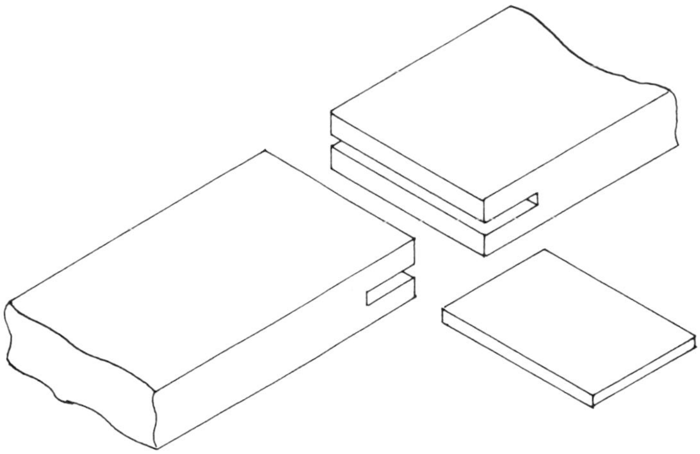

Fig. 61 Right *Spliced joints.*

Fig. 62 Below right *Mortise and tenon joint.*

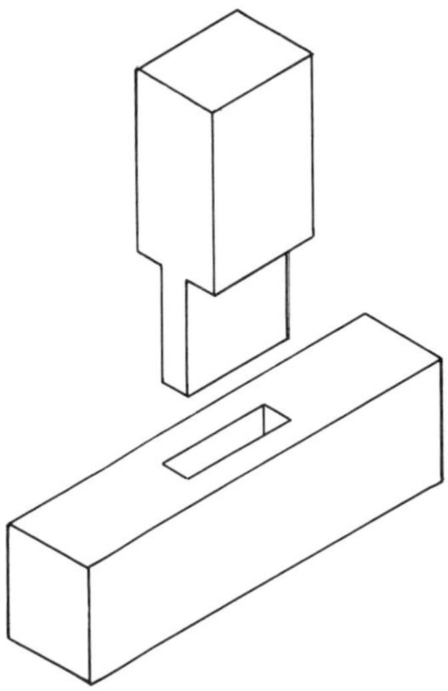

most usual problem is the tongue in the spliced joint; this should be a push fit when dry. Do not force the tongue into the joint as you are liable to split the timber of the frame. Check also that no parts of the frame near the new section are under undue strain caused perhaps by badly fitted joints or the new section being forced into place. When you are satisfied that all is well, the joints can be reassembled with glue and firmly screwed together.

One point to remember when using screws is to put the screws into the wood at a slight angle. Not only does this improve the strength of the joint by increasing the leverage required to pull the screws out of the wood; if they are angled towards the shoulders of the joint they will pull the shoulders closer together as they are tightened.

Another type of joint found in some body frames

An Alvis 12/50 body frame undergoing restoration (L. Eccles)

is the mortise and tenon joint (see Fig. 62), usually used to join centre rails to outside rails. To enable you to mark out the joint accurately you will need a mortise gauge. It is possible to manage without one but accuracy is likely to be lost.

First decide the thickness of the tenon; one-third of the thickness of wood is considered correct. This then has to be matched to the nearest mortise chisel size, usually ¼ in (6 mm), 5/16 in (8 mm), ⅜ in (10 mm), or ½ in (12 mm).

The length of the tenon which is equal to the width of the wood containing the mortise is marked around the end of the piece of wood. The mortise gauge points should now be set to the chisel that is going to be used to cut the mortise, then the stock of the mortise gauge set so that the pins are equidistant from either edge of the wood. Place the stock of the gauge against the face side of the timber and scribe the lines right around the end of the timber.

The position of the mortise should then be marked out on the other piece of timber. First mark the length of the mortise and then the width, using the mortise gauge from the face side of the timber.

Once the frame is finished or repaired, it is important to consider how to protect the timber from the effects of the weather. In my opinion there is only one effective method of protection and that is a complete and thorough application of exterior grade paint. As with all types of finish, careful preparation is the key to success. It is best that all the metal work (hinges, brackets, etc) on the body frame should be removed and the timber rubbed down with fine glass paper to provide a key for the primer. Two coats of aluminium wood primer should be applied and left for two or three days to thoroughly harden. Next apply at least two coats of undercoat to make sure that every section of the frame is adequately covered. This should also be left for two or three days to harden off properly. When you are sure it is hard, it can be rubbed down with fine carbide paper. Do not use any water with the paper; undercoat is not waterproof, and if water soaks into it, this will prevent the top coat from adhering to it. After rubbing down, use a tacky cloth to remove any dust particles. Tacky cloths are available from good accessory shops or paint factors. The top coat can be applied by brush and if done carefully you can obtain a good finish, although to achieve the best possible result the top coat should be sprayed on.

It is not advisable to use cellulose paints for the timber of a frame. Cellulose is very brittle and is more than likely to crack as the frame flexes when the car is driven or when the timber moves, as all timber does, in reaction to the weather.

Laminating and steam bending

On many original body frames, curved pieces of timber were cut from wide boards. Not only was this wasteful and expensive but the short grain on parts of the curve meant weak areas in the timber. A much more satisfactory method of producing curved pieces of timber is to laminate them up from thin strips of wood glued and clamped to a suitable former. This produces an extremely strong and stable body component, much stronger than the original piece.

Ash, elm and beech are all suitable timbers for laminating and will bend around a surprisingly tight radius, depending on the thickness of the laminates. For curves whose radius is less than 12 in (300 mm) the laminates should be ⅛ in (3 mm) in thickness. For curves whose radius is greater than this, ¼ in (6 mm) laminates will be satisfactory. The laminates should be wider than the finished size required to allow for

The body frame of the 12/4 Riley showing the use of plywood to produce a rigid frame. (N. Tidd)

planing up afterwards. Extra length is also needed to allow for cutting to length. It also saves the needless problems of trying to get the ends of the laminates neatly together and also of remembering that the laminates on the outside of the curve are longer than those on the inside of the curve.

A circular saw or large bandsaw will be needed to cut the laminates out of a board, for there is no point attempting such an exercise by hand. Once the laminates have been cut, some people advocate that they should be planed to produce as smooth a finish as possible to obtain a stronger join line. In my experience if the saw has a tungsten-tipped blade, the finish will be very nearly as good as that of a plane, and will produce a perfectly good lamination. Should your ability to produce a perfectly flat surface with a plane over a long piece of timber be in doubt, leave the wood as it came from the saw. If the saw has left a rough surface, the laminates will have to be planed. Perhaps the easiest way of holding thin pieces of timber for planing is to pin them to the bench top and punch the heads of the pins well below the surface. When that face has been planed, the laminate can be carefully levered up from the bench, turned over and the process repeated.

The jig around which the laminates are formed must be an accurate copy of the inside shape of the final component. For one-off or short runs of laminations, the jig can be easily made from fairly heavy sections of scrap wood. The thickness of the timber for the jig should be the same as the width of the laminates; this makes it easier to check that the laminates are lying flat together. If you are producing a long lamination, you may find it easier to bolt the jig to a large board. This makes clamping the laminates easier as they can rest on the board instead of flapping about in mid-air.

The outside laminate should be protected from the cramps by either a steel strip or a wooden former that corresponds to the outer shape of the component. Naturally the surfaces of the formers must be smooth, without any bumps or hollows, as these will cause uneven pressure under the cramps, weakening the glue line. Notches should also be cut, where necessary on the inside of the former, to allow the cramps to grip without sliding.

The formers and the board, if they are fitted to one, must be protected from the glue used on the laminates. It would be extremely frustrating to find your perfectly laminated component stuck fast to the former. A couple of coats of varnish will prevent the glue sticking to the former. As an extra precaution, a layer of polythene or aluminium cooking foil can be placed between the former and the laminates.

Before glueing the laminates together, cramp them up dry on to the former. I have found it easier to mark each laminate halfway along with a pencil and then start at the middle of the former and work towards

Fig. 63 Laminating wooden frame parts. The jig is screwed to the baseboard while the outer glue blocks are clamped to the laminates by G-cramps. In practice more G-cramps would be required than the number shown here.

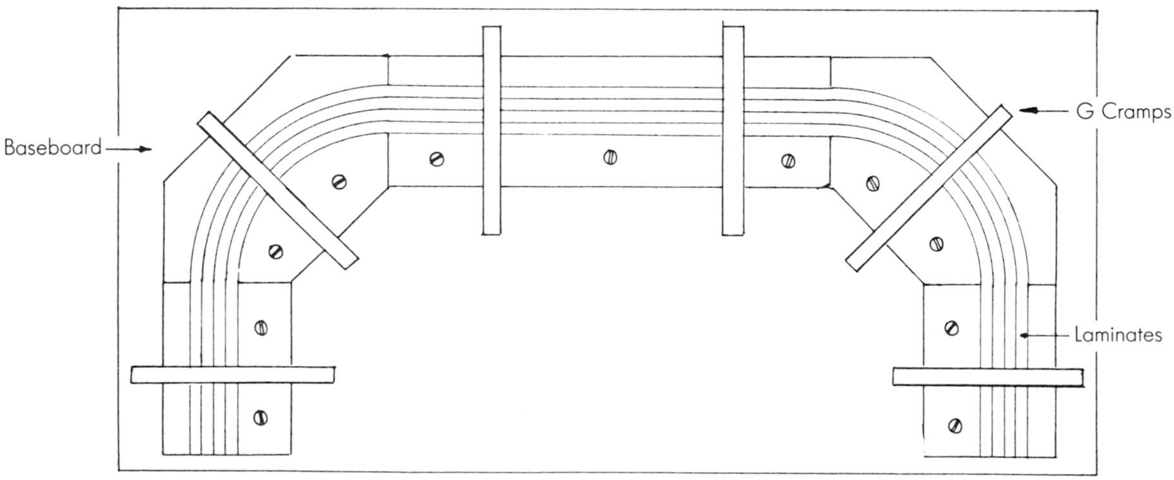

the ends. This method also needs less physical space in the workshop. Cramping them together dry will show up any problems you may have with the jig and also how many 'G' cramps you will need to pull the laminates together evenly. When the laminates are all cramped in place, check the join line between each piece; it should be tight together around the whole of the former. When you are satisfied that everything is right, the laminates can be glued and cramped back onto the former. Use either 'Cascamite' or one of the 'Aerolite' glues for laminating; the glue must be strong and waterproof. On long laminations, use a paint brush to apply the glue and make sure you cover all the mating surfaces. When the laminations have been cramped onto the former, remove as much of the surplus glue as you can. A damp cloth will remove the glue easily, and make cleaning up much easier. Glue, especially 'Cascamite', is extremely hard to remove when it has fully cured.

Should you want to bend timber above ¼ in (7 mm) in thickness, you will have to use steam to make the wood pliable enough to bend around the former. Ash, beech and elm are all suitable for steam bending. To make a steam chest, you will need a vessel of some kind in which to boil the water. This can range from an electric kettle to a special steaming pan which has a conical lid with a funnel for the steam to escape. I have seen an old tea urn pressed into service and an excellent job it did too! You will also need a length of pipe slightly longer than the longest piece of timber you wish to steam. P.V.C. pipe is ideal, but any waterproof pipe will do. The lid of your steamer must have a hole cut in it so that the pipe can be fitted there. The piece of timber should be suspended from the top of the pipe and the outlet sealed with polythene. The steam chest can then be filled with water and heated, so that the steam will rise up the pipe and saturate the timber. Check the water level regularly to prevent the chest boiling dry; much of the steam will condense on the polythene and return to the bottom.

The length of time the timber will require to be left in the steam chest will depend on the thickness of the component and the efficiency of the steam chest. Several hours may be needed but an occasional test will help you to discover how long is necessary. The timber should bend easily, without strain, around the former; if it doesn't, steam it for a further period and try again.

Once the timber is ready, cramp it to the jig as quickly as possible. Naturally you do not use glue yet if you are building up a component from laminates. The timber will take a couple of days to dry out and you must resist the temptation to remove it too soon. If you are using laminates, they should be marked with a pencil to show their relationship to each other and to the jig, before being removed. This will prevent the individual laminates becoming a sticky puzzle if you forget which went where after they have been coated with glue. They should then be cramped back onto the former and left while the glue cures.

One word of warning — use only the best quality timber for laminating and steam bending. Reject anything that has any defects such as knots, shakes or uneven grain. These will almost certainly break when they are bent.

Exterior fabric

Should your car have a body frame or roof covered in fabric, it is likely, if the covering is old, to be porous or starting to crack in many places. It is really pointless to try patching this type of covering. Only a total strip down and re-covering will prevent water seeping in and rotting the framework underneath. In the case of more modern cars with a fabric cover over a standard steel roof, leaking will allow rust to develop.

When dealing with a fabric body, the only satisfactory way of working is to remove the body from the chassis and if possible set it up on trestles at a suitable height. Before removing any of the fabric from any part of the vehicle, make a careful note of the position of any beading or joins in it. Use sketches or photographs; do not rely on your memory, otherwise problems may arise at a later stage. During the removal of the old fabric you should also note how the fabric has been taken round, or under, body fittings and what treatment has been used on the edges of the fabric.

Once all the old fabric, wadding and any other materials have been removed, it is essential to go over the whole area of the body or roof and remove every single tack remaining. This is time-consuming and possibly boring, but at the end of the process you will have accumulated a vast number of tacks and an intimate knowledge of the state of the woodwork under the fabric.

Any rot that is found in the wooden framework must be removed, either by replacing the whole frame member, or by cutting out the rot and joining in a new section as described in Chapter 17. Once the woodwork has been repaired, it should be rubbed down with glass paper until there are no raised pieces that will show through the final covering. Finally, the frame should be painted as described in Chapter 17 to ensure its survival for a considerable number of years.

When a fabric roof is being replaced, now is the time to decide whether to keep the sliding roof, if one has been fitted, or to fill it in for good. If the sliding roof is going to be retained, the mechanism should be carefully checked together with the runners and drainage tubes. The blocking of these, which causes leakage and rot, is the most common form of trouble with sunshine roofs. Should you decide to fill in the roof, the interior head lining will have to be removed so that the necessary woodwork can be installed and a new lining fitted to finish the job.

When the frame is ready, the recovering can begin. You may, as some manufacturers did, use a layer of sail cloth over the entire body frame, pulled taut and tacked down to provide a smooth surface. If the body frame is panelled with plywood or metal, this isn't really necessary. Place a thin and even layer of wadding on the surface of the cloth. Glue the wadding in place with a suitable adhesive such as 'Bostik' along all the edges, using some additional patches of glue on the main body to hold it in place. The edges of the wadding can be trimmed with scissors on the top and bottom of the body frame. Where joins occur on the surface of the body, the edges must be torn, otherwise a hard line will show through the top fabric where the wadding has been cut.

I have used, with success, ⅛ in (3 mm) thick foam sponge as a substitute for the wadding. It can be bought from a wide roll cut to any length, which obviates the need for unnecessary joins. Sponge is also easier to handle because of its light weight.

Once the wadding or sponge has been applied, the leathercloth can be fitted. Do not attempt to rush this part of the operation, otherwise the final finish will look very poor. The leathercloth should be cut roughly to size, leaving enough extra to get hold of to pull out the wrinkles that form. Tack the cloth into position but do not drive the tacks right in as they will need to be removed as the wrinkles are pulled out. The cloth must be pulled taut all over the frame to prevent creases forming after the edges have been finally tacked down. When you are satisfied with the appearance of the cloth, the excess should be trimmed off and 'Bostik' applied under the edge of the fabric. The tacks or gimp pins can then be hammered home, spaced at about ⅝ in (16 mm) intervals.

Convex curves require patience and some strength to pull the material round and remove all the wrinkles that occur. Hot water applied with a sponge while the fabric is being stretched will make the job easier, although an extra pair of hands will be required for this. Concave corners or curves will need to be cut to pull the fabric over. Make sure that the cuts are not too long and do not show on the finished exterior. The cut must not be left under tension otherwise it may, in time, form a split which will creep across the fabric.

Where the fabric is joined, it should be overlapped so that the beading will cover it completely. It is essential that the join is adequately waterproofed with adhesive before the beading is replaced. Fresh beading can be bought in various widths and it should be covered with the cloth butt-jointed on the underside of the beading. When the glue is dry, the beading can be hammered into place using thick card under the hammer to prevent damage to the leathercloth.

Once the body frame or roof is covered, the cappings or trim parts can be replaced to cover the gimp pins and raw edge of the fabric. It is particularly important that all the edges of the roof are sealed correctly and it is worth taking time to ensure that this is done properly. Neglect at this stage will allow water to quickly seep in and spoil an otherwise successful job.

CHAPTER 18

Inside the motor car

Interior woodwork

The woodwork used in the interior of a car often poses a different set of problems to the woodwork used for the body frame. For a start it is always visible and sets the seal on the appearance of the interior of the car. The dashboard is constantly on view and seen every time you look at the instruments, so it is important that it should be right.

The first thing to do is to carefully inspect all the interior woodwork, taking note of what goes where. Photographs taken of the interior of the car before dismantling can be a godsend some months later when you are trying to remember where everything went. Next, remove all parts that need attention. In my opinion, it is best to treat all the woodwork at the same time, particularly where the varnish has darkened with age, otherwise it is very difficult to match the colouring and you will be left with two different shades of woodwork in your car.

After removing the woodwork, check to see whether solid wood or a veneered panel has been used, as the treatment of the two types will be different. All the old varnish must be removed before any repairs can be made. I would advise against any mechanical method of removing the varnish, particularly in the case of veneered panels. The sheets of veneer are very thin and a scraper or similar tool is likely to cut straight through the top surface. A good quality paint stripper is the best method to use but do check the instructions carefully. Some paint strippers are liable to turn certain hardwoods either green or purple. If there are any such warnings on the container, avoid using its contents.

There are now many paint stripping firms that specialise in stripping household furniture; some of these provide an excellent service but once again check carefully with the operators that the process is suitable for your type of wood. If you have a piece of the interior woodwork that has got to be replaced, have that piece stripped to test the process.

Whether you strip off the varnish yourself or use the services of a strip shop, you will find that the surface of the wood will have become slightly rough, a normal consequence of the top layer of wood absorbing moisture. You may also find open pores in the grain of the wood, where the paint stripper has also removed the grain filler that was used to achieve a smooth surface quickly for production purposes. Unless time is very important to you, I would not recommend re-using grain filler. A much better result can be achieved with successive coats of varnish. This method will also never show the white hairlines that can appear when prolonged sunlight bleaches out the colour in the grain filler.

Any repairs that need doing can be tackled once the wood is stripped of varnish. Solid wood is easier to work on in many respects than veneered wood. Scratches in solid wood can be removed with either a cabinet maker's scraper or glasspaper. On veneered surfaces check whether the scratch has penetrated through the veneer. If it hasn't, glasspaper carefully to avoid removing the veneer altogether. Scratches that have cut through the veneer will require a new section of veneer inserted into the panel and I will deal with this and all veneering later in this chapter.

Dents in the surface of the wood can often be removed by using a wet cloth and a hot iron. Place the wet cloth over the dent and press down with the iron; the steam produced will swell the grain and lift the dent. It may take several attempts before the surface is level and the wood will be roughened and need glasspapering smooth. Cigarette burns or areas where the wood has actually been removed cannot be cured by steam. Burn marks should have the charred wood carefully scraped away and the blackened surface treated with ordinary household bleach applied with a small brush. Once the wood around the burn has been bleached back to approximately the right colour, the depression can be filled. Whatever filler you decide to use, test some on a spare piece of wood, to check the effect of stain and varnish on it once it has dried. Some fillers will absorb stain or varnish which can alter their colour; others are impervious to both and will stay their natural colour whether you want them to or not.

It is possible to fill a depression by melting shellac into it and then scraping the surface flat after the shellac has hardened. Sticks of coloured shellac are available from craft shops or possibly shops that cater for furniture restorers. Shellac can also be used for filling small holes left by screws or nails; these should not be filled with plugs of wood as the end grain will always show up against the rest of the wood. It may be difficult to see the plug when the wood has been sanded down prior to varnishing, but end grain will soak up varnish more readily than the surrounding wood and become darker, which will make it stand out like a sore thumb.

Small splits in wood can cause problems. It is almost impossible to close them up by cramping the wood together and even harder to get glue into them. They can be filled with shellac or wood filler or by inserting a thin piece of veneer into the split. If you use this method, the split will need to be enlarged very slightly in width by using a small pointed tool. A strip of veneer about ½ in (12 mm) wide should be cut and the edge and ends that are going into the split glasspapered to a feather edge. Coat the surface with clear glue and force it into the split, trim it off so it is still proud of the wood, then gently tap it down level with the surface. Once the glue has dried, it can be glasspapered smooth.

Should your car be fitted with veneered panels that have been damaged by the veneer being cut through, with pieces missing, you are faced with two choices — either to try to repair the damage by using inlaid patches or by re-veneering the panel.

Whichever method you choose you will need to buy some fresh veneer. For small amounts the local craft shop may prove the best bet, particularly if it deals with marquetry work. If the shop does not stock it, try the craft magazines for addresses or your local hardwood timber merchants. If you have already stripped the varnish off the wood, it will be easier to match veneers. If you have not, damp the veneer slightly so that it will give a better indication of the colour it will assume when varnished.

When an inlaid patch is needed, it is difficult to disguise it completely. Cuts across the grain of the wood will show up badly when the panel is varnished. To help eliminate this a long narrow diamond of veneer should be cut and the corners of its shorter axis rounded off. This can then be placed over the damaged area of veneer and cut around with a sharp knife. The old veneer can be lifted out and the new patch inserted. Take time and care to make sure the patch is a good fit; a badly fitting patch can look worse than the damage it was supposed to repair. If the damage is very bad, re-veneering is the only possible solution, not a difficult task on flat surfaces providing you take care. When veneering both the edge and face of a panel, the edge should be treated first, then the face, so that the veneer used on the face can overlap the edge veneer and prevent it from showing as a dark line.

The panel must be carefully prepared by either stripping off all the old veneer or patching it where necessary to present a smooth flat surface to which the new veneer can adhere. The first method is the best as this will prevent any problems with the original veneer lifting off the surface at a later date. When the surface has been prepared by removing all the varnish, glue, etc and by rubbing down to a smooth finish with glass paper, the veneer should be cut roughly to size leaving about ½ in (12 mm) overlap all the way round. This will allow for any slight movement of the veneer as it is cramped to the panel. Apply the glue with a paint brush to ensure that the surface is covered with an even layer of glue, paying particular attention to the edges to prevent dry spots where the veneer will lift from once the panel is in use. For saloon cars P.V.A. glue is suitable but for open cars a waterproof glue is essential. Place the veneer onto the panel and cover it with a layer of polythene; this will act as a barrier against any glue that is squeezed through the veneer during cramping. Next place a sheet of hard rubber or metal on top of the polythene. The surface which is in contact with the polythene must be clean and smooth otherwise the surface of the veneer will be damaged. On top of this, place a thick board and clamp them all together, starting from the middle and working towards the ends. Don't forget to put clamping blocks behind the panel to protect the wood from the shoe of the cramp. When the glue has set, trim the veneer carefully to within a 1/16 in (1.6 mm) of the edge of the panel, using a craft knife or similar tool. Lay the panel veneer side down on a clean, smooth surface, and cut round it, to help prevent the veneer splitting. The last small overlap can be finished off with fine glasspaper wrapped round a block; work downwards from the top of the veneer to prevent it lifting from the panel.

Before the veneer is ready for varnishing it must be smoothed down with glasspaper. Always glass-paper along the grain of the wood otherwise the scratch marks from the glasspaper will show up badly on the smooth panel. It is at this stage you have to decide whether to stain the wood or leave it its natural colour. Stains are very useful for matching up the various parts of the interior woodwork, particularly where the colour of the wood was achieved mainly by the use of a coloured varnish. Once the varnish is removed, the variation in colour can be considerable. Follow the maker's instructions carefully and you will be able to achieve an even match. Most dyes can be mixed together to alter the shade to suit your requirements, but do remember to try the stain on a spare piece of wood as it is almost impossible to remove if it is wrong.

The type of varnish to use is a matter of personal choice. My preference is for a polyurethane varnish as I feel it stands up to effects of sunlight better than an oil-based one. Whether you use a clear or satin finish, the method of application is the same — a large number of thin coats always achieves a better finish than one or two thicker coats. Varnish applied too thickly always reminds me of toffee apples and lacks depth of shine.

Always follow the maker's instructions carefully. The first few coats can be mixed with the correct thinners. This helps to penetrate the grain of the wood and gives a sound base for further coats. When you have built up enough layers so that the varnish is drying on top of the wood, it should be left to dry for at least 24 hours. After this it can be cut back to a smooth surface with some fine garnet paper. If you cannot obtain garnet, use some well-worn fine glasspaper.

The gloss coats can now be applied, thinned or at full strength, but make sure each coat is dry before the next is applied. At least three coats are needed to achieve a good body of varnish. After the final coat has been left to dry and harden for at least two days it should be rubbed down lightly to remove the nibs and dust marks which will have formed.

The final polish can be achieved with rubbing compound, followed by metal polish and a final coating of wax. This should give a deep shine showing the grain of the wood to perfection.

Wood graining by hand

Many pre-war cars used screen printed wood graining on dashboards and door cappings; this process was continued by some manufacturers until quite recently. Another form of artificial woodgrain involved the use of a plastic film with a grain pattern on it. This material was called 'Di-Noc', produced by the 3M Company until the end of 1982. Now there is little or no stock left unless you are lucky enough to find a stockist with some on the back of a shelf.

If your car was one of those that used either of these processes and the original is well worn, you have one of two options. Either paint all the metalwork involved to match the interior of the car or take the plunge and try artificial woodgraining yourself. Should you fail with the latter approach, all you will have lost is some time and small expense for materials involved. You can still paint the panels involved knowing that at least you had a go.

The metal must first be prepared so that it is smooth and free from flaws. It isn't necessary to go down to bare metal, though producing a smooth finish on 'Di-Noc' may be difficult without cutting through it. Another point to bear in mind with 'Di-Noc' is that, being a plastic, some types of paint may react with it, producing a sticky mess. Should this happen, you will have to remove all of it before you can continue.

Once the metal has been prepared, a coat of primer must be applied. When it has dried, rub it down gently to a smooth finish. Next apply the base colour; if you can discover the original base colour that was used on your car, use that one. If you are not successful, the choice is yours. Most base colours vary from a muddy yellow to an orangy brown. When it has dried thoroughly, lightly sand with wet and dry paper but only enough to remove any excess roughness, because the graining paint needs a roughened surface to which to adhere.

The graining paint can be either acrylic, enamel or water-based, or you can use black or brown printer's ink suitably thinned. Two points to remember when deciding what to use are, firstly that it must not dry too quickly, and secondly that it must not react with the base colour that has already been applied.

A layer of graining paint should be applied over the base and the grain effect produced by the use of various implements wiped over the surface. You can buy grainer's brushes which look like ordinary household paint brushes with shorter, stiffer bristles, and may have notches cut in them. Obviously you could make your own but many experts use a wide variety of odds and ends for producing the pattern; bits of sponge, plastic combs with some teeth bent or removed, rubber dog combs or even bits of screwed-up newspaper. The important thing is that the grain should flow from one end of the panel to the other. Look at the grain flow on household furniture and try to copy what you see. Experiment to your heart's content until you are pleased with the results. If you use a water-based paint it is a simple matter to wash off the failures and try again.

When you are satisfied with the results, your work will need a coat of clear varnish to protect the grain from wearing off very quickly. The varnish must be sprayed on otherwise a brush would soon destroy your painstaking creation. Don't forget to test that the varnish will not react with the paint or base colour.

Carpets and upholstery

The material used for upholstery will fall into three main types: hide, cloth and P.V.C. and all will respond to cleaning with possibly some extra treatment to bring out their best qualities.

The decision whether to renovate or replace is one that only you can make, but there are one or two points to consider. If only part of the interior is replaced, it can make everything else look much worse than it did before. Total replacement can be very expensive and may not justify its cost when compared to the total value of your car. Personally, I believe that older cars often look better with careworn interiors to match their age rather than looking as if they had just rolled off the production line, but that is a matter of opinion. Owners of more modern or classic cars may find it possible to buy replacement seats in better condition from breakers' yards or cars that are being sold for spares. If that is not possible, there are firms that sell seat covers for many cars which will not look out of place on one that is more modern.

Seats with cloth upholstery can be cleaned with any proprietary cloth cleaners. The main thing to avoid is soaking the upholstery with too much water which will take a long time to dry out and may also make the dye run from any backing material underneath the upholstery. It is advisable to test an area that is out of sight before starting on the whole of the upholstery. Taking off the cloth cover to wash it separately is not a good idea as the fabric could easily shrink and be impossible to replace.

Small splits or tears should be sewn together using small stitches with thread the same colour as the material to hide the join as much as possible. Where a panel of cloth is badly worn it may be possible to replace it, though problems can occur where the seat is a mixture of cloth and P.V.C. Joining the two can be difficult if the P.V.C. has started to break up. In this case a replacement seat or seat cover is probably the easiest answer.

P.V.C. or its forerunner Rexine are both man-made materials. P.V.C. can be cleaned and if necessary recoloured with a variety of products manufactured for the purpose, but be cautious about using these on Rexine since some of them may soften the surface of the material and leave a sticky mess. As with the cloth upholstery, try out the preparation on a part that does

The interior of the Alvis being re-upholstered. This shows what a skilled and careful amateur can achieve. (L. Eccles)

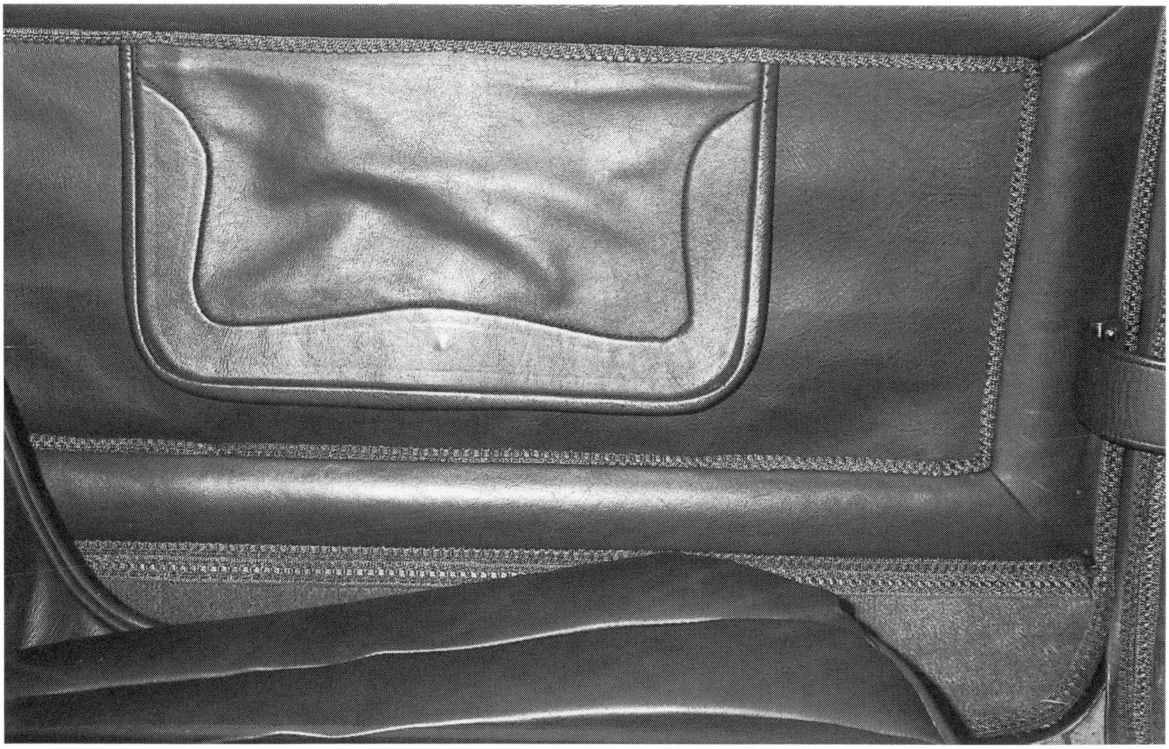

not show. One method of determining whether the upholstery is Rexine or P.V.C. is to cut off a small piece where it will not show (e.g. underneath the seat) and put a lighted match to it. If it is Rexine or some other nitro-cellulose cloth it will burn quickly and smell of burning castor oil. If it burns very slowly or not at all it will be P.V.C.

Nitro-cellulose material can be painted with 'leatherpaint', which is available in a variety of colours and usually sold in craft and D.I.Y. shops. Follow the maker's instructions carefully and it will do a good job on the upholstery.

Many cars were fitted with leather upholstery and though this is a very hardwearing material it does need periodic attention to keep it in the best condition possible. Connolly Brothers Ltd, who have supplied the majority of motor manufacturers in this country with upholstery hide, recommend that their leather be cleaned with a damp cloth dipped in a solution of mild soap and water or with 'Connolly Leather Cleaner'. After cleaning, a light application of their 'CeeBee Hide Food' should be given to help maintain the supple feel of the leather.

If the leather has faded or there is minor damage to the surface, Connolly's will supply their 'Connollising Kit' to rectify the trouble. They will need a small piece of unfaded hide cut from somewhere where it will not show, to use as a colour match for a range of dyes.

After the seat has been cleaned, the dye should be sponged onto the leather using long, even strokes, and left to dry. Once the dye has dried thoroughly, hide food can be rubbed into the surface and buffed with a soft cloth.

Carpets should be removed and given a good shake or beating before using a vacuum cleaner to remove the fine dust. Grit is the major cause of carpet wear, because the sharp edges of the grit cut into the fibres of the carpet and weaken them. Once all the loose dirt has been removed from the carpet, it can be cleaned with a proprietary carpet shampoo and left to dry.

If the carpet is sound but faded in parts it can be dyed to a uniform colour by using a suitable dye. Carpets with frayed edges will be improved greatly in appearance if the edging or binding is renewed.

Should the carpets be beyond redemption or missing altogether, it may be possible to buy a replacement set ready tailored for your car. If this is not possible there are several firms that will supply suitable carpet from a roll in a large variety of colours.

Where you have the remnants of carpets from which to take measurements it is best to lay them out on a large flat area having first made a careful note, with sketches or photographs if possible, of their position in the car. Make sure the pile of the carpets is running in the same direction and then take your measurements, making an allowance for cutting and seaming. If any of the carpets are made up of two or more pieces, check carefully how the pieces are joined together and make a note before taking them apart to use as patterns for cutting the new carpet.

If the carpets for your car are missing altogether and it isn't possible to buy ready-made replacements, patterns made from thick paper will have to be produced. Make sure that the patterns are large enough; skimping on the material will leave unsightly gaps around the edges of the carpet.

Make sure you buy carpet that does no fray as soon as it is cut, and bind the edges unless they are fitted underneath the sill plates or similar fastenings. Where new carpets are going to be fitted to existing fixing studs in the floor, chalk the top of the stud and press the new carpet down on to it. This will show clearly where to put the other half of the fastening in the new carpet.

CHAPTER 19

Fibreglass and other plastics

In recent years glass fibre — fibreglass — or glass reinforced plastic (G.R.P.) as it has become known, has come into wide-spread use by low volume producers, kit car manufacturers and for many replacement body panels.

The glass in GRP is strands of silicon which are bonded together or reinforced by the plastic, which is a resin. When the resin is mixed with a hardener or catalyst, the resin will cure and set solid.

Glass fibre is sold either as mat, woven roving, tissue or tape. Resin is sold as general lay up or gel coat resin which has an additive included to make it thixotropic or non-drip. The hardener is usually supplied in the correct quantities when you purchase the resin.

When working with fibreglass there are some important points to remember for health and safety. Many people find that working with glass fibre mat will produce a localised rash on their hands and arms. If you are affected, wear gloves or use a barrier cream. Some people are very allergic to the glass fibres and suffer such painful rashes and swellings that they would be well advised to ask someone else to do the job for them.

Always work in a well-ventilated area because the resin gives off styrene vapour which is highly inflammable and can cause drowsiness. Acetone used for cleaning purposes is also inflammable so the rule must be no smoking or naked lights when working or while the fibreglass is curing.

Apart from the obvious crash damage, the most common cause of deterioration in fibreglass is stress cracks in the laminate, which can be caused by a variety of things.

Whatever the cause, the remedy is the same. The paint layers must be ground away, then the gel coat of the resin and into the top layer of laminate. The ground-out area should extend 1 in - 2 in (25-50 mm) beyond the crack and the edges of the area should be angled rather than vertical. Always remember to wear a face mask when grinding fibreglass or bodyfiller.

Once the grinding is finished, the edge of the area should be feathered with abrasive paper, used dry. This will remove the grinding marks which would otherwise show after re-painting.

Cut a piece of tissue large enough to cover the area of the cracks and after applying a thin layer of mixed resin, place the tissue over the cracks. This should now be brushed gently with resin until it is thoroughly soaked, then left to cure.

The final stage necessitates completing the repair with filler paste, then smoothing it down to achieve the correct contour of the body panel.

Should the panel be cracked all the way through it will have to be repaired from both sides. The inside of the panel must be cleaned of any underseal, road dirt etc at least 4 in – 5 in (100–125 mm) beyond the split in each direction.

Two or three layers of mat should be laminated onto the back of the panel, after it has been lightly ground to form a key for the laminates. Make sure the repair is taken well beyond the split, to spread the load. When the repair has thoroughly cured, the outside of the panel can be treated in the same way as a stress crack.

If you want to make a new panel or some other article from scratch you will first have to make a mould. Moulds may be either male or female (a male mould is laid up on its outer surface, a female on its inside surface) and can be made from any rigid material. Porous materials such as wood or plaster must be sealed with varnish before use.

As with any other type of mould, you must ensure

that there are no re-entrant angles or curves on the mould which would prevent the finished moulding from being lifted off. If you do require such a shape, the mould must be designed so that it can be dismantled with the moulding in place, to allow it to be removed.

Male moulds are easier to make than female ones and for this reason it is often best to make a male mould first. When the mould is complete, it should be coated with a release agent, following the instructions on the tin carefully. A female mould can then be formed over the male one, using fibreglass. It may be necessary to incorporate strengthening ribs into the mould to prevent it flexing too much. These ribs can be made from any material such as wood strips or metal tube, providing they are clean. Wood bonds very well to fibreglass because its porous nature provides an excellent key for the resin. Best results are obtained if it is wiped over with acetone before laminating into the mould. When the laminate has cured, it can be removed and the inside face cleaned. It is now ready to be used as a mould.

Body panels can be used as moulds for producing fibreglass replacements. The master panel must be perfect in shape and surface finish. Any defects must be rectified before use, otherwise they will be reproduced on any subsequent mouldings.

One other use for the polyester resin which is used in G.R.P. work is the production of knobs for switches, window mechanisms, etc. Before you begin you will need an example of the knob you wish to reproduce. This must be cleaned and any scratches polished out before a mould can be made using the R.T.V. rubber process described in Chapter 11. If the knob has a threaded insert it can be hung in the mould box on a threaded rod. When the mould has cured, the knob used as the pattern can be removed. The resin should then be mixed according to the instructions and coloured pigment added. It may be necessary to experiment with varying amounts of the colour pigment to achieve the correct shade. A new insert can be made from either a brass nut if there is sufficient room in the mould, or a piece of brass rod drilled and tapped. File or machine grooves or notches into the rod to form a key for the resin. The insert can be hung on the threaded rod into the mould and the resin poured around it.

The polyester resins used in G.R.P. and casting work are known as thermosetting plastics. These cannot be re-shaped by the application of heat after they have been formed and the only way to shape them is with normal cutting tools. Thermoplastics on the other hand can be shaped by heating to the correct temperature and forming them by different methods.

Polymethyl Methacrylate (acrylic) is perhaps the best known under its I.C.I. trade name 'Perspex'. It has exceptional durability for outdoor use and in its clear form has excellent transparency. It has been used for many years as a substitute for glass in the windows of sports racing cars and for streamlined headlamp covers.

Perspex is available in sheets of varying thickness, rods or tube. The sheets are covered with protective paper and this should be kept in place as long as possible during working. Not only does the paper protect the surface of the sheet from being marked, it also makes marking out much easier.

Like other thermoplastics, acrylic can be cut and drilled with normal metal or woodworking tools. When sawing acrylic sheet, it is important that the saw is fed slowly and steadily into the sheet. This will prevent a build-up of heat which will soften the plastic. The sheet must be well-supported to avoid snapping and care is necessary to avoid splintering by over-vigorous sawing. The rough edge left by the saw can be smoothed with a file or, if it is a straight edge, a smoothing or block plane can be used. The blade of the plane must be sharp and set fine.

Normal drills are suitable for acrylic providing they are not run too fast and so generate excessive heat. Water or soluble oil can be used as a coolant. Make sure that the acrylic is clamped down onto a piece of wood, to prevent the sheet riding up the drill as the hole is completed and the bottom edge of the hole splintering.

It is possible to cut screw threads into acrylic using standard taps and dies. A coarse thread form will be the strongest and soluble oil or water should be used as a lubricant. Screw threads in acrylic will not last long if used frequently. In a situation needing regular dismantling, a metal insert should be used.

Acrylic rod can be turned on a lathe using H.S.S. tools. The tools should have zero top rake, 15°-20° front clearance and be kept sharp at all times. Coolant must always be used and the work should be held firmly and positioned correctly to prevent chatter. Rigid plastics can usually be machined using the same techniques as those used for light alloys.

Acrylic sheet can be bent easily if heated to 160°–170°C. For work at home the best heat source is the domestic oven. A polished sheet of metal should be used to support the plastic while it is being heated, otherwise it will sag between the bars of the oven shelf when it becomes soft. An approximate estimate of the time required to heat the sheet can be found with the following formula: time in minutes = 10 + 3 × thickness of the sheet in mm).

If only a simple bend is required in the sheet, a former made of wood or metal can be used around which to bend the sheet. The surface of the former must be clean and smooth otherwise the soft surface of the plastic will be damaged. Soft leather or cotton gloves should be worn when handling the heated plastic to prevent burns to the hands.

If a compound curve is required, a male and female mould can be made from wood or other rigid material. The surfaces of the mould must be perfectly smooth before use. The softened sheet of plastic, that has already been cut to shape, should be laid over the female mould and then pressed down into it with the male mould. Only hand pressure is required but the pressure must not be released until the plastic has cooled sufficiently to become rigid.

Any surface scratches can be removed using perspex polish or metal polish, though deeper scratches are best removed by using progressively finer grades of wet and dry paper before using the polish.

Nylon is another plastic that is being used more and more in the motor industry. It is a tough creep-resistant plastic that has an excellent resistance to oils, fuels and solvents. It is used for light engineering components such as gears, bushes and bearings where its major asset of not requiring lubrication can be utilised to the full.

There are a number of different types of nylon available but they all can be easily machined if the basic guide lines already mentioned for machining plastics are followed.

CONCLUSION

I hope that within this book you will have found that the processes described have enabled you to attempt work that in the past you have avoided, or sent out to the professionals.

Finally may I use a quote from one of the greatest engineers of the motor industry which may help give you confidence in your endeavours:

Whatever is rightly done, however humble, is noble.

Sir Henry Royce

List of suppliers

Adhesives.

Perma Bond Ltd,
Woodside Rd,
Eastleigh,
Hants, SO5 4EX.

Accessories.

The Complete Automobilist,
The Old Rectory,
Greatford,
Stamford,
Lincs, PE9 4PR.

Woolies,
Off Blenheim Way,
Northfields Industrial Est.,
Market Deeping,
Nr Peterborough, PE6 8LD.

Paul Beck,
Vintage Supplies,
Folgate Rd,
North Walsham,
Norfolk, NR28 0AJ.

Brakes.

Lancaster Vintage &
Classic Spares,
The Warehouse, Baxtergate,
Off Lord St.,
Morecambe, LA4 4HX

Bromley Brakes & Suspension,
Bromley,
Kent.

Padget's,
Vintage Spares Specialist,
Wisbech,
Cambs.

G. T. Classic Cars Ltd,
Rugby.

Carburettors.

Burlen Fuel Systems,
Spitfire House,
Castle Rd,
Salisbury,
Wilts.

Southern Careburettors,
Unit 14,
Oakwood Industrial Est.,
Gatwick Rd,
Crawley.

Gower & Lee,
24 Brook Mews North,
Paddington,
London, W2 3BW.

Chris Montague,
380/2 Finchley Rd,
London NW2 2HP.

Casting Supplies.

F. L. Hunt,
Salford,
Manchester.

Barretts,
1 Mayo Road,
Croydon,
Surrey CR0 2PQ.

Alec Tiranti Ltd.
70 High St,
Theale,
Berks, RG7 5AR.

Coachbuilders.

I Wilkinson & Sons,
Stafford St.,
Derby, DE1 1JH.

Rod Jolley,
37 Gordleton Industrial Pk.,
Sway Rd,
Lymington,
Hants.

Engine balancing & crack testing.

Mini Sport Ltd.
Thompson St,
Padiham,
Lancs, BB12 7AP.

Middleton Motors,
Coopers Lane,
Potters Bar,
Herts.

Basset Down Ltd,
Basset Down,
Swindon,
Wilts, SN4 9QP.

Engine components.

Peter Hepworth Components,
Bradgate House,
Chapel Lane,
Easingwold,
Nrth Yorks, YO6 3AE.

Sutton Re-Bore Service,
34-38 Lind Rd,
Sutton,
Surrey.

O. K. Pistons,
c/o 95 Billing Rd,
Brafield,
Northampton, NN7 1BL.

Engine rebuilding.

Sutton Re-Bore Service,
see above.
Stretton Summer,
Cleobury Garages Ltd,
High St,
Cleobury Mortimer,
Shropshire.

Engineering firms (one off or batch production).

Matley Tools Ltd,
Ryecroft Mill,
Smith St,
Ashton-Under-Lyne,
Lancs. OL7 0DD.

Tectus Engineering,
Mill Lane,
Hemingborough,
Nth. Yorks, YO8 7QX.

Exhaust manufacturers.

Mike Randell,
128 Stanley Park Rd,
Wallington,
Surrey.

Maniflow,
64-66 St. Pauls Rd,
Salisbury,
Wilts.

Cheesman Products,
6 Boundary Yard,
Woking,
Surrey.

P. D. Gough Associates,
The Old Foundry,
Common Lane,
Watnell,
Nottingham, NG16 1HD.

Instrument repairs.

Melvyn Rutter,
The Morgan Garage,
Little Hallingbury,
Nr Bishops Stortford,
Herts, CM22 7RA.

Bristol Instruments,
Templar House,
Temple Way,
Bristol, BS1 6HG.

Vintage Restorations,
The Old Bakery,
Tunbridge Wells,
Kent, TN2 4UU.

Interior trim.

Paul Beck
see above.

P. J. Donnelly (Rubber)
68 Lower City Rd,
Warley,
West Midlands, B69 2HL.

Creech Coach Trimming,
45 Anerly Road,
Crystal Palace,
London SE19 2AS.

Woolies Ltd.
see above.

Edgware Motor Accessories,
94 High St.,
Edgware,
Middx.

Coach Trimming Supplies,
111 Flaxley Rd,
Stechford,
Birmingham B33 9HR.

Standish Car Trim,
65a Bradley Hall Trading Estate,
Standish,
Nr Wigan,
Lancs.

Lamp repairs.

D. C. M. & Co,
94 Matilda St.,
Sheffield,
Yorks, S1 4QF.

Mickey Wraight Ltd,
9 Coniston Crescent,
Weymouth,
Dorset.

Metal cleaning, stoving & powder coating.

Sports & Vintage Motors,
Upper Battlefield,
Shrewsbury,
SY4 3DB.

P & J Powder Coatings,
17 Evanton Place,
Thornliebank Industrial Est,
Glasgow, G46.

Redditch Shotblasting Co,
Barleet Rd,
Washford West,
Redditch,
Worcs, B98 0DQ.

Nuts, bolts & other fixings.

Riveting Systems Ltd,
Harehill,
Tomorden,
Lancs, OL14 5JY.

Namrick Ltd,
124 Portland Rd,
Hove,
Sussex, BN3 5QL.

John Worrall,
12 Burntoak Drive,
Parkfield Rd,
Stourbridge, DY8 1HL.

K. Whistons Ltd,
New Mills,
Stockport.

CDS Screws,
Unit 2,
Warwick House Ind. Est.
Banbury Rd,
Southam,
Warwick, CV33 0HL.

Tectus Engineering,
see above.

Plating.

Dynic Sales (plating kits)
Bell View Cottage,
Ladbroke,
Leamington Spa
CV33 0DA.

Runcorn Metal Polishers,
Unit 27,
Percival Lane,
Runcorn,
Cheshire.

London Chroming Co,
735 Old Kent Rd,
London, SE15.

S & T,
Unit 15,
The Alpha Centre,
Great Western Business Park,
Yate,
North Avon.

Welding.

Cast-Iron Welding Services,
Unit 19,
Atlas Court,
Hermitage Ind. Est,.
Whitwick Rd,
Coalville,
Leics, LE6 3FL.

CRM Engineering Ltd,
Unit 5,
Martock Business Park,
Nr. Yeovil,
Somerset, TA12 6HA.

Wheels & Tyres.

Vintage Tyres,
12 Dalston Gardens,
Honeypot Lane,
Stanmore,
Middx HA7 1BY.

Longstone Garage.
Main St,
Great Longstone,
Bakewell,
Derbyshire.

Lambrook Tyres,
Lambrook Farm,
Colyton,
Devon, EX13 6DL.

Motor Wheel Service,
Jeddo Rd,
Shepherds Bush,
London, W12 9ED.

Ralph Wilde,
Lyric House,
off Church St.
Radford Semele,
Leamington Spa, CV31 1TN.

Specialised Autos,
Slack St,
off Bryons Lane,
Macclesfield,
Cheshire.

Rightwheel,
260 Church St,
Mitcham,
Surrey.

The inclusion of a firm in this list must not be considered as a personal recommendation by the author or publishers. Readers must satisfy themselves as to the suitability of the services offered.

Index

Page numbers in brackets refer to illustrations, diagrams or charts.